D1475911

Psychology & Christianity

with contributions by

GARY R. COLLINS, DAVID G. MYERS
DAVID POWLISON, ROBERT C. ROBERTS

*edited by Eric L. Johnson
& Stanton L. Jones*

InterVarsity Press
Downers Grove, Illinois

InterVarsity Press
P.O. Box 1400, Downers Grove, IL 60515
World Wide Web: www.ivpress.com
E-mail: mail@ivpress.com

InterVarsity Press® is the book-publishing division of InterVarsity Christian Fellowship/USA®, a student movement active on campus at hundreds of universities, colleges and schools of nursing in the United States of America, and a member movement of the International Fellowship of Evangelical Students. For information about local and regional activities, write Public Relations Dept., InterVarsity Christian Fellowship/USA, 6400 Schroeder Rd., P.O. Box 7895, Madison, WI 53707-7895.

All Scripture quotations, unless otherwise indicated, are taken from the Holy Bible, New International Version®. NIV®. *Copyright ©1973, 1978, 1984 by International Bible Society. Used by permission of Zondervan Publishing House. All rights reserved.*

Cover illustration: Roberta Polfus

ISBN 0-8308-2263-1

Printed in the United States of America ∞

Library of Congress Cataloging-in-Publication Data

Psychology & Christianity: four views/edited by Eric Johnson & Stanton L. Jones.
    p. cm.
   Includes bibliographical references.
   ISBN 0-8308-2263-1 (pbk.: alk. paper)
   1. Christianity—Psychology. 2. Psychology and religion. I. Title: Psychology and Christianity. II. Johnson, Eric L., 1956- III. Jones, Stanton L.
   BR110 .P77 2000
   261.5'15—dc21

                                         00-040951

19	18	17	16	15	14	13	12	11	10	9	8	7	6
16	15	14	13	12	11	10	09	08	07	06	05		

To my wife, Rebekah
Gift and Friend
With thanks for your
unending ministry
and encouragement
—Eric L. Johnson

To my sister Phyllis
with love and respect
—Stanton L. Jones

Acknowledgments

It is widely acknowledged that factions in American culture have been embroiled over the past two decades in a conceptual and political battle grounded in different views of morality, values, epistemology, and the role of religion in public life, a "culture war" of great importance to evangelicals. Less well-known are the similar battles waged *within* the evangelical community, one of which concerns the relation of psychology and Christianity. What has led to this particular conflict? There are at least two factors. Modern psychology has become enormously influential on our culture and on the American church. Yet for most of the twentieth century, modern psychology has been largely devoid of reference to religiousness, if not downright hostile to religion. As a result, Christians have taken different positions regarding the extent to which they should have anything to do with modern psychology, some embracing it wholeheartedly, others rejecting it just as vigorously, and many others falling somewhere between. Few opportunities have arisen for Christians to dialogue publicly about these differences, the value of psychology in general for Christians, and the problems involved in psychological study and counseling practice for people of faith.

We have been delighted to work on just such a dialogue. We wish to thank heartily our four main contributors. We have long felt a debt to them for their professional contributions on these matters, and we add to that a personal debt for their efforts in this project. It has been a privilege to work with such quality individuals.

In such a book as this, we want as well to thank a few of the many other individuals who have influenced us and the field of Christians in psychology and counseling with their work, and so contributed in different ways to this book: Arthur Holmes, C. Stephen Evans, Jay Adams, John Carter, Bruce Narramore, Mark McMinn, Larry Crabb, Mary Van Leeuwen, Malcolm Jeeves, Alvin Plantinga, and John Frame. We would also like to express our personal gratitude to some of those with whom we have dialogued over the years about the concerns dealt with in this book: George Marsden, Wayne Joosse, Mary Vander Goot, Michael Mangis, Rich Butman, Wade Wahl, and Don Johnson, as well as the many students we have been privileged to interact with and learn from.

We want also to state our gratitude to Sarah and Matt Collins, Joseph Biancardi, and Valerie Vincent for their help in composing the indexes.

Finally, we want to express our appreciation for the staff at InterVarsity, especially Andy LePeau for his guidance and support throughout the different stages of this project, as well as Drew Blankman for his grace and patience.

1 A History of Christians in Psychology

Eric L. Johnson & Stanton L. Jones

Followers of God have always been interested in his creation. After recounting the stars in the heavens, the bestowing of rain, the growth of vegetation and the feeding of wild animals, the psalmist cries out, "How many are your works, O LORD! In wisdom you made them all; the earth is full of your creatures" (Ps 104:24). But of all the things in creation, the greatest interest to most of us is our own nature, for we are fascinated with the wonder of ourselves. "For you created my inmost being; you knit me together in my mother's womb. I praise you because I am fearfully and wonderfully made; your works are wonderful, I know that full well" (Ps 139:13-14). As John Calvin (1559/1960) wrote, a human being is a microcosm of the universe, "a rare example of God's power, goodness, and wisdom, and contains within . . . enough miracles to occupy our minds" (p. 54). It should come as no surprise then to learn that Christian thinkers have also thought deeply about "psychology," psychology understood as the rigorous attempt to understand human character and behavior, one grounded in philosophical reflection and examination of the "data" of human experience.

Yet Christian interest in human nature has exploded in the last forty years of the twentieth century. Countless books have been written by Christians that describe and reflect on human beings: how we should be raised, the nature of our personalities, our development, our relationships, our inner well-being, and on and on. However, this explosion of interest has resulted in a major controversy within the church. Why? Because over the past century a complex and rich body of knowledge and practice has arisen that attempts to understand and treat human personality and behavior in ways which are usually disconnected from Christian perspectives on life, and sometimes in ways that seem to contradict what Christians have regarded as biblically grounded truth about humanity. Disagreement is rampant about how much and in what ways the theories and findings of this secular version of psychology should influence, be absorbed into, and even transform the way Christians think about persons.

Thus we are struggling as Christians with what seems like a new problem: How do we relate or connect our cherished Christian beliefs about persons to what this secular version of psychology tells us about them? This is reminiscent of an old problem: For centuries Christians themselves have thought about human beings in different ways. Christians have disagreed, for example, on the nature of human free will—Wesleyan and Reformed Christians believe differently about God's involvement in human actions. An even more complex problem is the focus of this book. Christians disagree about how we should understand and relate to the enormous, impressive body of knowledge and set of practices that have developed in the twentieth century known today as psychology, since it offers us a largely secular *version* of psychology. This book presents four of the most important approaches contemporary evangelicals use to relate their faith to the study and treatment of human nature (that is, psychology and counseling).

Some Christians believe there are marvelous things to learn from modern psychology, embracing psychological findings and theories with enthusiasm, while others approach secular psychology with great caution. There are even some who argue that *any* appropriation of secular psychology is heresy, that secular psychology is a poison which taints and infects all Christians who imbibe it. Think of a continuum: at one end are atheistic thinkers who believe that all religions, including Christianity, are false and that psychology is the only source of reliable knowledge about humanity; for these people "religious knowledge" means nothing and secular psychology means everything. At the other end of this continuum are Christians who might be called "fundamentalists," who believe Christians should only affirm what is in the Bible and reject any input from "worldly" sources, especially secular psychology; such critics go so far as to decry one-on-one counseling since it is not expressly taught in the Bible (cf. Bobgan & Bobgan, 1997). This book will examine neither of these extremes but instead will look at what lies between them—four constructive views of how Christians should understand psychology and counseling.

Before we learn about the four approaches themselves, let's take some time to trace the historical and intellectual background for the present debate.

Faith, Science, and Secularism

Over the past 150 years, revolutionary shifts have occurred in the fundamental ways we conduct our intellectual lives in the West. Though there were notable exceptions, Europeans and Americans of the early 1800s broadly agreed that Christianity provided the only legitimate view of reality. Most Westerners—common folk and scholars alike—thought within the framework of a biblical worldview. They assumed that God had created the world, that human beings were specially created in his image, that human reason could apprehend ultimate truth because God had made them capable of knowing truth, that biblical morality was universally true and invariant, that the biblical virtues depicted what it meant to be fully and perfectly human, and so forth.

Of course, the West is still commonly considered Christian, and a majority of Europeans and Americans would still label themselves Christian if asked their religion. Two significant changes, however, have occurred. Among this group of avowed Christians there is a relatively smaller percentage who would continue to hold to the traditional beliefs of classic Christianity and consistently practice their faith (perhaps 15 to 20 percent in America, maybe 5 to 10 percent in Europe [higher in Italy and Poland, lower in France, England, and Germany]). In addition, over the last 150 years an alternative worldview has competed for cultural influence, and over the course of this century it has become the dominant paradigm for understanding ourselves in Western culture, a worldview now called *modernism.*

A fuller description of modernism will be given below, but for now let's focus on one feature of modernism: its secularism; that is, its tendency to empty culture of its religious significance, discourse, and symbols. Because of this feature, Christianity and modernism have struggled in the West for cultural dominance. In the main, most contemporary Westerners have been shaped by both modernism and Christianity. However, the secularism that has pervaded the significant writings and major institutions of Western culture in the twentieth century is evidence that modernism has superseded Christianity in influence. Most of the influential authors, thinkers, scientists, and celebrities of the twentieth century were not religious, or if they were, their religion was not visible. Many of the most influential shapers of modern culture openly disparaged traditional religious perspectives (e.g., Marx, Nietzsche, Freud, H. G. Wells, John Dewey, Bertrand Russell, Samuel Beckett, Jean-Paul Sartre, Michel Foucault, and Richard Rorty, to name a few). Perhaps the most powerful and tangible example of this movement is the way that European and American institutions of higher learning have so remarkably moved from Judeo-Christian to secular sensibilities over the past 150 years. Institution by institution, colleges and universities have shed their original commitments to glorifying Christ and proclaiming the Christian gospel to embrace a secularized definition of mission and identity (a process in America that has been documented by Burtchael, 1998; and Marsden, 1994). Gradually, beginning in the early twentieth century, unwritten rules developed that excluded religious views from expression in the main forms of media, education, and science in the West. As a result, religious speech was relegated to private life and to religious institutions and media—churches, sectarian colleges, and religious broadcasting. Beyond that, with few exceptions religious considerations were dropped from public discourse.

Of course, there were benefits to Western culture that resulted from these modern requirements: it made possible a common educational system; it allowed people with different faith commitments (Christian, Jewish, agnostic) to talk with, work with, and learn from each other; and it allowed people to concentrate on those beliefs that most people hold in common rather than those that divide. However, in many ways the cost of this secularization has proven very high.

At the same time, this move away from a religious worldview to a secular one also happened to coincide with another very significant cultural development: the application of natural science methods to areas of the world to which they had not been previously applied. Intense quantification and controlled observation had proven successful in previous centuries in astronomy, physics, chemistry, and biology. Now these methods began to be applied to the study of society, human consciousness and behavior, economics and business, and education with notable results. Secularism combined with the methods of the natural sciences in the study of human nature resulted in a number of sciences being newly formed or reformed in ways that excluded reference to supernatural beliefs or assumptions. This mix of secularization and the application of scientific methods to the understanding of animal and human behavior, emotion, personality, and thought shaped the modern version of psychology. And it is this combination which has led to the present debate among Christians about how the findings and theories of *secular* psychology should relate to Christian belief and practice.

The History of Western Psychology and Counseling Before 1879

In thinking about how psychology and Christian faith should relate today, it is essential to recognize that the present state (one of tension and debate) is similar to and yet different from the state of psychology through much of the history of the church. According to most contemporary introductory textbooks in psychology, psychopathology, and counseling (and even some history of psychology texts), the founding of psychology is believed to have occurred in the mid to late 1800s. Nevertheless, there *was* counseling, psychological theorizing, reflection, writing, and in some cases research prior to this time, even centuries prior (Brett, 1912; Diamond, 1974; Leahey, 1997; Robinson, 1981; Watson & Evans, 1991). Unquestionably, the form of this work was different in many respects from twentieth-century psychology. Most importantly, it was far less empirically and quantitatively oriented, and much more reliant on the philosophical reflections of individuals. Still, genuine insights to psychological thinking can be found in pre-1879 texts, even if we must acknowledge that in most cases such insights were developed with less complexity than has been the case in the twentieth century.

Psychology in the West was first developed with unusual sophistication by Greek philosopher-therapists like Plato, Aristotle, and Epicurus. They attempted to describe human nature, including its fundamental ills and its reparation, on the basis of personal experience and rigorous reflection in light of prior thought (Nussbaum, 1994; Watson & Evans, 1991). These thinkers explored topics like the composition and "inner" structure of human beings—memory, reason, sensation, appetite, motivation, virtues and vices, and various ideals of human maturation. The Old and New Testaments themselves contain material of psychological import (and in the case of Paul, perhaps a strongly religious protopsychology; Brett, 1912). However these reflections belong under the category of "folk psychology," since they were not developed systematically for the express aim of contributing to psychological knowledge. Nevertheless, within the classic Christian tradition, the Bible's reflections on human nature have always been accorded a unique authority.

After the New Testament era it seems the Bible and the psychological contributions of Plato and Aristotle (and others) provided joint inspiration for and influence on the psychological theorizing of Christians for the next fourteen hundred years. With only a limited grasp of the value of actual empirical study, the major teachers and writers of the early church and medieval periods were convinced that philosophical reflection grounded in Scripture provided the surest route to knowledge. Not surprisingly then, the best psychological work by Christians was the result of personal reflection, not research. Though largely concerned with matters of faith and life, people like the desert fathers, Tertullian, Cassian, Gregory of Nyssa, and Gregory the Great wrote with sometimes penetrating insight into the nature of the soul and soul healing. However, it was Augustine, with his massive intellect, that provided the best example in the early church of psychological reflection (cf. Burnaby, 1938; Henry, 1960; Johnson, 1998; Wetzel, 1992). Steeped in the Scriptures and the thought of the earlier church fathers, Augustine's understanding was also influenced by the philosophical tradition inspired by Plato. He worked out a system of thought fundamentally shaped by scriptural categories, but with a Platonic flavor. Nevertheless, his work on love, sin, grace, memory, mental illumination, wisdom, volition, and the experience of time provide a wealth of suggestions for psychology.

Strongly influenced by Augustine but much more systematic (and therefore more directly helpful for developing psychological theory) was Thomas Aquinas (cf. Brennan, 1937; Cantin, 1948; Cross, 1998). Significantly, this great Christian thinker devoted his life to relating faith to the thought of another brilliant but secular philosopher. Aquinas unified the best of Augustinian and Aristotelian tradition and produced an influential body of psychological thought covering the appetites, the will, habits, the virtues and vices, the emotions, memory, and the intellect.

It is worth underlining that the two greatest intellectual lights of the church's first fifteen hundred years, Augustine and Aquinas, drew heavily in their theological and psychological work on the philosophical traditions of the two greatest (and non-Christian) Greek philosophers— Plato and Aristotle. And their distinct approaches contributed to genuine differences in thought (despite their shared faith). In a very real sense, then, the work of each of these two great Christian thinkers represents an "integration" of Christian and non-Christian thought, though Aquinas was engaged in such integration much more self-consciously than Augustine, who was more explicitly working out the differences between Christian and pagan thought, between the "city of God" and the "city of humanity."

Other Christians of the Middle Ages who wrote on psychological topics, including Bonaventure, Bernard of Clairvaux, Symeon the New Theologian, Anselm, Duns Scotus, and William of Ockham, typically focused on concerns like the structure of the soul, knowledge, and spirituality and spiritual development. Through the early church and medieval periods, these and other writers also studied the improvement of the soul. Pastoral care, counseling, and spiritual direction were of primary importance. Clearly, the healing of souls (and what we now call counseling) was central to the mission of the church long before modern psychotherapy came on the scene (Jones, 1985; McNeill, 1951; Oden, 1989; Stewart, 1998).

The Renaissance, Reformation, and Counter-Reformation released a new curiosity in things natural, including topics that we now consider psychology. For example, Catholics in the Counter-Reformation like Teresa of Avila and John of the Cross described spiritual development with unparalleled depth. Reformers like Luther and Calvin wrote only indirectly on psychology, but their reflections on sin, grace, knowledge, faith, and the nature of the Christian life contributed to the further development of a Protestant folk psychology largely shaped by biblical (and Augustinian) themes. However, similar to much of the work of earlier Christians, the main focus of this quasi-psychological writing was more pastoral: the cure and upbuilding of the Christian soul. In other words, their concern was most often directed toward the shaping of moral character and the enhancement or deepening of a believer's relationship with God, sometimes directed toward what we call "therapeutic" concerns (such as the resolution of severe "melancholy," seen as a normal part of pastoral care) and not at all directed toward what we call "self-actualization" or the enhancement of human potential. In the Reformation traditions this pastoral psychology reached its zenith in the Puritan and Pietist periods, when writers like Richard Baxter, John Owen, George Herbert, William Law, John Wesley, Jonathan Edwards, John Newton, and (later) Archibald Alexander developed sophisticated and nuanced understandings of the soul's spiritual development in Christ, considerations that have major implications for pastoral care and Christian counseling today.

In addition, Christian philosophers after the Middle Ages continued to reason about human nature in ways that shed light on psychology, including such luminaries as René Descartes, Giovanni Vico, John Locke, Bishop George Berkeley, Thomas Reid, Bishop Joseph Butler, Gottfried Leibniz, and Blaise Pascal, some of whom are universally recognized as important figures leading up to the founding of modern psychology. In the Americas a number of Christians also contributed works in psychology (the best of which probably include Edwards, 1754/1957; 1746/1959; McCosh, 1886, 1887; Porter, 1869; though probably only Edwards has more than historical interest). Possibly the most significant Christian psychology author since the Middle Ages was Søren Kierkegaard, who considered himself a Christian psychologist and who contributed some of the most profound theoretical psychological works ever written from a Christian or non-Christian standpoint (e.g., 1844/1980a; 1848/1980b; cf. Evans, 1990). Over the course of a decade he described with brilliance (in sometimes disturbing ways) the nature of personhood, sin, anxiety, the unconscious (before Freud was even born), subjectivity, human development, and spiritual development from a thoroughgoing Christian perspective. Kierkegaard is, as well, the only Christian thinker who can be considered a "father" to a major modern approach to psychological theory and therapy—existential psychology (though Kierkegaard would almost certainly be horrified to be considered the founding father of what is among the psychological approaches considered most alien and hostile to Christian faith; see Jones & Butman, 1991).

So while a certain form of psychology and therapy originated in the late 1800s, psychology (defined broadly as a disciplined, focused inquiry into human nature) and counseling (defined as an attempt to heal the soul and advance its well-being) have been practiced by Christians for centuries. Christians contributed novel and significant psychological insights in such areas as the nature of human reason, sensation, memory, attention, the appetites, the emotions, volition, and related subjects; the unconscious; the experience of time; moral, spiritual, and character development; the role of God and grace in human development; the nature and impact of sin; techniques for overcoming sin and brokenness (the spiritual disciplines, as well as herbal remedies and common sense helps); the psychology of religion; the relation of free will and determinism; biological versus environmental origins of psychological phenomena; body-soul relations; and some of the bases for scientific research (Brett, 1953; Robinson, 1981).

However, at the same time there is no question that the degree of complexity and accuracy in our understanding of human nature and the degree of rigor used in its investigation was with a few exceptions far below that of the twentieth century. The scientific revolution in the West contributed an amazing drive toward a detailed examination of phenomena unlike anything ever seen in history. Though the classical pastoral-care tradition may rival the work done on therapy in the twentieth century in certain respects, the sheer quantity of knowledge acquired in other psychological areas over the last one hundred years far outstrips the knowledge accumulated over previous centuries. Moreover, the simple truth is that pure philosophical and theological reflection about concrete matters of human life not clearly addressed in Scripture and unchecked by empirical research inevitably yields error as well as truth. Understanding human nature would advance only as human nature itself became the object of careful scientific investigation. We turn next to consider the Christian contribution to the scientific revolution.

Christian Influence on the Development of Modern Science

Secular thinkers and Christian fundamentalists often share a core conviction that we regard as substantially flawed: that "natural knowledge" (knowledge coming from sources other than the Bible, including scientific knowledge) is the enemy of faith. Admittedly, the church has long struggled with this issue. Here, we will not take on the task of outlining a justification for Christian engagement with "natural knowledge." We will presume the reasonableness of learning from sources other than the Scriptures.

Many secularists, however, claim that a clear lesson is learned from the historical relationship of science and religion. For many, the Galileo affair sums it all up: Religion has always stood for dogmatic certainty and superstition in the service of authoritarian control, while science has been on a noble quest for truth.[1] The two forces—superstitious religion and scientific rationality—have been locked in conflict since the emergence of modern science. By outlining how this conviction is mistaken, we hope to lay a better foundation for understanding how Christians can approach the scientific discipline of psychology.

Today, many people accept the "warfare" model of the relationship between science and religion. Several writers stand out in the last 150 years as proponents of this metaphor. Thomas H. Huxley, the popularizer of Darwin's thought (who was called "Darwin's bulldog," in his day), worked tirelessly to wrest control of nineteenth-century English universities away from the Church of England. He did so by painting Christianity as the enemy of the pursuit of knowledge. In one of his more flamboyant moments he wrote, "Extinguished theologians lie about the cradle of every science, as the strangled snakes beside that of Hercules;

---

[1]During the later years of the Inquisition, Galileo was threatened with imprisonment and excommunication by authorities in the Catholic Church if he did not retract his endorsement of a heliocentric planetary system, which was believed to contradict the teachings of the Bible and the authoritative views of ancient writers that the earth was at the center and was immovable. He did in fact recant in 1633 (Shea, 1986).

and history records that whenever science and orthodoxy have been fairly exposed, the latter have been forced to retire from the lists, bleeding and crushed; scotched if not slain" (Huxley, 1893, p. 52).

John W. Draper, a chemist and physiologist, wrote the highly influential *History of the Conflict Between Religion and Science* (1874, which is still in print today). It was essentially a diatribe against Roman Catholicism. Draper claimed that since its earliest years, the Roman Church had displayed "a bitter and mortal animosity" (p. 335) toward science that resulted in the brutal persecution of scientists and other nonconformists. He described the Church's hands as "steeped in blood" (p. 364). His revisionist history concluded that "Religion must relinquish that imperious, that domineering position which she has so long maintained against Science. There must be absolute freedom for thought. The ecclesiastic must learn to keep himself within the domain he has chosen, and cease to tyrannize over the philosopher [i.e., scientist], who, conscious of his own strength and the purity of his motives, will bear such interference no longer" (p. 367).

There is one small problem with such characterizations of the relationship between science and religion (particularly Christianity): they are tragic distortions of the truth. A summary of the many ways in which the "warfare" characterization is a distortion is beyond the scope of this introduction. All we can do here is highlight some crucial observations from recent scholarship. For more complete discussion, see the work of John H. Brooke (1991; see also Russell, 1985).

First, defining and distinguishing either religion or science is a challenge, especially when we are looking back in history through twenty-first-century eyes. Definitions of *science* and *religion* are profoundly complicated; both are dynamic and multifaceted human activities. The boundaries of each are both blurred and moveable. The term *science* was historically much broader than its use today. It was only since the mid-nineteenth century that science has become formally professionalized. Prior to this new era, scientists referred to themselves as "natural philosophers" and concerned themselves with many matters beyond what we would today regard as the narrowly scientific. Isaac Newton, perhaps the greatest scientific mind in history, seamlessly moved between interests in what we recognize as physics and chemistry, and interests in alchemy, biblical prophecy, and theology. "Newton himself remarked that it was part of the business of natural philosophy to discuss such questions as the attributes of God and His relationship to the physical world" (Brooke, 1991, p. 7). Neither science nor religion is a static "thing." "Because both are rooted in human concerns and human endeavor, it would be a profound mistake to treat them as if they were entities in themselves—as if they could be completely abstracted from their social contexts in which those concerns and endeavors took their distinctive forms" (Brooke, 1991, p. 8). Each is connected to the other as well as to politics (disciplinary and societal), culture, art, and daily life.

Second, religion has played complex roles in the rise of modern science. On balance, Christianity did much more to facilitate the development of science than to impede it. Brooke (1991) argued that Christianity has served or facilitated science in a number of ways, including the following three:

☐ It provided beliefs essential to the development of science that were not present or important in other religions. For example, Christianity suggested that we can expect uniformity in nature since one God created and sustained the entire cosmos, that the sovereign Creator decreed that the material cosmos would behave according to "laws," that human reason could understand the cosmos since our reason parallels that of its Creator, and that the created order is a suitable object of study since it is a created entity and not a part of God himself.

☐ Christianity provided personal motives for scientists, which include improving the world to bring glory to God and relieve suffering (note that the strength of the prescribed motive to alleviate suffering varies markedly among different religious systems), being able to more fervently praise God by the activities of the mind (thus Kepler spoke of the scientist "thinking God's thoughts after Him;" Brooke, 1991, p. 22), and the possibility of science serving the causes of natural theology and apologetics (respectively, the tasks of proving God's existence and attributes from study of the natural world, and the defense of faith against attacks by nonbelievers).

☐ Christianity "could reinforce prescriptions for an appropriate scientific method. Each science in its infancy has had to establish the assumptions and procedures by which it could claim to extend our knowledge of nature" (Brooke, 1991, p. 25). This foundation required justification *before* there was a substantial body of empirical product from the new science, and so justifications external to scientific inquiry itself had to be utilized. For example, "references to the freedom of the divine will were often used in the seventeenth century to justify attacks on rationalist theories of nature, whose authors presumed to know how God *must* have shaped the world" (Brooke, 1991, p. 26) and thus justifying observation and experimentation.

A third observation that has been made from history is that the best way to frame the evolving relationship of science and religion is not as one of "eternal conflict" but instead as a process of "gradual differentiation and divergence." There are three broad views of the proper relationship of science and religion: (1) never ending conflict (Draper and White), (2) complementarity or independence in which each asks different questions about reality in incommensurable ways (and hence really have little or nothing to do with each other), and (3) mutual interaction and constructive influence wherein certain types of religious belief may be more supportive of and conducive to science than others and where science and religion can work to mutual advantage. Brooke (1991) argues that a careful examination of the rich historical record reveals a complex interaction that belies quick summarization. If any broad generalization has gained acceptance, it is that religion and science have been undergoing a process of "gradual differentiation and divergence" (Rudwick, cited in Lindberg & Numbers, 1986, p. 9). If true, it would seem that the conflict hypothesis (view 1) is wrong historically. On the contrary, Christianity has been generally a positive influence on the development of science (view 3), but it would appear that that influence is steadily weakening as science becomes more and more independent of religion (view 2).

The fact that there is some general validity to this description does not necessarily mean that this is how it *ought* to be. Perhaps religious faith and scientific thought are at their best when they are connected and interrelated; the explosion of interest in the last decade in the relationship of science and religion may attest to this. If so, this may lend support to the current of Christian thought (traceable to Augustine) which has insisted that all of life is religious at core and therefore all human activity, including human knowing (as in the sciences), is fundamentally of a religious nature and necessarily involves faith. Such an approach sees humans as intrinsically religious beings (a function of being made in God's image), so that even atheists are seen as acting within the context of their "ultimate concerns," values, beliefs, and motives, which are functionally equivalent to explicitly religious (or we might say cultic) values, beliefs, and motives. This approach isn't surprised when explicit religion is seen as a constructive force in human life, believing that humans were made for true religion. This in turn would suggest that religion plays an essential role in the science of psychology (and the practice of psychotherapy; cf. Johnson & Sandage, 1999).

But even if we don't subscribe to a more Augustinian view of the relation of faith and understanding given the history of the relationship of science and religion, we can still argue that religion may have a useful role to play internally to less mature sciences, a characterization which certainly fits psychology. Further, there may be special characteristics of the scientific study of human beings which suggest that a more sustained relationship with religion is advisable or permissible—humanity is, after all, a special concern of religion. The profoundly complex subject matter of the human sciences may serve as a justification for a sustained dialogue with religion on the strengths and weaknesses of the assumptions scientists bring to the study of persons.

Finally, an observation of the relationship of science and religion: Conflict between science and religion, when it has occurred, has largely been a function of factors that have been peripheral to rather than at the heart of both scientific inquiry and the core of religious doctrine.

When specific historical cases that supposedly stand as prototypes of the science-religion conflict are carefully examined, they no longer can serve as simple "conflict stories." Sometimes, historians have actually fabricated conflicts where there were none; for example, it is often stated that Luther and Calvin condemned Copernican cosmology (the idea that the earth moves around the sun), but this appears to be completely untrue (Daub, 1978).

There have been many instances of actual conflict, but between whom was the conflict, and why? "Conflicts allegedly between science and religion may turn out to be between rival scientific interests, or conversely between rival theological factions. Issues of political power, social prestige, and intellectual authority have repeatedly been at stake" (Brooke, 1991, p. 5). The best contemporary understandings of the Galileo incident illustrate this point. Far from being a simple tale of the Catholic Church seeking to suppress scientific progress while defending simplistic biblical interpretation, it appears instead that Galileo fell afoul of a complex tangle of ecclesiastical, political, personal, social, and theological forces (described beautifully in a dramatic screenplay; Goodwin, 1998).

"Conflict historians" often harshly judge the actions or pronouncements of church representatives without proper distinction between those actions and judgments that flowed from grounded theological dogma, for instance, in creeds (this occurred rarely) and when the church officials were simply reflecting the common pagan knowledge of the day. For example, anti-Copernican sentiments have been attributed to Calvin, apparently grounded on Calvin's remark in one sermon that the idea of the earth in motion was offensive to common sense and experience. But Calvin made no sustained argument against Copernicanism based on theological premises (Daub, 1978). We must distinguish, in other words, between a religious figure saying, "This new scientific hypothesis is a heresy!" and the same figure saying, "This new scientific hypothesis is ridiculous; everyone knows that can not be true!" Calvin's statement appears to be the latter, not the former.

In conclusion, Christians should strongly contest the idea that religion and science, and particularly Christianity and science, can be shown from history to be mortal enemies and incompatible entities. History suggests instead that it is possible for Christian faith to facilitate the progress of science and for science to coexist peacefully with Christianity. We can even claim on good historical evidence that Christianity facilitated the development of modern science. Many core Christian beliefs (e.g., that the world has an independent existence from the divine, is orderly and rule-governed, and that humanity was created capable of knowing and exercising dominion over the world) form the ideal foundation for scientific thought.

We turn next to an examination of the movement of psychology and counseling from its pastoral and philosophical contexts into the modern, more empirically based form in which we find it in America today.

Christianity and the Origins of Modern American Psychology

So, contrary to the allegations of some secularists, Christians and their beliefs actually provided a strong justification for modern science's *empirical* approach to the natural world, which strives for an accurate and detailed understanding based on actual research. And this Christian-inspired impetus for empirical validity eventually influenced the study of human nature. As the standard histories of modern psychology have well documented (Boring, 1950; Brett, 1953; Hearnshaw, 1987; Hothersall, 1984; Leahey, 1997), the success of natural science methods in astronomy, physics, chemistry, and especially biology led gradually in the 1800s to their application to the study of human phenomena.

Yet it would be going too far to say that Christianity had a direct role in fostering empirical psychology. For one thing, as noted above, the essentially Christian psychological work of the early church, medieval, and early modern periods had been based largely on various combinations of reason, speculation, and human tradition accumulated over previous centuries. While Christianity inspired the rise of the natural sciences, the human sciences (being more abstract) arose somewhat later, at a time when Western culture happened to be moving away from Christianity. Moreover, it must be conceded that the application of natural science methods to human beings was facilitated by a shift in viewpoint regarding human beings: they had to be construed as a type of "thing," an "object of study," to which such methods could be rightly applied. It seems likely that the erosion of Christian belief in the West (particularly its high view of human nature) and the ascendancy of Darwinian and other materialistic views of persons contributed to this shift in views of human beings. It should be added, however, that in hindsight Christianity per se is not inconsistent with empirical study of the human being; Aquinas, for example, was convinced that humans were animals. Nevertheless, it is clear that Darwinism and the growing success of natural science methods together made it easier to treat human beings as empirical objects of study.

Beginning in the early to mid 1800s, European studies on the nervous system and sensory experience by diverse people like Müller (a devout Catholic), Helmholtz (a materialist), and Fechner (a pantheist) demonstrated that human experience could be objectively studied and measured, and that lawful relationships between stimuli in the world and our experience of it could be discerned. This proved that natural science methods could be used on that which hitherto was thought beyond their reach: inner human experience. In 1879 Wilhelm Wundt, the great German founder of modern psychology, was the first to develop a laboratory for the specific purpose of studying immediate human experience, commonly understood as the birth of modern psychology.

Once this empirical drive touched psychology, a profusion of articles and books begin pouring from the major universities in Europe and America that documented, through research, the structures and processes of the mind, emotions, and behavior. Our understanding of mind and behavior has increased a thousandfold over the 120 years since then, due to the raising of the standards of scholarship about human beings and the new requirement of empirical validity that revolutionized the field of psychology.[2]

Early on, some Christians were interested and in some cases participated in these developments. Some of the phrenologists, for example, were Christians who sought to understand the relation of the brain to the personality (Vande Kemp, 1998). And the devout scholar-president of

---

[2]The value of applying natural-science methods (observation and quantification) to the social or human sciences is beyond dispute given the enormous body of research it has yielded. However, critics have rightly recognized the limitations of using methods derived from the study of the natural world (physics, chemistry, biology) to study human beings, given that some of the features of human nature are not found in the natural world (e.g., the experience of self-awareness, freedom, morality, and values) (Dilthey, 1989; Giorgi, 1970; Harré, Clarke, & De Carlo, 1985; Maslow, 1968). Though things like morality and values can be observed and measured (e.g., Kohlberg), critics have argued that natural-science methods inevitably lead to a truncated body of psychological research since they cannot "pick up" that which is most distinctive about human beings (reality from the "inside"). As a result, they have advocated using alternative methods to augment natural science research (e.g., phenomenological study, participant observation, discourse analysis, narrative psychology) that at-tempt to take into account the perspective and self-understanding of the person(s) being studied. Though these methods are becoming more widely used (e.g., feminist and postmodern researchers are particularly open to them), mainstream psychology continues to use natural sciences approaches in most of its research. Christians, of course, have a stake in such issues since we assume that adult humans are persons: self-aware, responsible, relatively free and moral beings, and therefore, not mere mechanisms or computing organisms (Farnsworth, 1985; Van Leeuwen, 1982, 1985).

Princeton James McCosh (1886) published a work on cognition that was, though still heavily influenced by philosophy, perhaps the first work of psychology in America that took seriously the role of physiology in the mind (Roback, 1952). Shortly after that, the Protestant liberal theologian-turned-psychologist G. T. Ladd (1887; also the second president of the American Psychological Association [APA], before William James!) wrote the most important work on physiological psychology written in English for the next twenty years.

Christian openness to the latest research at this time was likely due to the influence of Common Sense Realism on the preeminent evangelical scholars and administrators of the 1800s (Marsden, 1994; Spilka, 1987). This philosophy, broadly accepted as the Christian approach to learning of its day (originated by the eighteenth-century Christian philosopher Thomas Reid), provided justification for a confidence in the abilities of normal humans to know truths regarding the natural order. These abilities, it was believed, were universally bestowed by the Creator on all normal persons; hence these thinkers saw science as an ally to theology by providing evidence of God's design (Spilka, 1987). So this philosophy encouraged Christians to trust the research and theorizing of intellectuals, whether Christian or not. Unfortunately, Common Sense Realism did not predispose them to think critically regarding the influence of non-Christian assumptions on science. Consequently, such Christians tended to readily accept the latest findings of non-Christians without a full and proper appreciation of the extent to which nonreligious and antireligious biases were built into the very fabric of the work (Marsden, 1994).

At the same time that the methods of the natural sciences were being so powerfully extended to psychological phenomena, a major intellectual-cultural movement was beginning to take root in American soil: secular modernism. Descended from the Enlightenment exaltation of reason and rejection of tradition, and newly empowered by the quest for objective, scientific knowledge, twentieth-century modernism seems to have been characterized by the following features: (1) a repudiation of tradition, dogma, and revelation, which are assumed to be impediments to the attainment of true knowledge, and a corollary reliance on human reason and scientific research to provide truth about reality; (2) a pervasive secularism which rejects claims about the supernatural and generally excludes religious discourse from the public square; (3) an ethic rooted in an individualism in which the highest value is the pursuit of one's own happiness, so long as it does not infringe on the pursuits of other individuals; (4) an optimistic belief in the improvability of humankind; (5) the goal of a universal understanding of things that all intelligent parties can agree to; and (6) a tendency to analyze (break down into fundamental elements), categorize, and specialize, resulting in the distinguishing and separation of each discipline from all other disciplines (MacIntyre, 1990; Pippin, 1991; Rosenau, 1992; Ward, 1996). This last feature resulted in theology and philosophy being demoted from their standing as premier, overarching disciplines, at first placing them alongside other disciplines of higher learning but increasingly leading to the rejection of any claims of something real beyond the senses.

By the turn of the century many American intellectuals were becoming disenchanted with traditional Christianity and the supernaturalism it represented (Hitchcock, 1982; Marsden, 1994; Turner, 1985). Gradually the notion that we could make metaphysical claims about the nature of things beyond what sense experience or research could ascertain was rejected. (This is the essence of positivism, a philosophical approach that has pervaded modernism.) Recognizing the significance of evolutionary theory and encouraged by its optimism, which easily combined with the optimism of the scientific and industrial revolutions, these intellectuals were eager to develop and advance an alternative framework to that offered by the Judeo-Christian religions for making sense of life and offering solutions to life's problems. And if science was going to be instrumental in providing better solutions than those offered by the traditional religions, the actual scientific study of human nature would have to be pivotal.

In this milieu, psychology came to be seen by many of its participants, and increasingly by the culture at large, as providing an authoritative replacement for the pronouncements of the Bible, the pope, and church tradition (cf. Watson, 1925).[3] Gradually, the "new psychology," the study

---

[3] A striking similarity of many of the leaders of modern psychology was the common familial heritage in Christian or Jewish faith and their subsequent rejection of at

of human nature based on natural science methods alone, began to develop a substantial and respectable body of research and theory, and came to be recognized as the only psychology to be taken seriously. All the while, psychology's participation in and contribution to the West's movement away from Christianity remained largely tacit and therefore largely unnoticed. No doubt this motive was an ambiguous influence and is difficult to interpret, but it is easy to document the pervasive positivism and naturalism (and increasing intolerance of metaphysical commitments of any kind, e.g., reference to a "will") that came to dominate the institutions and journals of early modern psychology.[4]

The only place where religion was allowed in psychology was as an object of study—the psychology of religion. Oriented by modernist assumptions, a number of psychologists living in a culture still largely religious were led to study religion supposedly without assuming any stance toward the phenomenon itself. Religion was merely a fascinating, perplexing human phenomenon to be explained. As a result many studies of religious behavior and phenomena were published around the turn of the century (e.g., Coe, 1900; Leuba, 1912; Pratt, 1907; Starbuck, 1899), the most important being *The Varieties of Religious Experience* by William James (1903). James, the father of American psychology, was an unusual hybrid: not an orthodox Christian, he was nevertheless somewhat scandalously open to "the supernatural" (Allen, 1967). Regardless, as a good modernist he insisted that religious experience be studied "objectively"—that is, without assuming its reality. Aside from a few such notable exceptions, among intellectuals the tide was turning against belief in anything metaphysical or supernatural. As a result, as the first generation of American psychologists died out, few of the next generation were drawn to study religious experi-

---

least the orthodox versions of that faith. This can be seen in the lives of G. Stanley Hall, John Dewey, William James, Joseph Jastrow, James Rowland Angell, James Mark Baldwin, J. B. Watson, William McDougall, B. F. Skinner, Carl Rogers, and Abraham Maslow, as well as Europeans like Freud, Jung, and Piaget.

[4]The topic of the human will is illuminating, for it was a major controversy around the turn of the century because of a clash between religious (or metaphysical) and "agnostic" worldviews (e.g., see James, 1890). But it is clear which worldview won out; by 1930 there was virtually no reference to the human will in mainstream psychological literature, a neglect that has continued to the present, though over the past fifteen years *action* has again become a focus of some research..

ence, and the field virtually died out for nearly a half century.

Simultaneous with these developments was a veritable revolution in the treatment of the soul: psychoanalysis. Whereas pastors, priests, spiritual directors, and rabbis had cared for the souls of Christians and Jews for centuries, this controversial new approach to the soul offered a disturbing but profound analysis of what was wrong with humans and how to help. Besides its intellectual complexity, sophistication, and alluring examination of the mysterious unconscious realm, this approach distinguished itself from pastoral care with its alleged empirical basis and by its lack of reference to supernatural causes or cures. Though increasingly criticized in coming decades, psychoanalysis was originally viewed by modernists as consistent with natural scientific methods and so was seen as largely compatible with the secular clinical psychology that was just getting started in America (in the work of people like Witmer, 1907; Beers, 1908; Munsterberg, 1909; and Prince, 1908, 1913). All of this was also occurring during the time when the modern American university was coming into its own and developing its own curriculum. Given the educational, social, and intellectual forces working at the time, the "new psychology," a modern, secular form of psychology and psychotherapy based ideally on empirical research alone, became institutionalized within the major academic settings of the day and accepted as the only legitimate versions of psychology and treatment for the soul (Danziger, 1979).

Christians and the New Psychology of the Twentieth Century

The "new" or *modern* psychology, then, was birthed through the union of a legitimate quest for empirically validated truth with a modernist worldview that separated psychology from theology and philosophy. This modern psychology strove to have all its assertions based on empirical research alone (Toulmin & Leary, 1985). As in many disciplines, Christians in psychology had to come to terms with this new, social-intellectual context. At first it took time for the new psychology to become widely recognized as a distinct discipline. However, psychology gradually became a part of the core curriculum in the social sciences at all major colleges and universities. Christian colleges participated in this change and typically began to offer courses in psychology in the 1920s and 1930s.

For the most part it appears that Christians offered few alternatives to these larger trends. Perhaps due to Common Sense Realism, Christians involved in psychology apparently shared some of the assumptions of modernism and practiced psychology according to the new rules. Probably the most distinct group of Christians in early modern psychology in America were Catholic. The earliest notable Catholic in the field was Edward Pace, a founding member of the APA, who began teaching psychology courses at the Catholic University of America in 1891, after having studied with Wundt (Misiak & Staudt, 1954; Roback, 1952). Catholics were apparently the first identifiable Christians who sought to provide texts that *supplemented* the literature of empirically based psychology with religiously grounded discussions on the person or soul (e.g., Brennan, 1937; Maher, 1918; Moore, 1924, 1939), though some Catholic voices rose in protest to the new psychology (Misiak & Staudt, 1954, pp. 4-7).

This supplemental activism was likely due in part to the Thomistic revival that began in the last decades of the nineteenth century and continued throughout the first half of the twentieth. The fact that Thomas Aquinas's corpus is psychologically rich, explicitly open to empirical research (à la Aristotle) and yet requires the use of philosophy (or reason) to deal with human nature in all its fullness led Catholics to augment the field of empirical psychology with additional philosophical considerations regarding topics like the will and soul-body relations.[5]

Protestants also gave some attention to psychology. But compared with conservatives (or fundamentalists), liberal Protestants (or modernists) appear to have been much more open to reflecting on the relation of psychology and the faith. G. T. Ladd (1915, 1918) may have been the first theological liberal to develop a body of work that explored religion in light of

---

[5]The Catholics Misiak and Staudt (1954) defend this approach, agreeing with modern disciplinary divisions and seeing psychology, philosophy, and theology as methodologically distinct, though forming a hierarchy of knowledge. On that basis they argue against a specifically Catholic (and by implication, Christian) psychology: "When psychologists confine themselves to the study of human behavior, as it can be experimentally studied, they are merely restricting their field of inquiry; they are not necessarily denying the existence of the soul" (p. 13). However, they also state that Catholics "will always endeavor to integrate psychology, philosophy, and theology" (p. 14). But since the three disciplines all seek the truth from different vantage points (theology through revelation, philosophy through reason, and psychology through observation), there will be no genuine contradiction between them.

the new psychology, but his work appears to have had little influence. Within a few decades mainline Protestants (most notably Boisen [1936, 1955]) began to explore the value of depth psychologies for the church. At the same time they also felt called to undermine the pervasive naturalism out of which modern psychology originated, eventually forming a large literature (e.g., Clinebell, 1966; Hiltner, 1943, 1958; Oates, 1962; Thornton, 1964). The Clinical Pastoral Education (CPE) movement that was inspired by this work has trained thousands of mainline ministers in pastoral care from mid-century to the present. Generally speaking, however, liberal Protestants who had been shaped by and supportive of some of the themes of modernism in practice seemed to view the relation of faith and psychology as largely one-directional. They saw modern psychology as aiding in a reconstruction of the faith along the lines suggested by modern values (greater individualism, softened personal morality, reason/science more authoritative than biblical revelation)[6] (cf. Oden, 1984). This general orientation has continued to the present (e.g., Browning, 1966, 1987; Capps, 1990; Howe, 1995), with greater sophistication and more willingness to critique mainstream psychology (e.g., Browning, 1987) but still with a greater openness to contemporary values and thought and a greater skepticism toward the Bible than seems compatible with historic Christianity.

During the first half of this century, there is not much evidence of conservative Christians thinking distinctively about psychology. Fundamentalists by and large were not interested in cultural issues, higher learning, and scholarship (Noll, 1994). A few Christians criticized the new psychology for its materialism and agnosticism (e.g., Wickham, 1928). And a few isolated works can be found that take the new psychology seriously but argue for a Christian perspective (e.g., Murray, 1938; Norlie, 1924). But for the most part conservatives were moving away from intellectual engagement with the wider culture, which they saw as spiritually blind. In addition, fundamentalists tended to be practice-oriented if not anti-intellectual, more interested in soul-winning

---

[6]Interestingly, the founding members of the editorial board of the journal that originated out of this movement, *Pastoral Psychology*, included Hiltner and Oates as well as Rollo May and Carl R. Rogers, neither of whom could be considered orthodox Christians at the time, suggesting a kind of breadth unusual for a journal for pastors (editors are listed in Vande Kemp, 1984).

and missions than in claiming culture for Christ. They were for the most part separationists, desiring to avoid contamination by the world (including the world of ungodly thinking, e.g., at the universities). For most fundamentalists, learning the Bible is the primary goal of higher education (rather than learning about things like psychology). As a result, these Christians turned away from the more established colleges that had been Christian, but by the 1920s and 1930s were becoming more modernist in orientation, and began to form their own postsecondary educational institutions: Bible colleges.

Another factor that helps explain the lack of fundamentalist interest in psychology and counseling is that the movement had little interest in inner matters of the soul and its well-being. Though there are exceptions (e.g., in some of the movement's hymns), the bulk of fundamentalist publishing and church life focused more on cognitive (belief) matters and evangelism. The state of one's soul (so important to the Puritans) was largely overlooked. As a result, for decades pastoral care was left to more liberal Christians.

It really wasn't until after World War II that conservative Protestants began to move out of their cultural ghettos and think more seriously about how their faith bears on the sciences and arts. A group of fundamentalists began to grope for a more activist role in culture and higher learning, calling themselves evangelicals (Carpenter, 1997). And it was only in the 1950s that we find evangelicals beginning to engage psychology in any concerted way.

Early Evangelical Activity in Psychology

Hardly a revolutionary thinker, Hildreth Cross, head of the psychology department at Taylor University, in 1952 published *An Introduction to Psychology: An Evangelical Approach,* presenting psychology positively but "screened through the Word of God" (preface). Though simplistic by most standards, it nonetheless provided a text combining information from modern psychology with Christian interpretation and evaluation. Critical of evolution, it included many citations from the Bible and an affirmation of supernatural reality in human life while presenting somewhat superficially some of the main topics covered in any introduction to psychology: the nervous system, sensation, learning, motivation, maturation, and individual differences. The book concluded with a study of the "dynamic Christian personality," in which the influence of redemption on the human personality is described with explicit dependence on theology and Scripture.

A group of conservative Christians, practicing psychologists mostly from a Reformed theological persuasion, got together in 1954 and 1955 for conferences that explored the relation of psychology, psychiatry, and religion. In 1956 they formed the Christian Association for Psychological Studies (CAPS), continuing to hold conferences (which are still held annually) that explored how a person's faith relates to psychology, with most of the interest directed toward counseling. The identity of CAPS has broadened substantially beyond its original roots in the Reformed community.

Also in 1954, Clyde Narramore began a radio program called "Psychology for Living" that eventually played on over two hundred Christian stations nationally. In 1960 he published an influential book outlining a Christian approach to therapy that incorporated a high view of Scripture along with a Christianized form of the person-centered counseling of Carl Rogers. Even more explicit in his appreciation for a model of therapy that originated outside Christianity, Tweedie (1961) wrote a book critiquing but largely supportive of the view of persons and therapy found in the work of Viktor Frankl. Both of these books argue that psychotherapy has something to offer Christians and can be critically received in light of a Christian worldview.

Also around this time the works of Paul Tournier (1963, 1965) were being translated into English. Tournier was a physician-psychotherapist from Switzerland who was schooled in the Freudian and Jungian traditions and had converted to Christianity in midlife. The writings of this wise, seasoned Christian therapist proved to be eye-opening for many evangelicals hungry for literature that helped to sort out the deep goings-on in the soul from a Christian perspective (e.g., Collins, 1980).

Eventually, a number of evangelicals began to sense the need for advanced training in psychology shaped by a Christian worldview. Fuller Theological Seminary was the first evangelical school to begin a doctoral program in clinical psychology (1964), and Rosemead School of Psychology followed within a few years (1970) with impetus from Clyde Narramore and under the leadership of Bruce Narramore, his nephew.

Rosemead also initiated the *Journal of Psychology and Theology* in 1973, providing the first academic forum for evangelicals in psychology. In some ways the 1970s were a turning point for evangelicals in psychology. Increasingly, books were being written by evangelicals that dealt with psychological topics or counseling, applying insights and techniques derived from modern psychology to such topics as child-rearing, marriage, self-esteem, and personal and spiritual growth (e.g., Collins, 1972, 1976; Dobson, 1974; LaHaye, 1971; Narramore, 1978; Schuller, 1978; Wagner, 1975; Wright, 1974).

The Biblical Counseling Model
Yet the decade began with a dark cloud over this whole endeavor. Jay Adams, professor of practical theology at Westminster Theological Seminary, published the widely read *Competent to Counsel* (1970) in which he severely criticized psychiatry and psychotherapy, suggesting that they provided approaches to counseling that were radically secular and fundamentally opposed to Christianity. Adams therefore urged Christians to repudiate such humanistic methods. In his own model, "nouthetic counseling" (Greek *noutheteō*, "to admonish"), he taught that genuine Christian counseling is based solely on the Bible and focused on sin (the cause of most psychological problems). He also believed that pastors should be the primary counselors in the Christian community. Adams founded the Christian Counseling and Educational Foundation in 1968 and the *Journal of Pastoral Practice* in 1977, to help the church meet counseling needs biblically.

His numerous books (e.g., 1973, 1977, 1979) and their aggressive style stimulated some and enraged others. They mobilized still others to counsel in strict accordance with Scripture, devoid of the influence of secular thought (at least ostensibly). This latter group also criticized the efforts of Christian counselors who they felt were synthesizing Christianity with secular thought (Bobgan & Bobgan, 1979, 1987; Ganz, 1993; MacArthur, 1991; MacArthur & Mack, 1994). Supportive organizations developed, like the National Association of Nouthetic Counselors and the International Association of Biblical Counselors, and a number of seminaries began offering counseling programs that centered on the use of the Bible in counseling theory and practice (e.g., The Master's College and Seminary). Eventually the movement made more clear its central focus by changing the name of the approach from "nouthetic" to simply "biblical" counseling (indicated by the name change of the *Journal of Pastoral Practice* to *Journal of Biblical Counseling* in 1993 and books like MacArthur & Mack, 1994). The movement is by no means monolithic; differences of approach and substance are obvious from a casual reading of these authors.

Nevertheless many Christian psychologists, counselors, and therapists continued to find this initiative unpersuasive. For one thing, many of them were doing their counseling outside the church, often working with individuals with little or no religious faith and on problems that seemed to receive scant treatment in the Scriptures; they found the challenge to use the Bible *alone* unhelpful. For another, most of these Christians had enough exposure to modern psychology to conclude that it had some value. Christian psychology teachers and researchers in particular saw in modern psychology much validity in its attempts to describe human nature. Therefore they found the biblical counseling critique overly biased or simplistic. This led some Christians to label the biblical counseling movement "antipsychology" (e.g., Beck & Banks, 1992). Moreover, some have seen firsthand that Bible-believing churches have not always cared well for the souls of its people (something also acknowledged by those in the nouthetic movement). They were appreciative of the help being offered by modern therapy.

Two other evangelical approaches were articulated during the 1970s. One was developed by Christian psychological professionals who sensed some truth in the critiques of the biblical counseling movement. They too were concerned with the naturalism and secular humanism that shaped the psychological and counseling literature, and knew Christianity (and its theology) had something unique to contribute to psychology and counseling, but they believed that modern psychology also had real value and that therefore the fields of theology and psychology needed to be related. The second group, composed largely of researchers and professors, were more uniformly appreciative of modern psychology as it is. We'll begin with this latter approach.

The Levels-of-Explanation Model

The "levels-of-explanation" approach underscores the distinction between the domains (or "levels") of psychology and theology (Jeeves, 1976;

Mackay, 1979; Myers, 1978). Influenced by the physicist Richard Bube (1971), they maintain that all levels of reality are important (the physical, chemical, biological, psychological, social, and theological), that each dimension or level of reality is uniquely accessible to study by the unique methods used in each discipline and that the boundaries of each should not be blurred. To confuse these levels of reality results in a misunderstanding of reality and a confusion of things quite different. Furthermore, the understanding of each of the different levels is assumed to offer a distinct perspective that is essentially independent of the understandings of other levels. Hence, this approach is often called perspectivalism (Evans, 1977). Theology and psychology, in particular, use different methods of investigation, have different objects of study and answer different questions. Confusing them would distort both (though its proponents encourage interdisciplinary dialogue "after hours" in order to get the fullest picture of human nature possible). They are also less concerned with the effects of secular modernism on psychology, for they believe strongly that science properly conducted goes a long way toward eliminating such bias. To bring theological matters into the science of psychology would only undermine the objectivity and integrity of the scientific method.

Significantly, most of the proponents of this approach have been academics, Christians teaching at both Christian and non-Christian colleges and universities. Some of them have done research on subjects like the human brain, where it is hard to conceive of a distinctly Christian approach that would make any difference. On the contrary, there has been concern in this group that true science will be impeded by the intrusion of faith beliefs from *any* quarter that cannot be empirically documented. Science can only proceed on the basis of an objective study of reality that is accessible to direct observation which can be replicated by any interested investigators.[7]

The Integration Model
The other approach alluded to above, more common among those

---

[7]Recently Jeeves (1997) has published his latest thoughts, *Human Nature at the Millennium*, continuing to use this approach. Also of interest, Hunsberger (1995) has written a book in pastoral care that essentially assumes a levels-of-explanation position.

involved in applied psychology, sought to underscore what the domains of psychology and theology hold in common. In different ways, both disciplines cover the nature of human beings, how humans develop, what has gone wrong with humans and how humans can overcome what has gone wrong. So some of these authors attempted to study the overlap between the domains, while others more ambitiously attempted to *integrate* the two where possible (Carter & Narramore, 1979; Collins, 1977, 1981; Crabb, 1975, 1977). In the latter approach, the goal of the Christian psychologist is "to combine the special revelation of God's word with the general revelation studied by the psychological sciences and professions" (Narramore, 1973, p. 17), or to place psychology on a different foundation, one that is "consistent with and built upon the Bible" in order to develop a "biblically based psychology" (Collins, 1973, p. 26). As a result, contrary to the levels-of-explanation approach, the integration approach tends to be more willing to criticize psychology in its modern form and to ask whether its findings are genuinely compatible with Scripture.

In the context of both these kinds of intellectual support, Christians began flocking to psychology, with most going to secular graduate programs but many attending Christian institutions (including newer programs at the Psychological Studies Institute, Trinity Evangelical Divinity School, Wheaton College, George Fox College, Geneva College, and many others). By the 1980s Christian books in psychology were all the rage. Christian publishers were putting out ever more books dealing with psychological topics, especially "recovery" issues. Christian radio programs by evangelical psychologists like James Dobson, and Frank Minirth and Paul Meier were becoming popular and influential. In addition, Christian counseling and treatment centers quickly spread across America during this time. The CAPS organization also grew in numbers (from over one thousand in 1980 to about two thousand today) and in 1982 began producing its own scholarly publication, the *Journal of Psychology and Christianity* (a prior version called the *CAPS Bulletin* began in 1975). However, while CAPS membership originally was largely composed of evangelicals, some of the issues that the CAPS leadership wrestled with in the 1980s (e.g., homosexuality and male references to God) led a group of Christian counselors to start an organization that focused exclusively on counseling, and that was theologically more conservative—the American Association of Christian Counselors. Membership in this group has exploded to its present size of more than twenty-five thousand.[8]

The Christian Psychology Model

The most recent evangelical approach to relating one's faith to psychology was foreshadowed by Mary Stewart Van Leeuwen (1985), an academic social psychologist who offered strong criticism of mainstream psychology from a Christian standpoint, arguing for a psychology of human nature derived from a Christian view of the person rather than simply taking modern psychology "as it is." With a very different agenda but the same willingness to approach psychology Christianly, Catholic psychologist Paul Vitz (1987) did a thorough study of the letters and essays of Sigmund Freud, only to radically reinterpret Freud's story in light of Christian assumptions.[9] However, philosopher C. Stephen Evans (1989) was the first to argue for the development of a psychology substantively reshaped according to Christian character, beliefs, and goals (p. 132). Pointing to the recent renewal of Christian philosophy, he suggested that the field of psychology could be similarly transformed.[10]

Within the Christian counseling arena, Larry Crabb has seemed to be moving away from the integration approach found in his earlier work to embrace more fully the themes of a Christian theology of sanctification in his writing about psychological and spiritual growth (1987, 1993, 1999). In the same vein Crabb's former colleague Dan Allender has worked together with Old Testament theologian Tremper Longman III (1990, 1994, 1998) to produce three popular books that have explored psycho-

---

[8]CAPS has remained essentially an evangelical organization, but with a tolerance for some theological diversity.

[9]Vitz (1977) had earlier subjected some major modern personality theories to a radical Christian critique. However, contrary to authors of the biblical counseling movement, Vitz's work has always demonstrated a willingness to work within the larger discipline of psychology and psychotherapy.

[10]Alvin Plantinga is one of many contemporary Christian philosophers to advocate for a specifically Christian philosophy. See his "Advice for Christian Philosophers" (1984), *The Twin Pillars of Christian Scholarship* (1990), and *Warranted Christian Belief* (2000).

logical topics with an unusually strong theological underpinning. Crabb and Allender typify those who strive to have a Christian theological framework that more radically sets the agenda of their understanding of psychology and counseling without entirely repudiating a psychological focus (cf. also Langberg, 1997; Payne, 1995, 1996; White, 1982, 1987).

So this book provides an opportunity to explore four major positions evangelicals have taken regarding the relation of psychology and the Christian faith. Admittedly, there are many Christians in psychology who do not neatly fit into one of these categories. Nevertheless, these four approaches seem to represent the most distinctive, clearly articulated evangelical approaches to date.

One more thing should be said before concluding this historical section. A significant shift in the stance of American secular psychology toward religion occurred in the 1990s: religion has again become respectable. For example, increasingly, psychologies of religion are being published again, and topics like forgiveness, prayer, and religious values in counseling are being researched and reported in mainstream journals. Perhaps most significantly the American Psychological Association itself has recently published two books that vigorously make the case for dealing with religious issues in therapy (Richards & Bergin, 1997; Shafranske, 1996; notably, a number of evangelicals contributed chapters to the Shafranske book). What all this portends for the future of evangelicals in psychology is hard to say. At the very least, it suggests that in the twenty-first century it may be more acceptable to acknowledge one's own religious beliefs and perspective in psychological discourse than it was throughout most of the twentieth century (at least as long as these beliefs do not too seriously offend the postmodern sensibilities that have contributed to this new openness).

For the Student: Issues That Distinguish Christian Approaches to Psychology

There are at least three main issues that distinguish the approaches toward psychology and counseling represented in this book. Look for evidence of these topics as you read the chapters and responses. Perhaps the main issue concerns the possible *sources* of psychological knowledge: empirical research, Scripture and theology, philosophy, and history. Modern psychology self-consciously moved away from reliance on nonempirical sources (philosophy, theology, and Scripture) and redefined itself by restricting itself to the actual study of human beings (and animals). So while reading the following chapters, consider the extent that empirical research shapes the thinking of the author. How seriously does the author take psychological research, and does it inform his conclusions about things? What is the author's understanding of the role of the Bible and theology within psychology and counseling? All evangelicals affirm the value of the Bible for Christian belief and practice. However, differences exist in terms of (1) whether the Bible is relevant to the theory and practice of psychology and counseling and (2) if so, the extent to which the Bible's teachings should be allowed to shape psychological theories, research, and counseling practice. So ask yourself what role the Bible and theology actually play in the author's understanding of psychology and counseling. A similar but less prominent issue for evangelicals involves the explicit use of philosophical or historical reasoning in psychology. Is this even appropriate for a science like psychology, and if so, how much?

A second distinguishing theme is the degree to which the contributors are critical, even suspicious, of non-Christian psychologists and their work. Some Christians are very concerned about the influence of non-Christian thinking on Christians and work hard at uncovering the underlying secular biases they discern in the non-Christian texts they read. Other Christians are more trusting of non-Christian authors, emphasizing that truth can be discovered by anyone (particularly if the research is done with proper controls), so they reserve their Christian critique for explicit, antireligious statements. See if such differences in a "hermeneutics of trust and of suspicion" distinguish the contributors.

Third, does Christianity provide a distinctive view of human nature that should bear on psychological theory-building, research, and counseling practice? The goal of modern science has been to construct a universal understanding of things (like human nature) that can be agreed to by all interested parties willing to do the research and replicate studies. However, Christian phenomena like the image of God, sin, and the role of Holy Spirit in spiritual development cannot be studied by neutral observation; it requires faith to "see it." Consider how the contributors differ on whether there should be a distinctive Christian approach to psychology and counseling or whether Christians should work together with non-Christians.

One other point to keep in mind: As you read, notice *where* the disagreements between the contributors occur. Most Christian psychologists and counselors don't dispute the more basic observations of psychology (e.g., brain structure, visual perception, or animal learning; we might say, the first half of an introduction to psychology course) (Larzelere, 1980). Most of the disagreement concerns the more complex aspects of human nature: motivation, personality, psychopathology, psychotherapy, and social relations (the last half of the course). Why is that? How does this fact bear on the debate?

Introduction of the Authors

David G. Myers, psychology professor at Hope College, is the representative of the levels-of-explanation approach. Early in his career Dr. Myers won the Gordon Allport Prize for his studies of group influence. His scientific research has appeared in two dozen periodicals, from *Science* and the *American Scientist* to the *American Psychologist* and *Psychological Science*. Myers also has digested psychological research for the lay public through many articles and eleven books, the most recent of which is *The American Paradox: Spiritual Hunger in an Age of Plenty* (2000). Among students of psychology Dr. Myers is best known for his introductory psychology and social psychology texts, both of which are the best-selling texts in their fields. However, Myers has also given much thought to the relation between faith and psychology, writing *The Human Puzzle: Psychological Research and Christian Belief* (1978) where he developed the levels-of-explanation approach with reference to psychology. He later collaborated with Malcolm Jeeves on *Psychology Through the Eyes of Faith* (1987), published by the Coalition of Christian Colleges and Universities in their series of Christian supplemental texts for various college disciplines. He has also written other articles further developing this approach to psychology (1987, 1991, 1996).

For the integration position, Gary Collins was recruited. Since 1969 Dr. Collins has written over forty books exploring psychology from an integrationist standpoint. He was a contributor to the first issue of the *Journal of Psychology and Theology* (1973), and two of the most important books explaining the integration model were penned by him: *Rebuilding the Foundations: An Integration of Psychology and Christianity* (1977) and *Psychology and Theology: Prospects for Integration* (1981). He has edited a major series on counseling topics from a Christian standpoint, a thirty-volume set entitled Resources for Christian Counseling. He was, until recently, the executive director of the American Association of Christian Counselors, the largest group of evangelical counselors in the world.

Robert C. Roberts, distinguished professor of ethics at Baylor University, is the exponent of the Christian psychology approach. Previously he taught for sixteen years at Wheaton College in Illinois, where he was a member of both the philosophy and psychology departments. Dr. Roberts has written or edited seven books and over thirty-five articles in philosophy and Christian psychology journals, becoming recognized as an authority on the virtues and vices, and on Søren Kierkegaard. In 1993 he wrote *Taking the Word to Heart: Self and Other in an Age of Therapies,* which constructively engaged a number of secular therapies and offered some correctives from a decidedly Christian perspective. In 1994 he was awarded a Pew grant to work on topics like the personality, emotions, and virtues from a Christian standpoint and has since been writing a major work on the emotions that is just now nearing completion. More recently he edited (with Mark R. Talbot) *Limning the Psyche: Explorations in Christian Psychology* (1997) in which he also contributed three chapters, one of which outlines the major themes of what a distinctively Christian psychology would look like.

Finally, the biblical counseling approach has David Powlison for its spokesperson. Dr. Powlison has been the editor of the *Journal of Biblical Counseling* since 1992. Besides contributing many articles to that journal, he has also written chapters for a number of books, making advances in the theory of biblical counseling and enriching its critique of secular psychology and Christian counseling. He has also written *Power Encounters: Reclaiming Spiritual Warfare* (1995), which attempts to expound a biblical approach to spiritual warfare while raising questions about the ways some Christians have dealt with the topic in our day. Powlison has taught biblical counseling at Westminster Theological Seminary for nearly twenty years and has counseled at the Christian Counseling & Educational Foundation even longer. He also serves as a board member of the National Association of Nouthetic Counselors.

These, then, are the contributors. We hope you enjoy their conversation.

References

Adams, J. E. (1970). *Competent to counsel.* Phillipsburg, NJ: Presbyterian & Reformed.

Adams, J. E. (1973). *Christian counselor's manual.* Phillipsburg, NJ: Presbyterian & Reformed.

Adams, J. E. (1977). *Lectures on counseling.* Grand Rapids, MI: Baker.

Adams, J. E. (1979). *More than redemption.* Grand Rapids, MI: Baker.

Allen, G. W. (1967). *William James.* New York: Viking.

Allender, D. B., & Longman, T., III. (1990). *Bold love.* Colorado Springs, CO: NavPress.

Allender, D. B., & Longman, T., III. (1994). *The cry of the soul: How our emotions reveal our deepest questions about God.* Colorado Springs, CO: NavPress.

Allender, D. B., & Longman, T., III. (1998). *Bold purpose.* Colorado Springs, CO: NavPress.

Amsel, A. (1969). *Judaism and psychology.* New York: Philipp Feldheim.

Beck, J. R., & Banks, J. W. (1992). Christian anti-psychology: Hints of an historical analogue. *Journal of Psychology and Theology, 20,* 3-10.

Beers, C. (1908). *A mind that found itself.* London: Longmans Green.

Bobgan, M., & Bobgan, B. (1979). *The psychological way/The spiritual way.* Minneapolis: Bethany Fellowship.

Bobgan, M., & Bobgan, B. (1987). *Psychoheresy: The psychological seduction of Christianity.* Santa Barbara, CA: Eastgate.

Bobgan, M., & Bobgan, B. (1997). *Against biblical counseling: For the Bible.* Santa Barbara, CA: Eastgate.

Boisen, A. T. (1936). *The exploration of the inner world.* Chicago: Willett, Clark.

Boisen, A. T. (1955). *Religion in crisis and custom.* New York: Harper & Bros.

Boring, E. G. (1950). *A history of experimental psychology.* New York: Century.

Brennan, R. E. (1937). *General psychology: An interpretation of the science of mind based on Thomas Aquinas.* New York: Macmillan.

Brett, G. S. (1912). *A history of psychology: Ancient and patristic.* London: George

Allen.

Brett, G. S. (1953). *Brett's history of psychology* (R. S. Peters, Ed.). London: George Allen & Unwin.

Brooke, J. H. (1991). *Science and religion: Some historical perspectives.* Cambridge: Cambridge University Press.

Browning, D. S. (1966). *Atonement and psychotherapy.* Philadelphia: Westminster.

Browning, D. S. (1987). *Religious thought and modern psychotherapies.* Philadelphia: Fortress.

Bube, R. (1971). *The human quest.* Waco, TX: Word.

Burnaby, J. (1938). *Amor Dei.* London: Hodder & Stoughton.

Burtchaell, J. T. (1998). *The dying of the light: The disengagement of colleges and universities from their Christian churches.* Grand Rapids, MI: Eerdmans.

Calvin, J. (1960). *Institutes of the Christian religion* (Vol. 1). (F. L. Battles, Trans.). Philadelphia: Westminster.

Cantin, S. (Ed.). (1948). *An outline of Thomistic psychology.* Quebec: Laval University Press.

Capps, D. (1990). *Reframing: A new method in pastoral care.* Minneapolis: Fortress.

Carpenter, J. (1997). *Revive us again: The reawakening of American fundamentalism.* New York: Oxford University Press.

Carter, J. D., & Narramore, B. (1979). *The integration of psychology and theology: An introduction.* Grand Rapids, MI: Zondervan.

Clinebell, H. J., Jr. (1966). *Basic types of pastoral counseling.* Nashville: Abingdon.

Coe, G. A. (1900). *The spiritual life: Studies in the science of religion.* New York: Fleming H. Revell.

Collins, G. R. (1972). *Effective counseling.* Carol Stream, IL: Creation House.

Collins, G. R. (1973). Psychology on a new foundation: A proposal for the future. *Journal of Psychology and Theology, 1,* 19-27.

Collins, G. R. (1976). *Living and growing together: Today's Christian family.* Waco, TX: Word.

Collins, G. R. (1977). *The rebuilding of psychology: An integration of psychology and Christianity.* Wheaton, IL: Tyndale.

Collins, G. R. (1980). Tournier's dialogue counseling. In G. Collins (Ed.), *Helping people grow: Practical approaches to Christian counseling* (pp. 55-80). Santa Ana, CA: Vision House.

Collins, G. R. (1981). *Psychology & theology: Prospects for integration.* Nashville: Abingdon.

Copenhaver, B. P. (1990). Natural magic, hermetism, and occultism in early modern science. In D. C. Lindberg and R. S. Westfall (Eds.), *Reappraisals of the scientific revolution* (pp. 261-302). New York: Cambridge University Press.

Crabb, L. J., Jr. (1975). *Basic principles of biblical counseling.* Grand Rapids, MI: Zondervan.

Crabb, L. J., Jr. (1977). *Effective biblical counseling.* Grand Rapids, MI: Zondervan.

Crabb, L. J., Jr. (1987). *Inside out.* Colorado Springs, CO: NavPress.

Crabb, L. J., Jr. (1993). *Finding God.* Grand Rapids, MI: Zondervan.

Crabb, L. J., Jr. (1999). *The safest place on earth.* Waco, TX: Word.

Cross, H. (1952). *An introduction to psychology: An evangelical approach.* Grand Rapids, MI: Zondervan.

Cross, R. (1998). Aquinas on psychology. *Journal of Psychology and Christianity, 17,* 306-318.

Danziger, K. (1979). The social origins of modern psychology. In A. R. Buss (Ed.), *Psychology in social context* (pp. 27-46). New York: Irvington.

Daub. E. E. (1978). Demythologizing White's warfare of science with theology. *The American Biology Teacher, 40,* 553-556.

Diamond, S. (Ed.). (1974). *The roots of psychology: A sourcebook in the history of ideas.* New York: Basic Books.

Dilthey, W. (1989). *An introduction to the human sciences.* Princeton, NJ: Princeton University Press.

Dobson, J. (1974). *Hide or seek.* Old Tappan, NJ: Fleming H. Revell.

Draper, J. W. (1874). *History of the conflict between religion and science.* New York: D. Appleton.

Edwards, J. (1754/1957). *Freedom of the will* (P. Ramsey, Ed.). New Haven, CT: Yale University Press.

Edwards, J. (1746/1959). *Religious affections* (J. E. Smith, Ed.). New Haven, CT: Yale University Press.

Evans, C. S. (1977/1982). *Preserving the person: A look at the human sciences.* Grand Rapids, MI: Baker.

Evans, C. S. (1989). *Wisdom and humanness in psychology: Prospects for a Christian approach.* Grand Rapids, MI: Zondervan.

Evans, C. S. (1990). *Søren Kierkegaard's Christian psychology.* Grand Rapids, MI: Zondervan.

Farnsworth, K. E. (1985). *Whole-hearted integration.* Grand Rapids, MI: Baker.

Ganz, R. (1993). *Psychobabble: The failure of modern psychology—and the biblical alternative.* Wheaton, IL: Crossway.

Giorgi, A. (1970). *Psychology as a human science.* New York: Harper & Row.

Goodwin, R. N. (1998). *The hinge of the world: A drama.* New York: Farrar, Straus, Giroux.

Gregory the Great. (1950). *Pastoral care* (H. Davis, Trans.). Westminster, MD: Newman.

Harré, R., Clarke, D., & De Carlo, N. (1985). *Motives and mechanisms: An introduction to the psychology of action.* London: Methuen.

Hearnshaw, L. S. (1987). *The shaping of modern psychology.* London: Routledge & Kegan Paul.

Henry, P. (1960). *Saint Augustine on personality.* New York: Macmillan.

Hiltner, S. (1943). *Religion and health.* New York: Macmillan.

Hiltner, S. (1958). *Preface to pastoral theology.* Nashville: Abingdon.

Hindson, E., & Eyrich, H. (Eds.). (1997). *Totally sufficient: The Bible and Christian counseling.* Eugene, OR: Harvest House.

Hitchcock, J. (1982). *What is secular humanism?* Ann Arbor, MI: Servant.

Hothersall, D. (1984). *History of psychology.* Philadelphia: Temple University.

Howe, L. T. (1995). *The image of God: A theology for pastoral care and counseling.* Nashville: Abingdon.

Hunsberger, D. V. D. (1995). *Theology and pastoral counseling: A new interdisciplinary approach.* Grand Rapids, MI: Eerdmans.

Huxley, T. H. (1893). The origin of species. In T. H. Huxley (Ed.), *Collected essays, Volume II, Darwiniana* (pp. 22-79). London: MacMillan.

James, W. (1890). *Principles of psychology.* New York: Henry Holt.

James, W. (1903). *The varieties of religious experience.* New York: Longmans, Green.

Jeeves, M. (1976). *Psychology and Christianity: The view both ways.* Downers Grove, IL: InterVarsity Press.

Jeeves, M. (1997). *Human nature at the millennium: Reflections on the integration of psychology and Christianity.* Grand Rapids, MI: Baker.

Johnson, E. L. (1998). Some contributions of Augustine to a Christian psychology. *Journal of Psychology and Christianity, 17,* 293-305.

Johnson, E. L., & Sandage, S. (1999). A postmodern reconstruction of psychotherapy: Religion, orienteering, and the healing of the soul. *Psychotherapy, 36,* 1-15.

Jones, A. (1985). *Soul making: The desert way of spirituality.* San Francisco: HarperCollins.

Jones, S. (1994). A constructive relationship for religion with the science and profession of psychology: Perhaps the boldest model yet. *American Psychologist, 49* (3), 184-199.

Jones, S., & Butman, R. (1991). *Modern psychotherapies: A comprehensive Christian appraisal.* Downers Grove, IL: InterVarsity Press.

Kierkegaard, S. (1844/1980a). *The concept of anxiety* (R. Thomte & A. B. Anderson, Trans.). Princeton, NJ: Princeton University Press.

Kierkegaard, S. (1848/1980b). *The sickness unto death* (H. V. Hong & E. H. Hong, Trans.). Princeton, NJ: Princeton University Press.

Ladd, G. T. (1887). *Elements of physiological psychology.* New York: Charles Scribner's Sons.

Ladd, G. T. (1915). *What may I hope? An inquiry into the sources and reasonableness of the hopes of humanity, especially the social and religious.* New York and London: Longmans, Green.

Ladd, G. T. (1918). *The secret of personality: The problem of man's personal life as viewed in the light of an hypothesis of man's religious faith.* New York and London: Longmans, Green.

LaHaye, T. (1971). *Transformed temperaments.* Wheaton, IL: Tyndale House.

Langberg, D. M. (1997). *Counseling survivors of sexual abuse.* Wheaton, IL: Tyndale House.

Larzelere, R. E. (1980). The task ahead: Six levels of integration of Christianity and psychology. *Journal of Psychology and Theology, 8,* 3-11.

Leahey, T. H. (1997). *A history of psychology: Main currents in psychological thought* (4th ed.). Upper Saddle River, NJ: Prentice Hall.

Leuba, J. H. (1912). *A psychological study of religion: Its origin, function, and future.* New York: Macmillan, 1912.

Lindberg, D. C., & Numbers, R. L. (1986). Introduction. In D. C. Lindberg & R. L. Numbers (Eds.), *God and nature: Historical essays on the encounter between Christianity and science* (pp. 1-18). Berkeley: University of California Press.

MacArthur, J. (1991). *Our sufficiency in Christ.* Dallas: Word.

MacArthur, J., & Mack, W. A. (Eds.). (1994). *Introduction to biblical counseling.* Dallas: Word.

MacIntyre, A. (1990). *Three rival versions of moral enquiry: Encyclopaedia, genealogy, and tradition.* South Bend, IN: University of Notre Dame Press.

Mackay, D. M. (1979). *Human science and human dignity.* London: Hodder & Stoughton.

Maher, M. (1918). *Psychology: Empirical and rational* (9th ed.). Longmans, Green.

Marsden, G. (1994). *The soul of the American university.* Oxford: Oxford University Press.

Maslow, A. (1968). *Toward a psychology of being.* New York: D. Van Nostrand.

McCosh, J. (1886). *Psychology: The cognitive powers.* New York: Charles Scribner's Sons.

McCosh, J. (1887). *Psychology: The motive powers.* New York: Charles Scribner's Sons.

McNeill, J. T. (1951). *A history of the cure of souls.* New York: Harper & Row.

Misiak, H., & Staudt, V. G. (1954). *Catholics in psychology: A historical survey.* New York: McGraw-Hill.

Moore, T. V. (1924). *Dynamic psychology.* Philadelphia: Lippincott.

Moore, T. V. (1939). *Cognitive psychology.* Philadelphia: Lippincott.

Munsterberg, H. (1909). *Psychotherapy.* New York: Moffat, Yard.

Murray, J. A. C. (1938). *An introduction to a Christian psycho-therapy.* Edinburgh: T & T Clark.

Myers, D. G. (1978). *The human puzzle: Psychological research and Christian belief.* New York: Harper & Row.

Myers, D. G. (1987). Yin and yang in psychological research and Christian belief. *Faith and Thought, 13,* 33-52.

Myers, D. G. (1991). Steering between the extremes: On being a Christian scholar within psychology. *Christian Scholar's Review, 20,* 376-383.

Myers, D. G. (1996). On professing psychological science and Christian faith. *Journal of Psychology and Christianity, 15,* 143-149.

Myers, D. G. (2000). *The American paradox: Spiritual hunger in an age of plenty.* New Haven, CT: Yale University Press.

Myers, D. G., & Jeeves, M. (1987). *Psychology through the eyes of faith.* San Francisco: Harper & Row.

Narramore, B. (1973). Perspectives on the integration of psychology and theology. *Journal of Psychology and Theology, 1,* 3-17.

Narramore, B. (1978). *You're someone special.* Grand Rapids, MI: Zondervan.

Narramore, C. M. (1960). *The psychology of counseling: Professional techniques for pastors, teachers, youth leaders, and all who are engaged in the incomparable art of counseling.* Grand Rapids, MI: Zondervan.

Noll, M. (1994). *The scandal of the evangelical mind.* Grand Rapids, MI: Eerdmans.

Norlie, O. M. (1924). *An elementary Christian psychology.* Minneapolis, MN: Augsburg.

Nussbaum, M. C. (1994). *The therapy of desire: Theory and practice in Hellenistic ethics.* Princeton, NJ: Princeton University Press.

Oates, W. (1962). *Protestant pastoral counseling.* Philadelphia: Westminster Press.

Oden, T. C. (1984). *Care of souls in the classic tradition.* Theology and Pastoral

Care (D. S. Browning, Ed.). Philadelphia: Fortress.

Oden, T. C. (1989). *Pastoral counsel.* Classical Pastoral Care (Vol. 3.) New York: Crossroad.

Payne, L. (1995). *The healing presence: Curing the soul through union with Christ.* Grand Rapids, MI: Baker.

Payne, L. (1996). *Healing homosexuality.* Grand Rapids, MI: Baker.

Pippin, R. B. (1991). *Modernism as a philosophical problem: On the dissatisfactions of European high culture.* London: Basil Blackwell.

Plantinga, A. (1984). Advice to Christian philosophers. *Faith and Philosophy, 1,* 253-271.

Plantinga, A. (1990). *The twin pillars of Christian scholarship.* Grand Rapids, MI: Calvin College and Seminary.

Plantinga, A. (2000). *Warranted Christian belief.* New York: Oxford University Press.

Porter, N. (1869). *The human intellect, with an introduction upon psychology and the soul.* New York: Charles Scribner.

Pratt, J. B. (1907). *The psychology of religious belief.* New York: Macmillan.

Prince, M. (1908). The unconscious. *Journal of Abnormal Psychology, 3,* 261-297.

Prince, M. (1913). *The dissociation of a personality: A biographical study in abnormal psychology.* London: Longmans, Green.

Richards, P. S., & Bergin, A. E. (1997). *A spiritual strategy for counseling and psychotherapy.* Washington, DC: American Psychological Association.

Roback, A. A. (1952). *History of American psychology.* New York: Library Publishers.

Robinson, D. N. (1981). *An intellectual history of psychology* (2nd ed.). New York: Macmillan.

Rosenau, P. M. (1992). *Post-modernism and the social sciences.* Princeton, NJ: Princeton University Press.

Russell, C. A. (1985). *Cross-currents: Interactions between science and faith.* Leicester, England: Inter-Varsity Press.

Schuller, R. (1978). *Discover self-love.* Eugene, OR: Harvest House.

Shafranske, E. (Ed.). (1996). *Religion and the clinical practice of psychotherapy.* Washington, DC: American Psychological Association.

Shea, W. R. (1986). Galileo and the church. In D. C. Lindberg & R. L. Numbers (Eds.), *God and nature: Historical essays on the encounter between Christianity and science* (pp. 114-135). Berkeley: University of California Press.

Spilka, B. (1987). Religion and science in early American psychology. *Journal of Psychology and Theology, 15,* 3-9.

Starbuck, E. D. (1899). *The psychology of religion: An empirical study of the growth of religious consciousness.* New York: Scribners.

Stewart, C. (1998). *Cassian the monk.* Oxford: Oxford University Press.

Thornton, E. E. (1964). *Theology and pastoral counseling.* Engelwood Cliffs, NJ: Prentice-Hall.

Toulmin, S., & Leary, D. E. (1985). The cult of empiricism in psychology, and beyond. In S. Koch & D. E. Leary (Eds.), *A century of psychology as science* (pp. 594-617). New York: McGraw-Hill.

Tournier, P. (1963). *The strong and the weak.* Philadelphia: Westminster.

Tournier, P. (1965). *The healing of persons.* New York: Harper & Row.

Turner, J. (1985). *Without God, without creed: The origins of unbelief in America.* Baltimore: Johns Hopkins University Press.

Tweedie, D. F., Jr. (1961) *Logotherapy and the Christian faith: An evaluation of Frankl's existential approach to psychotherapy from a Christian viewpoint.* Grand Rapids, MI: Baker.

Vande Kemp, H. (1984). *Psychology and theology in western thought: 1672-1965: A historical and annotated bibliography.* Millwood, NY: Kraus.

Vande Kemp, H. (1998). Christian psychologies for the twenty-first century: Lessons from history. *Journal of Psychology and Christianity, 17,* 197-204.

Van Leeuwen, M. S. (1982). *Sorcerer's apprentice: A Christian looks at the changing face of psychology.* Downer's Grove, IL: InterVarsity Press.

Van Leeuwen, M. S. (1985). *The person in psychology.* Grand Rapids, MI: Eerdmans.

Vitz, P. (1994). *Psychology as religion: The cult of self-worship.* Grand Rapids, MI: Eerdmans.

Vitz, P. (1987). *Sigmund Freud's Christian unconscious.* New York: Guilford.

Wagner, M. (1975). *The sensation of being somebody: Building an adequate self-concept.* Grand Rapids, MI: Zondervan.

Ward, S. C. (1996). *Reconfiguring truth: Postmodernism, science studies, and the search for a new model of knowledge.* Lanham, MD: Rowman & Littlefield.

Watson, J. B. (1925). *Behaviorism.* New York: People's Institute.

Watson, R. I., & Evans, R. B. (1991). *The great psychologists: A history of psychological thought.* New York: HarperCollins.

Wetzel, J. (1992). *Augustine and the limits of virtue.* Cambridge: Cambridge University Press.

White, A. D. (1896). *A history of the warfare of science with theology in Christendom* (2 Volumes). New York: D. Appleton.

White, J. (1982). *The masks of melancholy.* Downers Grove, IL: InterVarsity Press.

White, J. (1987). *Putting the soul back into psychology: When secular values ignore spiritual realities.* Downers Grove, IL: InterVarsity Press.

Wickham, H. (1928). *The misbehaviorists.* New York: Dial Press.

Witmer, L. (1907). Clinical psychology. *Psychological Clinic, 1,* 1-9.

Wright, H. N. (1974). *The living marriage: Lessons in love from the Living Bible.* Old Tappan, NJ: Fleming H. Revell.

2   A Levels-of-Explanation View

David G. Myers

During psychology's first century its definitions have varied. For William James (*The Principles of Psychology*, 1890) psychology was the science of mental life. By the mid-twentieth century it had become the science of behavior. Today we synthesize this history by defining psychology as the science of behavior and mental processes.

Across the waxing and waning of behaviorism these definitions of psychology have shared one thing in common: psychology is a *science*. After noting a kinship between the spirits of science and of faith, I will illustrate how psychological science has often affirmed and occasionally challenged biblical understandings of human nature and of the significance of faith.*

Science and Faith

Many secularists and Christians alike see science and faith as competing systems of explanation—natural versus supernatural. One side tells us to beware those skeptical, heathen scientists; the other, those naive, judgmental fundamentalists. When our ancestors came to see bolts of lightning as acts of nature, they ceased seeing them as acts of God. When our contemporaries came to see humans as a product of evolutionary history, they often ceased viewing them as special creatures of God. Science and

---

*Parts of this chapter are adapted from Myers (1991, 1994, 1995, 1996, 1999, 2000a, b) and Myers and Jeeves (1989).

religion, it seems, sit on opposite ends of an explanatory teeter-totter.

Actually, say some historians of science, many of the founders of modern science were people whose religious convictions made them humble before nature and skeptical of human authority (Hooykaas, 1972; Merton, 1938). The Christian convictions of Blaise Pascal, Francis Bacon, Isaac Newton, and even Galileo led them to distrust human intuition, explore God's creation, and submit their ideas to the test. Whether searching for truth in the book of God's Word or the book of God's works, they viewed themselves in God's service. Speaking on my campus, Francis Collins concluded his explanation of the Human Genome Project, which he directs, by quoting Copernicus: "To know the mighty works of God; to comprehend His wisdom and majesty and power; to appreciate, in degree, the wonderful working of His Laws, surely all this must be a pleasing and acceptable mode of worship to the most High, to whom ignorance cannot be more grateful than knowledge."

If, as previously supposed, nature is sacred (e.g., if nature is alive with river goddesses and sun gods), then we ought not tamper with it. But if, as the scientific pioneers assumed, it is an intelligible creation, a work to be enjoyed and managed, then let us seek its truths by observing and experimenting. And let us do so freely, knowing that our ultimate allegiance is not to human doctrine but to God alone. Let us humbly test our ideas. If nature does not conform to our presumptions, so much the worse for our presumptions. Disciplined, rigorous inquiry—checking our theories against reality—is part of what it means to love God with our minds.[1]

These attitudes of humility before the created world and skepticism of human ideas also underlie psychological science. The Christian psychologist, neuroscientist Donald MacKay argued, "is to 'tell it like it is,' knowing that the Author is at our elbow, a silent judge of the accuracy with which we claim to describe the world He has created" (1984). If God is the ultimate author of whatever truth psychological science glimpses, then I can accept that truth, however surprising or unsettling. Disciplined scientific inquiry becomes not just my right but my religious duty.

---

[1]"You shall love the Lord your God with all your heart, and with all your soul, and with all your mind" (Mt 22:37 NRSV).

Psychological science and hidden values. Many postmodernists, Marxists, and fundamentalists resist such openness to psychological science. They say that psychology is so ideologically loaded that we should not swallow it uncritically. Being wary of hidden presuppositions and values, they would prefer we squeeze psychology into the contours of feminist, Marxist, or Christian ideology. Rather than mirroring the real world, say postmodernists, scientific concepts are socially constructed fictions. Intelligence, for instance, is a concept we humans created and defined. Because personal values guide theory and research, truth becomes personal and subjective. In questing for truth, we follow our hunches, our biases, our cultural bent.

Psychological scientists agree that many important questions lie beyond the reach of science, and they agree that personal beliefs often shape perceptions. But they also believe that there is a real world out there and that we advance truth by checking our hunches against it. Madame Curie did not just construct the concept of radium, she *discovered* radium. It really exists. In the social sciences, pure objectivity, like pure righteousness, may be unattainable, but should we not pursue it as an ideal? Better to humble ourselves before reliable evidence than to cling to our presumptions.

The list of popular beliefs that have crashed against a wall of observations is long and growing. No longer do many of us believe that sleepwalkers are acting out their dreams, that hypnosis uncovers long-buried memories, that our two cerebral hemispheres are functionally equivalent, that newborns are dumb to the world, that traumatic experiences tend to be massively repressed but recoverable much later, or that electroconvulsive therapy is a barbaric and ineffective treatment for profound depression.

Still, psychology's critics score points. Although psychological science helps us answer some important questions, it cannot answer all questions. "Bear in mind psychology's limits," I remind students:

> Don't expect it to answer the ultimate questions posed by Russian novelist Leo Tolstoy (1904): "Why should I live? Why should I do anything? Is there in life any purpose which the inevitable death that awaits me does not undo and destroy?" Instead, expect that psychol-

ogy will help you understand why people think, feel, and act as they do. Then you should find the study of psychology both fascinating and useful. (Myers, 1998, p. 5)

Moreover, values indeed guide our research and reporting. Ironically, it is experiments—on "confirmation bias," "belief perseverance," "mental set," and the "overconfidence phenomenon"—that most convincingly demonstrate their point: *belief guides perception.* When first viewing the "canals" on Mars through telescopes, some astronomers and writers perceived them as the product of intelligent life. They were, but the intelligence was on the viewing end of the telescope. To believe is to see. Moreover, whether hidden or explicit, our values leak through our choice of topics, our examples and emphases, and our labeling of phenomena.

Consider the values hidden in our terminology. Should we call sexually restrained people "erotophobic" or "sexually conservative"? Should we label those who say nice things about themselves on personality tests as having "high self-esteem" or "defensive"? Should we congratulate socially responsive people for their "social sensitivity" or disparage them for their tractable "conformity"? (Reflecting our culture's individualistic values, American psychology values the independent self rather than the interdependent self valued in many Asian and Third World cultures.) Without discarding scientific rigor, we can rightly expose psychology's value-ladenness in our teaching.

Ergo, neither psychological science nor our reporting of it is dispassionate. Our preconceived ideas and values—our schemas—guide our theory development, our interpretations, our topics of choice, and our language. In questing for truth we follow our hunches, our biases, our voices within. Perusing our results we are at times like the many voters who while observing presidential debates perceive their own predebate views confirmed. As C. S. Lewis noted, "What we learn from experience depends on the kind of philosophy we bring to experience" (1947, p. 11). Similarly, we teachers and authors cannot leave our values at home. In deciding *what* to report and *how* to report it, our own sympathies subtly steer us.

Being mindful of hidden values within psychological science should motivate us to clean the cloudy spectacles through which we view the world. Knowing that no one is immune to error and bias, we can be wary of absolutizing human interpretations of either natural or biblical data. We can steer between the two extremes of being naive about a value-laden psychology that pretends to be value-neutral, and being tempted to an unrestrained subjectivism that dismisses evidence as nothing but collected biases. In the ever reforming spirit of humility we can put testable ideas to the test. If we think capital punishment does or does not deter crime more than other available punishments, we can utter our personal opinions, as has the U.S. Supreme Court. Or we can ask whether states with a death penalty have lower homicide rates, whether their rates have dropped after instituting the death penalty, and whether they have risen when abandoning the penalty. In checking our personal predictions against reality we emulate the empiricism of Moses: "If a prophet speaks in the name of the LORD and what he says does not come true, then it is not the LORD's message" (Deut 18:22 TEV).

Psychological science and spiritual awe. So far I have suggested that people of faith, mindful of the limits of human reason and intuition, can embrace psychological science as one way to explore the human creature. There is another reason why people of faith can welcome rather than fear the advance of psychological science. The sense of awe and wonder that is at the core of the religious impulse—that bewildered sense that, as J. B. S. Haldane (1928) said, "the universe is not only queerer than we suppose, but queerer than we can suppose"—comes more genuinely from science than pseudoscience.

Consider how we perceive the world. What is truly extraordinary is not extrasensory perception, claims for which inevitably dissolve upon investigation.[2] What is extraordinary is rather our very ordinary moment-to-moment sensory experiences of organizing formless neural impulses into colorful sights and meaningful sounds.

Think about it. As you look at someone, particles of light energy are

---

[2]The repeated scientific debunking of claims of paranormal, supernatural human abilities (including telepathy, clairvoyance, precognition, past-life regression, and out-of-body frequent flyer programs) provides our first example of the congeniality of psychological science and biblical faith. The scientific refutation of New Age ideas about humans as extensions of God supports biblical presumptions about our human limits as finite creatures of God.

being absorbed by your eyes' receptor cells, converted into neural signals that activate neighboring cells, which down the line transmit a million electrochemical messages per moment up to your brain. There, separate parts of your brain process information about color, form, motion, and depth, and then—in some still mysterious way—combine this information to form a consciously perceived image that is instantly compared with previously stored images and recognized as, say, your grandmother. The whole process is as complex as taking a house apart, splinter by splinter, transporting it to a different location, and then through the efforts of millions of specialized workers, putting it back together. Voilà! The material brain gives rise to consciousness. That all of this happens instantly, effortlessly, and continuously is better than cool; it is truly bewildering. In explaining such phenomena I empathize with Job: "I have uttered what I did not understand, things too wonderful for me" (Job 42:3 NRSV).

Psychological Research and Christian Belief

Faith connects to psychological science not only by motivating scientific inquiry and sensitizing us to implicit values, but, as table 1 indicates, in other ways as well. We can, for example, make religion a dependent variable by studying the psychology *of* religion. (Why do some people take the leap of faith, while others do not?) We can make religion an independent variable by asking whether it predicts attitudes and behaviors. (Are people of faith noticeably more or less prejudiced? generous? happy?) And we can ask how insights into human nature gleaned from psychological research correspond to biblical and theological understandings: as when boring a tunnel from two directions, the excitement comes in discovering how close the two approaches are to connecting.

In times past, scholars connecting faith and psychology drew on the old personality theories; for example, they suggested that Freud's ideas of aggressive, narcissistic motivations complemented Calvin's idea of original sin. A newer approach relates big ideas from research in various fields of psychology to ancient religious understandings. In any academic field the results of tens of thousands of studies, the conclusions of thousands of investigators, the insights of hundreds of theorists, can usually be boiled down to a few overriding ideas. Biology offers us principles such as natural selection and adaptation. Sociology builds upon con-

INTEGRATION STRATEGY	PERSONAL EXAMPLES
1. *Faith motivates science.* Believing that "in everything we deal with God" (Calvin), and aiming to worship God with our minds, we can rigorously search God's world, seeking to discern its truths, while recognizing the limits of science.	1. Experiments on "group polarization" (exploring how group discussion changes and strengthens attitudes) 2. Reviewing studies of subjective well-being (who is happy?)
2. *Faith mandates skeptical scrutiny.* In the ever-reforming spirit of humility, we put testable claims to the test. This is the empiricism advocated by Moses: "If a prophet speaks in the name of the LORD but the thing does not take place or prove true, it is a word that the LORD has not spoken" (Deut 18:22).	1. Scrutinizing claims of the efficacy of intercessory prayer and faith healing 2. Reporting tests of New Age claims of reincarnation, channeling, fortune-telling, aura readings, telepathy, clairvoyance, astrology (and their implications of human godlike powers)
3. *Being true to one's deepest convictions and values.* Like everyone, we infuse certain assumptions and values into our teaching, writing, research, and practice.	Writings for Christian and secular audiences (e.g., Myers, 1998, 1999; Myers & Jeeves, 1987)
4. *Giving psychology to the church.* We can also *apply* psychology's insights to the church's life. For some, this means merging Christian and psychological insights pertinent to counseling and clinical practice.	Showing how social influence and memory principles might be applied in creating memorable, persuasive sermons and undertaking effective evangelism
5. *Relating psychological and religious descriptions of human nature.* We can map human nature from two directions, asking how well psychological and biblical understandings correlate.	Relating psychological research (in biological, developmental, cognitive, and social psychology) to Christian belief
6. *Studying determinants of religious experience.* The psychology of religion can explore influences on spirituality, religious commitment, charismatic behavior, etc. Who believes— and why?	Exploring parallels between (a) research on the interplay between attitudes and behavior, and (b) biblical-theological thinking about the interplay between faith and action
7. *Studying religion's effects.* Is faith a *predictor* of people's attitudes? emotions? behavior?	Summarizing links between faith and joy (religious commitment and self-reported life satisfaction and happiness)

Table 1. Seven ways to relate faith and psychology (adapted from Myers, 1995)

cepts such as social structure, cultural relativity, and societal organization. Music exploits our ideas of rhythm, melody, and harmony.

In my specialty of social psychology, what are the really big ideas? And how well do these big ideas about human nature connect with Judeo-Christian understandings? I discern four truths, actually four pairs of complementary truths. As Pascal reminded us three hundred years ago, no single truth is ever sufficient, because the world is not simple. Any truth separated from its complementary truth is a half-truth.

Rationality and irrationality. How "noble in reason" and "infinite in faculties" is the human intellect, rhapsodized Shakespeare's Hamlet. In some ways, indeed, our cognitive capacities are awesome. The three-pound tissue in our skulls contains circuitry more complex than all the telephone networks on the planet, enabling us to process information automatically or with great effort, to remember vast quantities of information, and to make snap judgments using rules of thumb called heuristics. One of the most human tendencies is our urge to explain behavior and therefore to make it seem orderly, predictable, and controllable. As intuitive scientists, we make our attributions efficiently and with enough accuracy for our daily needs.

Yes, Jewish and Christian theologians have long said, we are awesome. We are made in the divine image and given stewardship of the earth and its creatures. We are the summit of the Creator's work, God's own children.

Yet our explanations are vulnerable to error, insist social psychologists. In ways we are often unaware, our explanations and social judgments are vulnerable to error. When observing others we are sometimes too prone to be biased by our preconceptions. We "see" illusory relationships and causes. We treat people in ways that trigger their fulfilling our expectations. We are swayed more by vivid anecdotes than by statistical reality. We attribute others' behavior to their dispositions (e.g., presuming that someone who acts strangely must *be* strange). Failing to recognize such error in our thinking, we are prone to overconfidence.

Such conclusions have a familiar ring to theologians, who remind us that we are finite creatures of the one who declares "I am God, and there is none like me" and that "as the heavens are higher than the earth, so are my ways higher than your ways and my thoughts than your thoughts" (Is 46:9; 55:9 RSV). As God's children we have dignity but not deity. Thus we must be skeptical of those who claim for themselves godlike powers of omniscience (reading others' minds, foretelling the future), omnipresence (viewing happenings in remote locations), and omnipotence (creating or altering physical reality with mental power). We should be wary even of those who idolize their religion, presuming their doctrinal fine points to be absolute truth. Always, we see reality through a dim mirror.

Self-serving bias and self-esteem. Our self-understanding is a fragile container of truth. Heeding the ancient admonition to "know thyself," we analyze our behavior, but not impartially. Our tendency to self-serving bias appears in our differing explanations for our successes and failures, for our good deeds and bad. On any socially desirable dimension, we commonly view ourselves as relatively superior—as more ethical, socially skilled, and tolerant than our average peer. Moreover, we justify our past behaviors. We have an inflated confidence in the accuracy of our beliefs. We misremember our own past in self-enhancing ways. And we overestimate how virtuously we would behave in situations that draw less-than-virtuous behavior out of most people. Researcher Anthony Greenwald spoke for dozens of researchers: "People experience life through a self-centered filter" (1980, 1984).

That conclusion echoes a very old religious idea—that self-righteous pride is the fundamental sin, the original sin, the deadliest of the seven deadly sins. Thus the psalmist could declare that "no one can see his own errors" and the Pharisee could thank God "that I am not like other men" (and you and I can thank God that we are not like the Pharisee). Pride goes before a fall. It corrodes our relations with one another—conflicts between partners in marriage, management and labor, nations at war. Each side views its motives alone as pure, its actions beyond reproach. But so does its opposition, continuing the conflict.

Yet self-esteem pays dividends. Self-affirmation is often adaptive. It helps maintain our confidence and minimize our depression. To doubt our efficacy and to blame ourselves for our failures is a recipe for failure, loneliness, or dejection. People made to feel secure and valued exhibit less prejudice and contempt for others.

Again there is a religious parallel. To sense divine grace—the Christian parallel to psychology's "unconditional positive regard"—is to be liberated from both self-protective pride and self-condemnation. To feel profoundly affirmed, just as I am, lessens my need to define my self-worth in terms of achievements, prestige, or material and physical well-being. It is rather like insecure Pinocchio saying to his maker, Geppetto, "Papa, I am not sure who I am. But if I'm all right with you, then I guess I'm all right with me."

Attitudes and behavior. Studies during the 1960s shocked social psychologists with revelations that our attitudes sometimes lie dormant, overwhelmed by other influences. But follow-up research was reassuring. Our attitudes influence our behavior—when they are relevant and brought to mind. Thus our political attitudes influence our behavior in the voting booth. Our smoking attitudes influence our susceptibility to peer pressures to smoke. Change the way people think and, whether we call such persuasion "education" or "propaganda," the impact may be considerable.

If social psychology has taught us anything it is that the reverse is also true: We are as likely to act ourselves into a way of thinking as to think ourselves into action. We are as likely to believe in what we have stood up for as to stand up for what we believe. Especially when we feel responsible for how we have acted, our attitudes follow our behavior. This self-persuasion enables all sorts of people—political campaigners, lovers, even terrorists—to believe more strongly in that for which they have witnessed or suffered.

The realization that inner attitude and outer behavior, like chicken and egg, generate one another parallels the Judeo-Christian idea that inner faith and outer action likewise feed one another. Thus, faith is a source of action. Elijah is overwhelmed by the holy as he huddles in a cave. Paul is converted on the Damascus Road. Ezekiel, Isaiah, and Jeremiah undergo an inner transformation. In each case, a new spiritual consciousness produces a new pattern of behavior.

But faith is also a consequence of action. Throughout the Old and New Testaments, faith is nurtured by obedient action. The Hebrew word for *know* is usually an action verb, something one does. To *know* love, one must not only know about love, one must *act* lovingly. Philosophers and theologians note how faith grows as people act on what little faith they have. Rather than insist that people believe before they pray, Talmudic scholars would tell rabbis to get them to pray and their belief would follow. "The proof of Christianity really consists in 'following,'" declared Søren Kierkegaard (1851). To attain faith, said Pascal, "follow the way by which [the committed] began; by acting as if they believed, taking the holy water, having masses said, etc. Even this will naturally make you believe" (1670). C. S. Lewis concurred:

> Believe in God and you will have to face hours when it seems *obvious* that this material world is the only reality; disbelieve in Him and you must face hours when this material world seems to shout at you that it is not all. No conviction, religious or irreligious, will, of itself, end once and for all [these doubts] in the soul. Only the practice of Faith resulting in the habit of Faith will gradually do that. (1960)

Persons and situations. My final two-sided truth is that people and situations interact. We see this, first, in the evidence that social influences powerfully affect our behavior. As vividly shown in studies of conformity, role-playing, persuasion, and group influence, we are the creatures of our social worlds.

The most dramatic findings come from experiments that put well-intentioned people in evil situations to see whether good or evil prevailed. To a dismaying extent, evil pressures overwhelmed good intentions, inducing people to conform to falsehoods or capitulate to cruelty. Faced with a powerful situation, nice people often do not behave so nicely. Depending on the social context, most of us are capable of acting kindly or brutally, independently or submissively, wisely or foolishly. In one irony-laden experiment, most seminary students en route to recording an extemporaneous talk on the Good Samaritan parable failed to stop and give aid to a slumped, groaning person—if they had been pressed to hurry beforehand (Darley & Batson, 1973). External social forces shape our social behavior.

The social psychological concept of powers greater than the individual parallels the religious idea of transcendent good and evil (symbolized in the creation story as a seductive serpent) powers. Evil involves not only individual rotten apples here and there. It also is a product of "principalities and powers"—corrosive forces that can ruin a barrel of apples. And because evil is collective as well as personal, responding to it takes a communal religious life.

Although powerful situations may override people's individual dispositions, social psychologists do not view humans as passive tumbleweeds, blown this way and that by the social winds. Facing the same situation, different people may react differently, depending on their personality and culture. Feeling coerced by blatant pressure, they will sometimes react in ways that restore their sense of freedom. In a numerical minority, they will sometimes oppose and sway the majority. When they believe in themselves (maintaining an "internal locus of control") they sometimes work wonders. Moreover, people choose their situations—their college environments, their jobs, their locales. And their social expectations are sometimes self-fulfilling, as when they expect someone to be warm or hostile and the person becomes so. In such ways, we are the creators of our social worlds.

To most religious traditions, that rings true. We are morally responsible, accountable for how we use whatever freedom we have. What we decide matters. The stream of causation from past to future runs through our choices.

Faced with these pairs of complementary ideas, framed either psychologically or theologically, we are like someone stranded in a deep well with two ropes dangling down. If we grab either one alone we sink deeper into the well. Only when we hold both ropes can we climb out, because at the top, beyond where we can see, they come together around a pulley. Grabbing only the rope of rationality or irrationality, of self-serving pride or self-esteem, of attitude-first or behavior-first, of personal or situational causation, plunges us to the bottom of the well. So we grab both ropes, perhaps without fully grasping how they come together. In doing so, we may be comforted that in both science and religion accepting complementary principles is sometimes more honest than an oversimplified theory that ignores half the evidence. For the scissors of truth, we need both blades.

Psychological Science and Christian Values

Christians are predisposed not only to certain understandings of human nature but also to values such as committed love, joy, peace, and other "fruits of the Spirit." As followers of the one who bade children to come to him, Christians also tend to have a concern for the well-being of children and for the social ecology believed to nurture them (intact families, responsible media, healthy faith communities). Social-science research findings generally affirm those values. To see how, consider some facts of contemporary life.

In many ways, these are the best of times. Since 1960, Americans have been soaring economically, especially at the upper levels. The average real income in the United States is twice as high as in 1960, and we have twice as many things to spend our money on. We have espresso coffee, the World Wide Web, sport utility vehicles, and caller ID. We eat out two-and-a-half times as often, enjoy a higher life expectancy, and offer expanded opportunities for ethnic minorities and women. As I write, welfare rolls are shrinking, inflation is at a thirty-year low, and the national budget has an unexpected surplus.

Had you fallen asleep in 1960 and awakened in the 1990s, would you—overwhelmed by all these good tidings—also feel pleased at the cultural shift? Here are some other facts that would greet you (see figure 1; and Myers, 2000b). Since 1960:

☐ The divorce rate has doubled and happiness in surviving marriages has slightly declined.

☐ Child abuse and neglect reports have soared.

☐ Cohabitation, which predicts increased risk of divorce, has dramatically increased.

☐ Teen sexual activity has doubled.

☐ The 5 percent of babies born to unmarried parents in 1960 has increased to 32 percent.

☐ In 1960 just over 1 in 10 children did not live with two parents. Today, 3 in 10 do not.

In a recent survey, American Psychological Association members rated "the decline of the nuclear family" as today's number one threat to mental health. Developmental psychologist Urie Bronfenbrenner describes the trends starkly: "The present state of children and families in the United States represents the greatest domestic problem our nation has faced since the founding of the Republic. It is sapping our very roots" (quoted in Clinton, 1996).

Moreover, family decline since 1960 has been accompanied by other social trends:

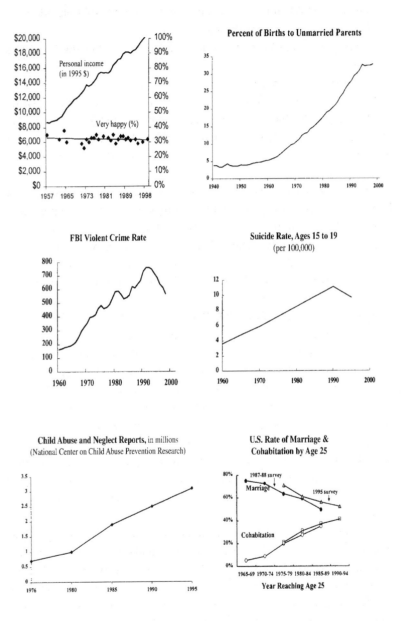

Figure 1. Indicators of social recession in the United States (from Myers, 2000b)

☐ The rate of child and adolescent obesity has more than doubled.

☐ The teen suicide rate has tripled.

☐ Reports of violent crime have quadrupled (even after the late 1990s decline).

☐ Depression rates have soared.

Christian family advocates believe that the ideal ecology for rearing children is two adults committed to each other and to their children. Are they right? Does family structure indeed affect children's well-being? Or is it simply a proxy for another factor such as poverty, race, or parental education?

Sociologists and psychologists have generated a mountain of data hoping to answer that question. One strategy has been to compare children of different family structures while statistically extracting the influence of other entangled factors. The best such data come from Nicholas Zill's summary of a 1981 child health survey of 15,416 randomly sampled children, conducted by the National Center for Health Statistics and from a 1988 repeat survey of 17,110 more children. Zill and his colleagues (Peterson & Zill, 1986; Zill, 1988; Dawson, 1991; Zill et al., 1993) recognized that intact and broken families differ in many ways: race, children's ages, parental education, family size, and income (poverty, we know, can be socially corrosive). To see if those were the only factors at work, he statistically adjusted scores to extract such influences. Even so, children of intact families were less likely to display antisocial and "acting out" behavior. Those living with both parents were half as likely as those living without fathers to have been suspended or expelled from school or to have had misbehavior reported by the school. In the 1988 national survey, children in intact families were half as vulnerable to school problems and were a third less likely to repeat a grade, regardless of their age or race.

The other strategy has been to follow children's lives through time, noting their well-being before and after parental divorce. A monumental but rarely discussed study by Andrew Cherlin and others (1991, 1995, 1998; Chase-Lansdale et al., 1995) began when researchers interviewed 17,414 women—the mothers of 98 percent of all British children born during the first full week of March 1958. British parents and teachers rated the behavior of nearly 12,000 of these children as seven-year-olds and again four years later, knowing that by then some would have experienced divorce. At the second rating, boys whose parents had divorced during the four years had about 25 percent more behavior problems than those whose families remained intact.

But were these children's postdivorce problems influenced by the marriage breaking up, or were they the result of the marital problems that preceded the divorce? "Staying in an unhappy marriage is psychologically damaging," asserts Pepper Schwartz, "and staying only for the children's sake is ultimately not in your interest or anyone else's" (1995). So rather than stay together for the sake of the children, should unhappy couples divorce for the sake of the children?

When the children had reached age twenty-three, the intrepid researchers traced and interviewed 12,537 of the original sample, enabling them to compare those who at age seven were living with two biological parents with those living with one, and to compare those whose parents had divorced with those whose parents had not divorced by age sixteen. Controlling for predivorce family problems did not weaken the divorce effect. Moreover, among children of divorce, 45 percent had cohabited—a rate more than double the approximately 19 percent among children of intact marriages. "Parental divorce seems to have stimulated a pattern of behavior characterized by early homeleaving due to conflict with parents and stepparents and early sexual activity outside marriage—leading, in this cohort, to a greater likelihood of premarital birth and cohabitation," said the researchers. Yet another follow-up, with 11,759 of the participants at age thirty-three, confirmed the emotional aftermath of the chain of events that often began with parental divorce. The bottom line from this important study is that by launching children into "negative life trajectories through adolescence into adulthood," divorce predicts increased social problems.

For victims of abuse, infidelity, alcoholism, or financial irresponsibility, divorce is sometimes the lesser of two evils. (If divorced people have participated in brokenness, who among us has not? We are all earthen vessels. We all at some time find ourselves broken, if not in our love life, then in our parenting, our friendships, or our vocations.) Moreover, most children of nonmarried or divorced parents thrive. Nevertheless, the results of these two national studies are confirmed by dozens of others that reveal the toxicity of family disruption for many children. Why this is so is a complicated story, apparently having less to do with parenting differences than with the poverty, broken attachments, dislocations, and altered peer relationships associated with family fracturing and parental absence. If normal variations in well-meaning parenting matter less than most people suppose, family collapse and its associated social ecology matters more than many suppose. (So too do the post-1960 increases in materialism, individualism, and media modeling of impulsive sexuality and violence. But those stories are for another bedtime.)

Faith and Well-Being

These findings are the tip of an iceberg of data that support the social and family values linked with religious faith. Does an active faith therefore enhance social and psychological well-being? Or is religion, as Freud surmised, corrosive to happiness by creating an "obsessional neurosis" that entails guilt, repressed sexuality, and suppressed emotions (1928, p. 71)?

Accumulating evidence reveals that some forms of religious experience correlate with prejudice and guilt, but that, in general, an active faith correlates with several mental health criteria. First, actively religious North Americans are much less likely than irreligious people to become delinquent, to abuse drugs and alcohol, to divorce, and to commit suicide (Batson, Schoenrade, & Ventis, 1993; Colasanto & Shriver, 1989). Thanks in part to their lesser rates of smoking and drinking, religiously active people even tend to be physically healthier and to live longer (Koenig, 1997; Matthews & Larson, 1997).

Other studies have probed the correlation between faith and coping with crises (Myers, 1993). Compared to religiously inactive widows, recently widowed women who worship regularly report more joy in their lives. Among mothers of developmentally challenged children, those with a deep religious faith are less vulnerable to depression. People of faith also tend to retain or recover greater happiness after suffering divorce, unemployment, serious illness, or a disability. In later life, according to one meta-analysis, the two best predictors of life satisfaction have been health and religiousness.

In surveys in various nations, religiously active people also report somewhat higher levels of happiness (Inglehart, 1990). Consider a Gallup (1984) U.S. survey. Those responding with highest scores on a spiritual commitment scale (by agreeing, for example, that "my religious faith is the most important influence in my life") were twice as likely as those lowest in spiritual commitment to declare themselves very happy. National Opinion Research Center surveys reveal higher levels of "very happy" people among those who feel "close to God." Self-rated spirituality and happiness may both be socially desirable responses, however. Would the happiness correlation extend to a behavioral measure of religiosity? As figure 2 indicates, it does. The evidence similarly indicates that strong religiosity predicts heightened generosity with time and money (Myers, 2000a).

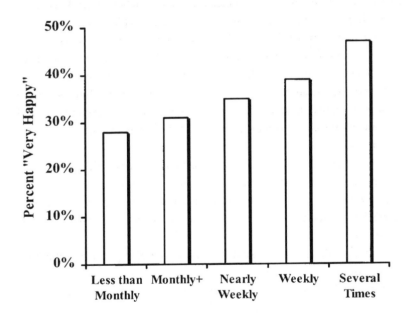

Figure 2. Religious attendance and happiness. Data from 34,706 participants in the General Social Surveys, National Opinion Research Center, 1972 to 1996.

What explains these links between faith and personal and social well-being? Is it the supportive close relationships—the "fellowship of kindred spirits," the "bearing of one another's burdens," "the ties of love that bind"—provided by faith communities? Is it the sense of meaning and purpose that many people derive from their faith? Is it a worldview that offers answers to life's deepest questions and an optimistic appraisal of life's events? Is it the hope that faith affords when facing "the terror resulting from our awareness of vulnerability and death" (Solomon, Greenberg, & Pyszczynski, 1991)? Such are among the proposed explanations.

When Psychological Science Challenges Faith

We have seen how psychological research affirms faith-rooted values and assumptions about human nature. Although psychological science is largely congenial to faith, it does, however, sometimes motivate us to rethink certain of our cherished ideas and to revisit Scripture. As ecological findings drove biblical scholars to reread the biblical mandates concerning our stewardship of the earth and its creatures, so recent psychological findings have stimulated new questions among people of faith. One example comes from research on illusory thinking, another from new information about sexual orientation. Such findings have prompted some of us to rethink our presumptions about both prayer and homosexuality—and to look more closely at what the Bible does and does not say.

Example 1: Testing prayer. We pray, asking in faith. Sick, we pray for healing. Fearful, we pray for safety. Hopeful, we pray for success. Suffering drought, we pray for rain. Sharing our prayer experiences, we may recall times when God has answered our petitions and our intercessions for others.

And then along comes a spate of psychological experiments showing that we humans

☐ perceive relationships where none exist (especially where we expect to see them)

☐ perceive causal connections among events that are only coincidentally correlated

☐ believe that we are controlling events that are actually beyond our control

These experiments have been extended to studies of gambling behavior, stock market predictions, clinical assessments of personality, superstitious behavior, and intuitions about ESP. The unchallenged verdict: We easily misperceive our behavior as correlated with subsequent events, and thus we easily delude ourselves into thinking that we can predict or control uncontrollable events.

Reading this research has provoked some of us to wonder whether illusory thinking contaminates people's beliefs regarding the power of their petitionary prayers. If indeed we are predisposed to find order in random events, to interpret outcomes guided by our preconceptions, to search for and recall instances that confirm our beliefs, and to be more persuaded by vivid anecdotes than by statistical reality, then might we not misunderstand the efficacy of petitionary prayer? Is prayer not a made-to-order arena for the operation of illusory thinking principles?

If that sounds heretical, it may be reassuring to remember that warnings about false prayer come more often from believers than from skeptics. There was no stronger skeptic of false piety than Jesus. If it is heretical to think too little of the power of our prayers, is it not more heretical to think of God as a sort of celestial Santa Claus who grants our wishes if we are good?

Well then, say some researchers from both the skeptic and believer camps, why not settle the issue empirically? Why not put prayer to the test? Recognizing the mixed results and design problems in prayer experiments to date, a massive and well-designed Harvard Medical School prayer experiment is currently underway (Roush, 1997). One large group of coronary bypass patients is being prayed for and one is not. These patients are participating voluntarily, but without knowing whether they are being prayed for or not. To assess a possible placebo effect, a third group is being prayed for and knows it. From a scientific perspective the study seems flawless. It exploits the methodology used in evaluating the healing powers of a new drug. (By keeping patients "blind" as to whether they are being prayed for, the experiment controls for various possible natural explanations that might explain any healing power of one's own meditative prayers.) Anticipating that the results of this study will be widely publicized and debated shortly after the publication of this book, what result do *you* predict?

As I report in my introductory psychology texts, we now have impressive evidence of links between faith and health (more good news from psychology for people of faith). Nevertheless, as a person of faith, I have three reasons for predicting that intercessory prayer will *not* exhibit significant healing powers for the cardiac care patients in this experiment. Indeed, along with many other Christians and Jews who worship the God of the Bible, my understanding of God and God's relation to the created world would be more challenged by positive than null results.

First, *the prayer concept being tested is more akin to magic than to a biblical understanding of prayer to an omniscient and sovereign God.* In the biblical view, God underlies the whole creation. God is not some little spiritual factor that occasionally deflects nature's course but the ground of all being. God works not in the gaps of what we do not yet understand but in and through nature, including the healing ministries that led people of faith to spread medicine and hospitals worldwide. Thus, while our Lord's model prayer welcomes our acknowledging our dependence on God for our basic necessities ("our daily bread"), it does not view God as a celestial vending machine, whose levers we pull with our prayers. Indeed, would the all-wise, all-knowing, all-loving God of the Bible be uninformed or uncaring apart from our prayers? Doesn't presuming that we creatures can pull God's strings violate biblical admonitions to humbly recognize our place as finite creatures of the infinite God? No wonder we are counseled to offer prayers of adoration, praise, confession, thanksgiving, dedication, and meditation, as well as to ask for what will (spiritually if not materially) be given. Prayer, J. I. Packer has written, "is not an attempt to force God's hand, but a humble acknowledgment of helplessness and dependence" (1961, p. 11).

Second, *even for those who believe that God intervenes in response to our prayers, there are practical reasons for expecting null effects:*

☐ The noise factor. Given that 95 percent of Americans express belief in God, all patients undergoing cardiac bypass surgery will already be receiving prayer—by spouses, children, siblings, friends, colleagues, and congregants or fellow believers, if not by themselves. Do these fervent prayers constitute a mere "noise factor" above which the signal of additional prayers may rouse God? Does God follow a dose-response curve (i.e., more prayers yield more response)? Does God count votes? Are the pleading, earnest prayers of patients and those who love them not sufficiently persuasive (as if God needs to be informed or persuaded of our needs)? Are the distant prayers of strangers participating in an experiment also needed?

☐ The doubt factor. To be sure, some Christians believe that prayers, uttered in believing faith, are potent. But how many people of faith also believe that prayers called forth by a doubting (open-minded, testing) scientist will be similarly effective?

☐ "God is not mocked." As Christians recalled during the great British prayer test controversy of 1872 (over a hypothetical proposal for a similar experiment), Jesus declared in response to one of his temptations that we ought not put God to the test. Reflecting on a proposal to test prayers for randomly selected preterm babies, Keith Stewart Thompson questions "whether all such experiments come close to blasphemy. If the health outcomes of the prayed-for subjects turn out to be significantly better than for the others, the experimenter will have set up a situation in which God has, as it were, been made to show his (or her) hand" (1996). C. S. Lewis observed, regarding any effort to prove prayer, that the "impossibility of empirical proof is a spiritual necessity" lest a person begin to "feel like a magician" (1947, p. 215). Indeed, if this experiment were to show that numbers of pray-ers matter—that distant strangers' prayers boost recovery chances—might rich people not want, in hopes of gaining God's attention, to pay indulgences to others who will pray for them?

Third, *the evidence of history suggests that the prayers of finite humans do not manipulate an infinite God.* If they could and did, how many droughts, floods, hurricanes, and plagues would have been averted? How many stillborn infants or children with disabilities would have been born healthy? And consider the Bible's own evidence: How should the unanswered prayers of Job, Paul, and even Jesus (in petitioning that the cup might pass) inform our theology of prayer? If the rain falls on my picnic, does it mean I pray with too little faith or that the rain falls both on those who believe and those who do not? Should we pray to God as manipulative adolescents—or as dependent preschoolers, whose loving parents, already knowing their children's needs, welcome the intimacy?

If my prediction of no demonstrable effect of experimental prayers proves correct, perhaps some good may come of this unprecedented, massive Harvard prayer experiment. The publicity and debate I expect will be generated by the experiment may stimulate healthy reflection on

God's relationship to the natural and human world. Moreover, as Henri Nouwen once suggested, clearing the decks of some of the false gods of popular religion may prepare our hearts for the God of the Bible. Although the Bible does not promise that we will be spared sorrow, humiliation, misfortune, sickness, and death, it does offer a perspective from which to view such events, a promise that God is beside us in our suffering and a hope that out of defeat and suffering and even death we may gain new life.

Example 2: The question of sexual orientation. I see myself as a family-values guy. In my psychology textbooks I document the corrosive effects of pornography, teen sexual activity, and family decline. I am on the advisory board of the National Marriage Project, whose recent cohabitation report concludes that trial marriages undermine marriage. I am participating in the new "communitarian" initiative to help renew society's moral roots. And I have invested a couple of thousand hours in writing a new book (*The American Paradox: Spiritual Hunger in an Age of Plenty,* Yale University Press, 2000b) that documents the post-1960 social recession and its roots in radical individualism, the sexual revolution, and the decline of marriage and the two-parent family.

Hearing me speak on such things, recently a friend remarked, "You've become more conservative." No, I said, I've always been pretty conservative on these family concerns, because the data are so persuasive.

Mindful of my "ever-reforming" Reformed tradition, new data have, however, dragged me along with other Christian thinkers such as Lewis Smedes (1994) and Letha Dawson Scanzoni and Virginia Ramey Mollenkott (1994) to revise my understanding of sexual orientation. Here are some of the observations that challenged my former assumptions (for documentation, see Myers, 1998):

There is no known parental or psychological influence on sexual orientation. Factors once believed crucial actually seem not to matter. Sexual orientation appears not to be influenced by child abuse, social example, overprotective mothering, distant fathering, or having gay parents. We may yet discover some parental or psychological influence. But for now if some new parents were to seek my advice on how to influence the sexual orientation of their newborn, I could only say, after a half century of research, that we are clueless. We simply do not know what, if anything, parents can do to influence sexual orientation.

Unlike sexual behavior and other moral tendencies, sexual orientation appears unaffected by an active faith. Earlier I noted that compared with people who attend church rarely, if at all, those who attend regularly are less likely to be juvenile delinquents, abuse drugs and alcohol, and divorce. In a recent National Opinion Research Center survey, they were also one-third as likely to have cohabited before marriage, and they reported having had many fewer sexual partners. Yet, if males, they are no less as likely to be homosexual (Smith, 1996). This unpublicized finding is worth pondering. If male sexual orientation is a spiritually influenced lifestyle choice, then should it not—like those other disapproved tendencies—be less common among people of faith?

Today's greater tolerance seems not to have amplified homosexuality. Homosexuals are a small minority, roughly two or three percent of the population, and their numbers appear not to have grown with the emergence of a gay rights movement or with the passage of gay rights laws. Contrary to the concern that gay role models would entice more people into homosexuality, surveys suggest no increase in the homosexual minority.

Biological factors are looking more and more important. This scientific story is still being written and the light is still dim, so we had all best be tentative. Nevertheless, we have learned, first, that biological siblings of gay people, especially their identical twins, are somewhat more likely than people without close gay relatives to themselves be gay.

Genetic instructions, if there are such, must be manifest in physiology. So it should not surprise us that new evidence points to both prenatal hormonal differences and to brain differences in a region known to influence sexual behavior. One scientific review concludes that "the emerging neuroanatomical picture is that, in some brain areas, homosexual men are more likely to have female-typical neuroanatomy than are heterosexual men" (Gladue, 1994). This may explain why homosexual men tend to have spatial abilities like those typical of heterosexual women. A newer report suggests that this female-typical pattern extends to a prenatally influenced fingerprint difference between gay and straight men (Hall & Kimura, 1994).

Homosexual women may likewise have more male-typical anatomy.

For example, the hearing systems of lesbian women appear to develop in a way that is "intermediate to those of heterosexual females and heterosexual males" (McFadden & Pasanen, 1998).

Although these findings suggest biological influences at work, we should be wary of an extreme biologism. As every psychology student knows, biologically disposed tendencies operate within an environmental context. Even tulips require hospitable soil and water. It may yet be shown that certain biological dispositions interact with particular environments to predispose sexual orientation.

Efforts to change a person's sexual orientation usually (some say, virtually always) fail. People who have experimented with homosexual behavior (as many heterosexual people do) can turn away from it. Homosexuals, like heterosexuals, can become celibate. Or they can marry against their desires and have children. But research on efforts to help people do a 180-degree reversal of their sexual orientation—their feelings and fantasies—reveals "no evidence indicating that such treatments are effective" (Haldeman, 1994). Many people have tried, hoping upon hope to escape their culture's contempt. Few, it seems, have succeeded.

Christian ex-gay organizations have had a go at this and may offer effective support to those seeking to leave the gay culture. But many, including thirteen such organizations affiliated with Exodus International (Leland & Miller, 1998), have been abandoned by their ex-gay founders. Two of Exodus's own cofounders, Michael Bussee and Gary Cooper, fell in love and left the organization. "I counseled . . . hundreds of people . . . who tried to change their sexual orientation and none of them changed," recalls Bussee (quoted in *Record*, 1990). "The bottom line is, it doesn't work."

Reading the ex-gay literature, one is struck by the admitted homosexual temptations many "ex-gays" still struggle with. "God does not replace one form of lust with another," explain Bob Davies and Lori Rentzel (1993, p. 27). Ex-gays commonly struggle with homosexual attractions. The ex-gay man "may never have the same level of raw sensuality in looking at his fiancée/wife" as he felt toward men and typically does "not experience sexual arousal solely by looking at [his] wife's body" (pp. 159, 162).

Sexual feelings are private (and it is, after all, the direction of one's lusts—one's feelings and fantasies—that define sexual orientation). Thus, short of physiologically measuring sexual responses to male and female sexual stimuli before and after sexual conversion programs, there can be no precise measure of the frequency of actual sexual orientation conversion. Such research has not yet been done, so it remains an open issue as to whether significant numbers of sexual conversion have occurred. For men, whose "erotic plasticity" is relatively low (Baumeister, in press), this may be an especially elusive goal.

But this much seems certain. Many gay and lesbian Christians have felt called to heterosexuality, but after years of effort, prayer, laying on of hands, Christian counseling, and searing guilt have found only misery, and in some cases have lost faith.

For all these reasons it becomes difficult to avoid the conclusion that sexual orientation appears not to be a choice. For most of us, the emerging scientific surmise rings true to our experience. Can those of us who are heterosexual recall a time when we *chose* to be so? Or is it just the way we are?

To suggest that sexual orientation may be disposed rather than chosen leaves one free to regard homosexuality as, like left-handedness, a natural part of human diversity or as a lamentable aberration such as dyslexia. Scientific evidence also does not decide personal values. Whether straight or gay, everyone faces moral choices over options that include abstinence, promiscuity, and permanent commitment.

Faced with the accumulating evidence and the experiences of gay and lesbian Christians, some people of faith have rethought their presumption that homosexuality is a lifestyle choice. Some biblical scholars are also reexamining and debating the half dozen or so scriptural passages referring to same-sex activity. Issues related to sexual orientation will surely challenge the church for some years to come. It therefore behooves us all to discern biblical mandates and priorities, critically evaluate and learn from the natural revelations of science, regard one another with love and grace, and learn from one another through open, honest dialogue.

What Psychological Science and Faith Share in Common

Psychological science and the spirit of faith, then, share similar ideals: humility before nature and skepticism of human presumptions. Psychological science enlivens ancient biblical wisdom about human nature. Psychological science documents the corrosion of family values and the toxic effects of that corrosion for children and civic life. Psychological science has shown the correlates between an active faith and human health and happiness. And psychological science challenges us to revisit certain of our assumptions, mindful that all truth is God's truth, and therefore to be welcomed rather than feared. This is not to say that psychological science, value-laden and limited as it is, should ever be the final word. Rather, by often affirming and sometimes challenging our prejudgments, it helps keep alive that "ever-reforming" Reformation spirit.

In that spirit we in this book lay our tentative and still-forming thoughts before one another, welcoming one another's reflections and critique. My surest conviction is that some of my ideas err. And that is why I welcome the correction and admonition of my esteemed colleagues.

References

Batson, C. D., Schoenrade, P. A., & Ventis, W. L. (1993). *Religion and the individual: A social-psychological perspective.* New York: Oxford University Press.

Baumeister, R. F. (in press). Gender differences in erotic plasticity: The female sex drive as socially flexible and responsive. *Psychological Bulletin.*

Chase-Lansdale, P., Cherlin A. J., & Kiernan, K. E. (1995). The long-term effects of parental divorce on the mental health of young adults: A developmental perspective. *Child Development, 66,* 1614-1634.

Cherlin, A. J., Chase-Lansdale, P. L., & McRae, C. (1998). Effects of parental divorce on mental health. *American Sociological Review, 63,* 239-249.

Cherlin, A. J., Kiernan, K. E., & Chase-Lansdale, P. L. (1995). Parental divorce in childhood and demographic outcomes in young adulthood. *Demography, 32,* 299-316.

Cherlin, A. J., et al. (1991). Longitudinal studies of effects of divorce on children in Great Britain and the United States. *Science, 252,* 1386-1389.

Clinton, H. R. (1996). *It takes a village.* New York: Simon & Schuster.

Colasanto, D., & Shriver, J. (1989, May). Mirror of America: Middle-aged face marital crisis. *Gallup Report, 284,* 34-38.

Darley, J. M., & Batson, C. D. (1973). From Jerusalem to Jericho: A study of situational and dispositional variables in helping behavior. *Journal of Personality and Social Psychology, 27,* 100-108.

Davies, B., & Rentzel, L. (1993). *Coming out of homosexuality: New freedom for men and women*. Downers Grove, IL: InterVarsity Press.

Dawson, D. A. (1991). Family structure and children's health: United States, 1988. *Vital and Health Statistics, Series 10: Data from the National Health Survey, No. 178*. Hyattsville, MD: National Center for Statistics, U.S. Department of Health and Human Services, DHHS Publication No. PHS 91-1506.

Freud, S. (1928/1964). *The future of an illusion*. Garden City, NY: Doubleday.

Gallup, G., Jr. (1984, March). Commentary on the state of religion in the U.S. today. *Religion in America: The Gallup Report, 222*.

Gladue, B. A. (1994). The biopsychology of sexual orientation. *Current Directions in Psychological Science, 3*, 150-154.

Greenwald, A. G. (1980). The totalitarian ego: Fabrication and revision of personal history. *American Psychologist, 35*, 603-618.

Greenwald, A. G. (1984, June 12). Quoted by D. Goleman, A bias puts self at center of everything. *New York Times*, pp. C1, C4.

Haldane, J. B. S. (1928/1971). *Possible worlds and other papers*. Freeport, NY: Libraries Press.

Haldeman, D. C. (1994). The practice and ethics of sexual orientation conversion therapy. *Journal of Consulting and Clinical Psychology, 62*, 221-227.

Hall, J. A. Y., & Kimura, D. (1994). Dermatoglyphic asymmetry and sexual orientation in men. *Behavioral Science, 108*, 1203-1206.

Hooykaas, R. (1972). *Religion and the rise of modern science*. Grand Rapids, MI: Eerdmans.

Inglehart, R. (1990). *Culture shift in advanced industrial society*. Princeton, NJ: Princeton University Press.

Kierkegaard, S. (1851/1944). *For self-examination and judge for yourself* (W. Lowrie, Trans.). Princeton, NJ: Princeton University Press.

Koenig, H. G. (1997). *Is religion good for your health? The effects of religion on physical and mental health*. Binghamton, NY: Haworth.

Leland, J., and Miller, M. (1998, August 17). Can gays convert? *Newsweek, 47*.

Lewis, C. S. (1947). *Miracles*. New York: Macmillan.

Lewis, C. S. (1960). *Mere Christianity*. New York: Macmillan.

MacKay, D. M. (1984, December). Letters. *Journal of the American Scientific Affiliation, 237*.

Matthews, D. A., & Larson, D. B. (1997). *The faith factor: An annotated bibliography of clinical research on spiritual subjects* (4 vols.). Rockville, MD: National Institute for Healthcare Research and Georgetown University Press.

McFadden, D., & Pasanen, E. G. (1998). Comparison of the auditory systems of heterosexuals and homosexuals: Click-evoked otoacoustic emissions. *Proceedings of the National Academy of Sciences, 95*, 2709-2713.

Merton, R. K. (1938/1970). *Science, technology and society in seventeenth-century England.* New York: Fertig.

Myers, D. G. (1991). Steering between the extremes: On being a Christian scholar within psychology. *Christian Scholar's Review, 20,* 376-383.

Myers, D. G. (1992). *The pursuit of happiness.* New York: William Morrow.

Myers, D. G. (1994). *Exploring social psychology.* New York: McGraw-Hill.

Myers, D. G. (1995). Teaching, texts and values. *Journal of Psychology and Theology, 23,* 244-247.

Myers, D. G. (1996). On professing psychological science and Christian faith. *Journal of Psychology and Christianity, 15,* 143-149.

Myers, D. G. (1998). *Psychology* (5th ed.). New York: Worth.

Myers, D. G. (1999). *Social psychology* (6th ed.). New York: McGraw-Hill.

Myers, D. G. (2000a). The funds, friends and faith of happy people. *American Psychologist, 55,* 56-67.

Myers, D. G. (2000b). *The American Paradox: Spiritual hunger in an age of plenty.* New Haven, CT: Yale University Press.

Myers, D. G., & Jeeves, M. A. (1987). *Psychology through the eyes of faith.* San Francisco: HarperCollins.

Packer, J. I. (1961). *Evangelism and the sovereignty of God.* Downers Grove, IL: InterVarsity Press.

Pascal, B. (1670/1965). *Thoughts.* (W. F. Trotter, Trans.) In M. Mack (Ed.), *World masterpieces.* New York: W. W. Norton.

Peterson, J. L., & Zill, N. (1986). Marital disruption, parent-child relationships, and behavior problems in children. *Journal of Marriage and the Family, 48,* 295-307.

Record (the Newsletter of Evangelicals Concerned). (1990, spring). p. 1.

Roush, W. (1997). Herbert Benson: Mind-body maverick pushes the envelope. *Science, 276,* 357-359.

Scanzoni, L. D., & Mollenkott, V. R. (1994). *Is the homosexual my neighbor? A positive Christian response* (Rev. ed.). San Francisco: HarperCollins.

Schwartz, P. (1995, April 4). When staying is worth the pain. *New York Times,* p. C1.

Smedes, L. (1994). *Sex for Christians: The limits and liberties of sexual living.* Grand Rapids, MI: Eerdmans.

Smith, T. W. (1996). American sexual behavior: Trends, socio-demographic differences and risk behavior. National Opinion Research Center GSS Topical Report No. 25.

Solomon, S., Greenberg, J., & Pyszczynski, T. (1991). A terror management theory of social behavior: The psychological functions of self-esteem and cultural worldviews. *Advances in Experimental Social Psychology, 24,* 93-159.

Thompson, K. S. (1996, November-December). The revival of experiments on prayer. *American Scientist,* 532-534.

Tolstoy, L. (1904). *My confessions.* Boston: Dana Estes.

Zill, N. (1988). Behavior, achievement and health problems among children in stepfamilies: Findings from a national survey of child health. In E. M. Hetherington & J. D. Arasteh (Eds.), *Impact of divorce, single parenting and stepparenting on children.* Hillsdale, NJ: Erlbaum.

Zill, N., Morrison, D. R., & Coiro, M. J. (1993). Long-term effects of parental divorce on parent-child relationships, adjustment and achievement in young adulthood. *Journal of Family Psychology, 7,* 91-103.

An Integration Response

Gary R. Collins

David Myers and I are both psychologists. We went to different graduate schools at different times, but we were both steeped in the view that psychology is science. Like Dr. Myers, I too had an interest in social psychology and studied it at the graduate level. But whereas I moved to clinical psychology, Myers went on to become a distinguished leader in the social psychology field.

I begin on this personal note to show that Myers and I have some similar professional roots and perspectives. I share his respect for science and for empirical data. I resonate with his awareness of social influences like postmodernism and the search for happiness. I appreciate his acknowledgment that values guide both our research and our reporting, that scientific studies are affected by human error and self-serving bias, and that religious beliefs influence many of our perceptions and behaviors. Myers's knowledge of social psychology and science enables him to present fascinating factual data that expands our understanding of the faith-psychology debate. As a fellow psychologist who respects data, appreciates research, and sees no conflict between solid scientific data and good biblical exegesis, I applaud Myers for his awareness of empirical studies and familiarity with the scientific literature.

Nevertheless, the social-scientific approach that I admire also causes my three greatest concerns with Myers's position. First, after honestly admitting its weaknesses, limitations, and potential for bias, the author seems to elevate empirical research into what might be called a scientific imperialism. Science becomes the preeminent standard against which everything else—including his own beliefs and values—are tested. He describes himself as a "family-values guy" and notes that he has always been "pretty conservative on . . . family concerns, *because the data are so persuasive*" (emphasis added). He then builds his case about sexual orientation on what he presumably views as "persuasive" data. In this discussion Myers seems to ignore the clear teaching of Scripture and the theological and ethical conclusions of the vast majority of classical Christianity in favor of what he judges to be the contemporary findings of science in the sexual orientation debates. Science appears to be the supreme determinant of Myers's position, the standard against which all else is measured.

This brings me to a second and even greater concern. Myers notes that "new data" have "dragged" him, along with other Christian thinkers, to revise his earlier assumptions and understanding of sexual orientation. It appears, however, that the reverse is true. The data have not dragged Myers into a new way of thinking about sexual orientation. His thinking seems to have led him to overemphasize evidence that supports his position even as he overlooks or ignores a substantial body of contradictory data. This is not good science, especially coming from one who has taken such pains to affirm the importance and value of the scientific method.

Consider the first statement that the author cites to support his new position. He notes authoritatively that there is *"no known parental or psychological influence on sexual orientation."* A few paragraphs later, however, he acknowledges (correctly) that the scientific story about the etiology of sexual orientation is "still being written and the light is still dim, so we had best be tentative." Myers cites two studies to show that "biological factors are looking more and more important," but he fails to mention other studies that challenge this view.

In a major, in-depth review of this research literature, literature undoubtedly familiar to Myers, psychologists Stanton Jones and Mark Yarhouse conclude that the "genetic, brain structure, and prenatal hormonal causation hypotheses are 'hot' right now. Although there is an impressive amount of research cited in favor of the former three hypotheses [relating to biological causation], the direct research in support of each is not conclusive. On the other hand, there is a substantive legacy of research on psychological/familial factors which is being generally ignored today despite the statistically significant findings represented in that literature. . . . In reality, the biologic theories at this point 'seem to have no greater explanatory value' than the psychosocial models they seek to displace" (Jones & Yarhouse, 1997, p. 465. See also Jones & Yarhouse, 1999, 2000; Schmidt, 1995).

In passing, it must be noted that this conclusion has nothing to do with the attitudes or the compassion (or lack of compassion) that we might feel toward people who are homosexuals. The Scriptures never give any justification for the insensitivity, gay bashing, or outright hatred that comes too often from people who name the name of Christ.

A third concern about this chapter relates to the author's selection of sexual orientation as an example of one way in which "psychological science challenges faith." He cites data showing that homosexuals are a small minority of our population and that the prominence of gay issues has not increased the number of homosexual persons. He states boldly that *"efforts to change a person's sexual orientation usually . . . fail,"* but he admits that scientific data in support of this conclusion is weak. Most of his arguments come not from empirical studies but from nonscientific anecdotal reports of people who have tried to change but did not succeed. Apparently Myers chose a case-study approach that allows him to express his emerging beliefs about sexual orientation, but it fails to demonstrate his goal of showing that psychological science challenges faith. By selecting this example, whatever the reason, Myers undercuts his own argument and detracts from his view that science, especially psychological science, has much to contribute to our understanding of faith issues.

Perhaps as much as anything else, this example illustrates the author's earlier statement that "personal beliefs often shape our perceptions." In this book the core issue is whether the Bible is the authoritative Word of God that transforms and becomes the standard against which we evaluate our psychology, or whether psychological science is the standard against which we evaluate our beliefs? I take the former stance. It appears to me that Myers leans toward the latter.

In my writings over the years I have sought to bring the latest scientific findings and good biblical exegesis to bear on a number of counseling issues, including anxiety, loneliness, guilt, marital conflict, and grief. Like many others, undoubtedly including Myers, I have found that carefully produced scientific data and the Christian worldview are complementary; there is no contradiction between good science and good theology. When apparent conflict appears, as we see in some contemporary discussions about homosexuality, we rest on the truth of our biblically based Christian worldview, but we also look more carefully at the data, realizing that the scientific evidence may be more complex than we originally thought.

I appreciated Myers's open spirit at the end of his chapter. He concludes that psychological science challenges us to revisit our assumptions and writes that he is *not* saying that "psychological science, value-laden and limited as it is, should ever be the final word." As I read his chapter, however, I wonder how much the author agrees with his own conclusion. To the extent that science is the major foundation for his psychological conclusions and worldview, in my opinion he is in danger of building on a bed of shifting sand.

And we all know what happens to houses that are not built on rock.

References

Jones, S. L., and Yarhouse, M. A. (1997). Science and the ecclesiastical homosexuality debates. *Christian Scholar's Review, 26,* 446-447.

Jones, S. L., and Yarhouse, M. A. (1999, October 4). The incredibly shrinking gay gene. *Christianity Today,* p. 53.

Jones, S. L., and Yarhouse, M. A. (2000). *Homosexuality: The use of scientific research in the church's moral debate.* Downers Grove, IL: InterVarsity Press.

Schmidt, T. E. (1995). *Straight or narrow? Compassion and clarity in the homosexuality debate.* Downers Grove, IL: InterVarsity Press.

A Christian Psychology Response

Robert C. Roberts

David Myers begins his chapter by referring to the twentieth century as "psychology's first century," thus expressing the viewpoint of what I call the "psychological establishment" in my chapter. He also says that the consensus of this establishment is that "psychology [is] the science of behavior and mental processes." A little later he warns that psychology in this sense of the word does not answer all questions. In particular, it does not answer "ultimate questions" about the meaning of life. In other words, it does not answer all psychological questions. Taking the broader historical view that I commend in my essay, one sees that the vast majority of psychologies and psychological writings have indeed sought to answer such ultimate questions. Christianity has certainly done that, but so did Aristotle and Plato, the Stoics, Epicureans, Confucians, and countless others who thought hard and carefully about the "soul," about mental health and pathology, about the nature of personality and personal relations, about psychological development, about what human behavior and emotions are and how they may be shaped, and the like. And this "psychology of the ultimate questions" is not restricted to the ancient world or to the time before controlled psychological experiments, careful data collection, and statistical construals of data. The twentieth century is full of major psychologists whose aim, in part, was to tell us the meaning of life, to point the way to fulfillment and the good life (or in the case of Freud, to the coping life, given that his answer to the ultimate question is that there is no ultimate meaning). Abraham Maslow, Fritz Perls, Carl Jung, Carl Rogers, Alfred Adler, Albert Ellis, and Rollo May are a few who come to mind.

In fact it seems when the human mind turns its attention to psychological questions, it takes tremendous discipline (though meanness of spirit may also help) to keep from touching on questions about the ultimately good life for human beings. David Myers, who is very disciplined and anything but mean of spirit, has not restricted himself to narrowly scientific explanations of "behavior and mental processes." A recurring topic in his work, which he touches on in his paper for the present volume, is the nature and causes of human happiness. This is certainly an "ultimate question"—one answered in a rather bewildering variety of ways in the psychologies, ancient and modern, that I referred to in the preceding paragraph.

In this response I want to ask to what extent we can answer questions about human happiness by the more narrowly scientific methods of twentieth-century psychology, or rather, what a scientific study of happiness would look like. Let us begin by asking whether happiness is either a behavior or a mental process, since these are the two kinds of things that scientific psychology supposedly explains. In his book *The Pursuit of Happiness,* Myers quotes research psychologist Jonathan Freedman as saying, "If you feel happy, you are happy—that's all we mean by the term" (Myers, 1992, p. 27). Now Freedman's conception of happiness does seem to make it into a mental process (or perhaps a mental state—or better yet, a summing of mental processes or states), something we might call "positive affective hedonic tone"—pleasant emotion(s) as opposed to unpleasant. On this conception, if a person's emotions are predominantly pleasant, he or she is happy. If they are predominantly unpleasant, the person is unhappy. If neither kind predominates, he or she falls somewhere in the middle of a continuum between happiness and unhappiness. If we can trust people's summary assessments of their own subjective emotional pleasures and pains, then they can be the final authority on whether they are happy or not. Happiness becomes a simple matter of "life satisfaction." And all the social scientific research that I know of trades on this conception of happiness (all that Myers cites does).

The life-satisfaction concept of happiness certainly prevails in contemporary American and European life. But a venerable older crosscultural tradition has a more complicated concept of happiness: the happy person has to have real well-being, not just a sense of well-being, and a person's sense of well-being is not always a reliable indicator of his or her happiness. Furthermore, in some versions of this older concept, a person can have well-being, and thus in a sense happiness, even though he or she is suffering pretty intense emotional pain. The Greek words *eudaimonia* and *makariotēs* tend to carry this richer meaning; the Latin *beatitudo* is similar. Let us call this older, classical conception the full well-being conception of happiness.

On Aristotle's and Plato's view, a fool might be highly satisfied with life, but being a fool he or she couldn't possibly be enjoying happiness *(eudaimonia)*. The reason is that genuine, human well-being, which is required for happiness, is not consistent with being a fool. In the Beatitudes, Jesus Christ pronounces people in various socially and psychologically painful conditions happy (that is, *makarioi).* In the circumstances of the present age these social and psychological conditions indicate that one is in a kind of harmony with God and his kingdom. And this is self-realization for creatures of God made in his image. Aristotle would resist ascribing happiness to people who are being persecuted for righteousness' sake, and Jesus explains their happiness by pointing out that they are citizens of the kingdom of heaven (presumably with the hope that that involves).

Thus happiness in these two ancient understandings does have a reference to life satisfaction. But the life satisfaction that constitutes *happiness,* rather than *mere* life satisfaction, is one that comes from being what one was designed to be or what is appropriate to human nature. Aristotle is quite explicit that happiness is enjoyed only by virtuous people—by those who have actualized their real human nature (as contrasted, say, with some erroneous conception of human nature). Aristotle and Jesus do not fully agree on the question of what human beings are. (Aristotle does not think we are created in the image of God for eternal fellowship with God, and his concept of God is very different from that of Jesus.) But the Christian psychology and the Aristotelian psychology share this formal similarity: happiness is not just feeling good about your life but also involves being what you were meant to be.

Twentieth-century psychologies are similar. Each of the major psycho-therapies and personality theories have a concept of human nature and a corresponding concept of what it is to live optimally as a human being. Sigmund Freud sees us as animals with certain biological drives, but different from animals in that we live within cultural forms that are designed to produce social harmony by impeding and shaping the expression of the drives. Maturity is a formation of character (defense mechanisms) such that the expression of these biological impulses is neither socially nor psychologically destructive. For Carl Rogers, the fact that we live in society is really accidental to our deepest nature. We are essentially self-transparent, freely developing, exploratory, experiencing, self-regulating, ever-expanding individual spirits; and as such, we need to declare independence from the cultural forms and expectations that will stifle our spirits if we internalize them. When we do this, we display a virtue that Rogers calls "congruence." (For other illustrations, see Roberts, 1993.)

Some of these psychologies may suppose that if a person is not in the prescribed state, he or she will always feel dissatisfied with life. But this seems implausible, and most of them have conceptual resources for explaining why people may feel satisfied even if they are not in the prescribed state (for example, that they are in a state of self-deception or at least self-opacity). If so, then like the ancient psychologies, they allow for a possible discrepancy between feeling happy and being happy. And so they imply that psychology is not just the science of behavior and mental states but is a normative discipline that makes prescriptions about some ultimate questions.

In the Aristotelian and Christian conceptions of happiness we see the following structure: first, the happy individual must be functioning as human nature dictates. This condition implies that proper mental and behavioral functioning must be indexed to some conception of human nature—Christian, Aristotelian, Confucian, Rogerian, Jungian, Freudian, or whatever. Thus we might say that happiness is "theory relative." Second, included in any conception of human nature is a conception of a proper operating environment. An individual pheasant might be everything that a pheasant can be—healthy and well developed according to the standards of pheasant nature. But we can hardly expect the pheasant to function well under water. Similarly, a finely formed human being can hardly be expected to function optimally in an environment that is very foreign to human nature. On Aristotle's conception of human nature, we should not expect well-formed persons (i.e., persons with all the Aristotelian virtues) to feel good if they are not citizens of a city-state with a good constitution or if they utterly lack some of the material conditions for expressing themselves in action. This is where life satisfaction comes in: life satisfaction indicates happiness only if one experiences it in the kind of environment in which human beings are naturally suited to function. A healthy pheasant can be expected to have life satisfaction when living in an appropriate plains habitat in Nebraska. Aristotelians will expect that a person with the Aristotelian virtues will have life satisfaction when living in a well-constituted city-state in which he or she has a certain amount of leadership. Christians will expect that a person with the Christian virtues will experience life satisfaction when living in the kingdom of God. This logic of happiness implies a test for conceptions of human nature. If, for example, persons who were optimally formed by Aristotelian standards did not experience life satisfaction in a well-constituted city-state, we would have reason to think that Aristotle's psychology is in some way incorrect or incomplete.

Leo Tolstoy's novel *Anna Karenina* supplies a nice illustration of some of my points. Constantin Levin is an unusually excellent person by Tolstoy's standards. Seriously concerned about family life, moral purity, religious questions, and the working of the land, he is a man of deep and significant feelings. His friend Stepan Oblonsky, by contrast, is a happy-go-lucky adulterer who neglects his family and plunges them into debt. He is not concerned whether his work is genuinely productive, if only he makes good money at it. He has a full range of emotions, but they are shallow. He lives for pleasures, especially those associated with pretty young women, hunting, and the life of high society. During much of the novel Levin is a tortured soul—tortured precisely about the really important issues that are also important for him in his capacity as a good man. He also has intensely positive emotions, for example when he goes mowing with the peasants and when he finally manages to get married and see a family growing up around him. But life is very much a mixture of "happy" and "unhappy" emotions. By contrast, Oblonsky is pretty much always cheerful, precisely because he is not deeply concerned about what is important, and the rather trivial pleasures that he loves are always forthcoming for him. At most points during the novel, Oblonsky would rate himself very high on a life satisfaction questionnaire, and at many points Levin would rate himself very low. On a life satisfaction conception of happiness, it is clear that Oblonsky is the happier of the two men. But there is something wrong with this conclusion. He is, as his wife comments at one point, "pitiful." That is, he is pitiful by Christian as well as Tolstoyian and Aristotelian standards, and probably also by the standards of most of the twentieth-century personality theories.

However, he is not pitiful by playboy standards. If we elevate the playboy philosophy of life to the status of a serious conception of human nature, then he is a well-formed human being, one who has actualized his deepest human nature. Furthermore, he has the good fortune to live in an environment that satisfies that nature—the life of wealthy, upper-crust, nineteenth-century Russian society. If we assume the playboy psychology, Oblonsky is thus a well-functioning person living in an environment that suits human nature. He is just about as happy as a human being can get. In that case, Levin is indeed an unhappy person, not just because he has low life satisfaction but also because he is ill formed as a human being. But he is not ill formed in Tolstoy's view. Some of Levin's suffering does come from his personal defects, but much of it comes from the fact that he lives in a world (namely, that frivolous upper-crust Russian society) not well suited to well-formed human beings. Oblonsky's life satisfaction arises from an accidental combination of being a poorly formed person and living in an environment that is well suited to the satisfaction of persons who are poorly formed in just his particular way.

What would the scientific study of happiness look like if we follow Aristotle and Christ on the nature of happiness? On the full well-being conception, collecting information about people's levels of life satisfaction at various ages and in various cultural and social and political settings would need to be set in a context of normative decisions. People can be determined to be happy or unhappy in the full sense only if a standard of self-realization (character-in-an-environment) is fixed upon. The standard might be hypothetical; it need not be one to which the researcher personally subscribes. But the research would need to be indexed to some particular conception or perhaps multiple specified conceptions of happiness: Christian, playboy, Aristotelian, Jungian, or whatever. To conduct such research it would be necessary to have ways of measuring people's character—their degree of conformity to the chosen standard of self-realization—as well as their life satisfaction. And the life satisfaction measure will vary, as an indicator of happiness, with the character of the environment the subjects are operating in (for example, in a Christian conception, life satisfaction is the more relevant to happiness the more the environment approximates the kingdom of God; it is less relevant in an environment of persecution [Mt 5:10]).

What implications have the foregoing considerations for the idea that psychology is the science of behavior and mental processes? Behavior and mental processes are central objects of psychology's investigations, but if it is to investigate happiness as full well-being, it must give full and explicit recognition to the norms of such well-being, and these are neither behaviors nor mental processes—at least they are none that belong to the objects of inquiry. Happiness in the full well-being sense is neither a behavior nor a mental process nor a combination of the two, but a complex norm-relative dispositional state of persons-in-environments. Or rather, the word *happiness* in the full well-being sense may refer to any number of different dispositional states of persons-in-environments, depending on the psychological norms governing the uses of the word.

This fact enormously complicates the scientific study of happiness, but it seems to me that psychology cannot dodge the complication, given the obvious inadequacy of the concept of happiness as mere subjective life satisfaction and the fact that the question of happiness is one of those "ultimate" questions that psychologists—even some very scientifically oriented psychologists like Myers—do try to answer (though often they hate to admit it). Christian psychologists have special reasons for not accepting the simplistic inference "If you feel happy, you are happy," because the psychology of our own tradition rules it out in favor of something much more profound. Scientific psychology is here to stay. It has taught us some things and promises to teach us more. But it cannot do this very well if it is philosophically naive, and it is certainly naive to think that a phenomenon as fraught with norms as human happiness can be properly studied without careful attention to the varying norms that govern its concept.

References

Myers, D. G. (1992). *The pursuit of happiness: Who is happy and why.* New York: William Morrow.

Roberts, R. C. (1993). *Taking the word to heart: Self and other in an age of therapies.* Grand Rapids: Eerdmans.

A Biblical Counseling Response

David Powlison

I like David Myers's vigorous confidence that God has made an intelligible creation and that there are many ways that human creatures can explore the human creature. We live in a real world, and our perceptual and mental apparatus correspond to what is. Of course, *nothing* made can be exhaustively comprehended. From galactic clusters to charmed quarks, from aesthetic experience to sin-twisted hearts, from the interpretation of Ephesians to the causes of war, there is no final knowledge or pure objectivity this side of the mind of God. Still, *everything* can be comprehended in part. And we can always learn more about anything and know more accurately what we now know partially.

I also appreciate the resistance of Myers to the epistemological skepticism of those who would deprecate the value of rigorous inquiry into what is. Awareness of how ideology colors and constructs human knowing should never obliterate knowing itself. To construe knowledge to be nothing but a tool of perverse self-interest is itself a form of perverse self-interest. *God* calls his creatures to be "receptively reconstructive" knowers, to think God's thoughts after him (Van Til, 1976, p. 49). At the same time, Myers's call to epistemological humility acknowledges that inquiry, interpretation, and application are shaped by values, beliefs, sympathies, and philosophies at every point. There is no dispassionate realm of "science," contrary to those echoes of positivism that still resonate within our culture's received wisdom.

On closer examination of this question of the role of assumptions, however, I find myself parting company with Myers. He states the principle of presuppositional effects, but he does not work the principle consistently. Remnant positivistic tendencies water down and sometimes distort Christian distinctives. Myers begins by accepting the definition of psychology taught by the psychological "establishment" (Robert Roberts's phrase): "psychology is the science of behavior and mental processes." He takes as self-evident a statement that is in fact prejudicial and controversial. From the Christian standpoint it would be more accurate to say that "most scientific psychology pursues a fully secularized and deterministic interpretation of behavior and mental processes."

According to Myers, psychology does not purport to answer the "ultimate questions." Then he immediately states that "psychology will help you understand *why* people think, feel, and act as they do" (emphasis mine). But the "why" question is surely one of the ultimate questions. It is the cornerstone that systematically aligns each differing conception of human nature. Questions of motivation happen to be exactly where modern psychology is the least helpful and most misleading. It is more accurate to say, "Psychology will help you understand *what* and *how* people think, feel and do. But one of the effects of sin on theorizing is that unbelieving thought always gets the *why* wrong." Myers's epistemology lacks fine-grained attention to the particular intellectual effects of sin and redemption. He joyously holds creation and common grace in view but misses the consistent disorienting effect that fallenness exerts on conceptual systems—and the consistent reorienting effect of redemption.

Myers's four pairs of complementary truths illustrate the problem. As broad generalizations they are true enough—truistic, in fact. In each case a somewhat pallid generalization substitutes for the vigor, nuance, penetration, and specificity of the Bible's treatment of the issue under consideration. His descriptions of correspondences between psychology and generic Judeo-Christian religion prove, on closer inspection, to exhibit only a formal similarity to the Faith, not a substantive resemblance. Functional equivalents operating within contrary models are indeed "parallel," but the significance of such observations is rather like the comparative religions scholar who notes, "Christians and Muslims are similar in that both pray to a monotheistic supreme being, and the imam of a mosque parallels the pastor of a church." The peculiar delights of our piquant and shining Faith are dulled. If the counterfeit did not parallel the true in some way, it would be wholly implausible. Myers's effort to identify parallels even leads him to make statements that are false from the distinctively Christian point of view. Consider two examples.

First, the discussion of our vulnerability to error and self-deception fails to express Christian convictions. Our deluded perceptions arise not because "we are finite creatures" nor because "we are swayed more by vivid anecdotes than by statistical reality." Finitude is no barrier to true knowledge, and *God* sways us with vivid anecdotes more often than with statistics. Our main problem is that we are sinful creatures whose gaze and intentions register the "madness in [our] hearts" (Eccles 9:3). Our Father's true stories keep us from being swayed either by manipulative anecdotes or by supposed statistical realities. Empiricistic methodology offers no reliable corrective to our liability to error, because self-deceiving people design studies, then collect and interpret data.

Second, is it true that the "sense of divine grace is the Christian parallel to psychology's 'unconditional positive regard' "? Or is grace the radical alternative to a rather crude counterfeit? The grace in Christ is remote from an all-tolerant acceptance that "affirms me, just as I am." Unlike unconditional positive regard, God's love is pursuing, jealous, rehabilitating, passionate, self-sacrificing, choosy, generous, tough, committed, evaluating, beckoning, and protective. Divine grace accepts me *despite* how I am, "just as I am, without a plea, but that thy blood was shed for me" (see Powlison, 1994). A mother at a soccer game might feel unconditional positive regard for all the children in general, on both teams. But she *loves* her own son, feeling fiercely protective if an opponent trips him, anguished concern if he gets hurt, ecstatic joy if he scores a goal, and appropriate anger if he backtalks the referee.

Myers's two extended case studies—the efficacy of prayer and the validity of homosexuality—further illustrate the problem of scientific psychology's lack of significant weight and substance when stacked up against the riches of the Faith's wisdom. Regarding the efficacy of prayer, Myers made a searching presuppositional criticism of the assumptions operative in that research study. He showed a priori, nonstatistically, that the study will prove inconclusive and wrong-headed because it contradicts the Bible. Here is an example of pastoral theological reflection, arising from careful pondering of the Faith and hard thinking about how to bring the mind of Christ to bear. I couldn't help but think that everyone involved in that massive, costly project—researchers, pray-ers, and patients—would benefit far more from spending two hours doing a Bible study on prayer.

The homosexuality case study went the other direction. It illustrates how an interpretive grid can introduce biases, propelling a scientist to do hard thinking with frail data in order to contradict the mind of Christ. The facts that "prove" the legitimacy of homosexual orientation—chiefly the experience of ongoing struggle and cases of recidivism among those who attempt to change—equally "prove" the legitimacy of the historic Christian view that homosexuality is a typical sin from which God progressively redeems his children.

It is no surprise that people being redeemed out of homosexual lust battle with temptations—and that some fall back. This is true of every pattern of sexual lust, not only homosexuality: a woman whose romantic-erotic fantasies are energized by reading romance novels, a man whose eyes rove for a voyeuristic glimpse down a blouse, a woman aroused by sadomasochistic activities and implements, a man obsessed with young girls. In each of these cases, *lust* has been patterned around a characteristic object; *love* will learn a different pattern in Christ's lifelong school for reorienting the disoriented.

But there is no reason that an energetic, ideologically committed researcher could not find some data that might suggest that each of these sexual disorientations might arise from some biological predisposition. What if future research suggests that a particular personality characteristic, brain structure, hormone level, and perceptual style correlates to adult-to-child homosexuality? To bestiality? To heterosexual promiscuity? The last mentioned might even prove the strongest case for the style of argument Myers makes. Would his argument generalize to these cases? He would have to say yes if the statistics seemed to tilt that way. If persons with any of the above problems continue to struggle or at some point slide back into old patterns, then it might mean that their particular morph of sexuality is innate and valid.

I'm not familiar with the studies of female homosexuality, but let me offer an "unscientific" observation arising from pastoral experience. I've known many lesbians driven more by "intimacy lusts" than by the unvarnished eroticism of many heterosexual or homosexual males. In fact, most of them had once been actively heterosexual, unsuccessfully looking for love from a man or men. They eventually found that other women were similarly wired to intimacy and companionship as the context for erotic feelings. An emotional closeness initially developed that was progressively sexualized during the process of redefining oneself as a lesbian. Such a process makes lucid sense on the Faith's analysis of the outworking and inworking of sin. And I've seen the fiercely tender grace of God break in, progressively rewiring some of these women. Statistics might give definition to words such as *most, many,* and *some.* But statistics could neither confirm nor disconfirm the point of view whose plausibility is established theologically, anecdotally, and pastorally.

Myers's biological data on homosexuality was admittedly rather dim light, not something that could drag a researcher along who was not otherwise willing. But let me offer another "unscientific" comment about data that might yet be discovered. If or when the "homosexuality gene" is discovered, I predict that the facts will be of the following kind. Among people *without* the H-gene, say 1.5 percent are oriented toward homosexuality, while among people *with* the H-gene, say 15 percent are oriented toward homosexuality. That would be a very significant statistical difference. But what would it prove? Only that characteristic temptations differ, that our bodies are one locus of temptation, that nothing is deterministic either way. It will be analogous to finding any other "gene for sin." Those with the "worry gene," the "anger gene," the "addictive pleasure gene," or the "kleptomania gene" will be prone to the respective sins. Such findings cause no problem for the Faith. They do trouble a Pelagian view that defines sin only as conscious "choice." But sin is an unsearchable morass of disposition, drift, willful choice, unwitting impulse, obsession, compulsion, seeming happenstance, the devil's appetite for souls, the world's shaping influence, and God's hardening of hard hearts. Of course biological factors are at work: we are *embodied* sinners and saints. That some people may be more prone to homosexuality is no more significant than that some may be more prone to worry.

Grace is similarly personalized. Some of God's children find Philippians 4:4-9 breathes particular comfort amid their besetting temptation to anxiety. Others find the Spirit pacifying their fierce temper and writing James 3:1—4:12 on their hearts. Still others find Proverbs 23:29-35 clobbers them about the madness of their heavy drinking and that they grow wiser as they quit hanging out with old drinking buddies and spend time with new, wiser companions (Prov 13:20). Still others experience a keen-edged joy in earning a paycheck, paying for things they once stole, and sharing money with people in need (Eph 4:28). Others find that Christ's comprehensive vision for rearranging *everyone's* sexuality—in the whole Bible, not just "a half dozen verses"—reaches into their particular form of disorientation, teaching them to love people, not lust after them. One and all, former neurotics, rageaholics, drunks, thieves, and gays find that truth rings true and rings with hope.

Each of us deals with what Richard Lovelace termed "characteristic flesh" (Lovelace, 1979, p. 110). Repeat temptations and instances of recidivism do not change the rules. Strugglers with indwelling sin genuinely grow in grace, but often the generic issue remains on stage in some manner throughout a person's lifetime. Abiding struggles are no reason to throw over the Christian life, which is defined as growth amid struggle unto a future perfection (1 Jn 3:1-3). Those being redeemed out of homosexualized lust are examples of the rule, not exceptions granted license to give up the fight and rationalize their sin. The way Myers handled this issue illustrates the Achilles' heel in his view of the relationship between the Faith and psychology.

References

Lovelace, R. (1979). *Dynamics of spiritual life.* Downers Grove, IL: InterVarsity Press.

Powlison, D. (1994). "Unconditional love"? *Journal of Biblical Counseling 12*(3), 45-48.

Van Til, C. (1976). *The defense of the faith.* Philadelphia: Presbyterian & Reformed.

3 An Integration View

Gary R. Collins

Mr. Green was my Sunday school teacher when I was a teenager growing up in Canada. I remember both his gentle spirit and his deep concern when he learned that I planned to study psychology in my freshman year at the university. For Mr. Green, psychology was suspect, maybe something from the devil, certainly not a wise course choice for a young Christian student with thoughts of someday entering the ministry. Mr. Green could never have predicted, and neither would I, that his former student would spend a lifetime committed to serving Christ as a professional psychologist.

My professors largely ignored religion, and whenever it was mentioned in our textbooks the references were always negative. We learned about the fears of demons and the witch-hunts in the Middle Ages. We read about bizarre religious hallucinations in hospitalized schizophrenics and were introduced to Freud's view that religion was an opiate, a crutch and an illusion that someday would be replaced by science. During those student years I enmeshed myself in psychology and tried to learn it well. I also maintained my devotional life and determined to walk with Christ. I read the Bible regularly, taught a Sunday morning Bible class for undergraduates, and did extracurricular reading in the early pastoral counseling literature. Most of it was written from a theological perspective more liberal than mine, but it was all we had.

In those days, less than forty years ago, I probably never saw the word *integration.* It seemed that relatively few Christians were in the field of psychology. Apart from a handful of controversial visionaries such as Gordon Allport (1950), Hobart Mowrer (1961), Abraham Maslow (1964), and Karl Menninger (1973), speakers never mentioned religion at the American Psychological Association (APA) conventions I attended. When I found a book written in part by a former APA president who identified himself as a Lutheran, I devoured its contents and drew a red line under these words:

> We simply take for granted the truth of revelation found in Scripture. . . . [W]e also take for granted the essential correctness of what is held, on experimental or clinical grounds, by students of physiology, psychology, and psychiatry. If these two belief systems are both true, we ask what possibilities are conceptually available for accommodating them to one another. (Meehl, 1958, p. 6)

The book described the Christian psychologist as one who

> takes it for granted that revelation cannot genuinely *contradict* any truth about man or the world which is discoverable by other means. If such appears to have happened, he [or she] must operate on the assumption that this is only an appearance. That being presupposed, he [or she] then seeks to resolve the contradiction. . . . If a resolution cannot be effected, the problem is put on the shelf as a mystery, not solvable by the lights of nature or of grace but only in the light of glory. (p. 181)

The authors added that they did "not expect the non-Christian reader to be pleased with this methodology or even to understand how anyone can unblushingly adopt it" (p. 181). But for a young Christian graduate student, these words were like refreshing rain in a theologically dry and thirsty academic land.

It is beyond the scope of this chapter to summarize developments in the field of integration since Meehl and his colleagues published their 1958 book. It is enough to say that in subsequent years thousands of Christians have entered the field of psychology (and related fields such as psychiatry, social work, and professional counseling), hundreds of books and articles on integration have appeared, and numerous academic institutions have promised prospective students that integration is at the core of their educational programs. The integration of psychology and theology has become a subject of much discussion and much condemnation among Christians.

Despite all of this activity, we Christians have widely different views on how to integrate or even on whether integration is worth the effort. And we still don't agree on what the word *integration* means!

Waves of Integration

Everett Worthington (1994) has suggested that writings about the interdisciplinary integration of psychology and theology have occurred in three waves. The first was prior to 1975 and included Paul Meehl (1958), Paul Tournier (1964), Richard Bube (1971), and Gary Collins (1973). Worthington's list also should have included Clyde Narramore (1960), whose lonely pioneering efforts set the stage for much that would follow in the United States. Narramore's contribution has been lost in discussions of integration, perhaps because he was not a scholar writing for professional publications. Instead he worked as a practitioner and popularizer, becoming the first to make psychology respectable in the evangelical Christian community. Although Swiss physician Paul Tournier had no formal training in psychology or psychiatry, he began writing in 1940 with descriptions of how his faith was being integrated into his counseling-oriented medical practice.

The founding of the *Journal of Psychology and Theology* and the development of the Fuller and Rosemead graduate schools of psychology inspired a second wave of integrationists who, according to Worthington, addressed the integration of psychology and theology with vigor. During this period from 1975 to 1982, John Carter, Richard Mohline (Carter & Mohline, 1976), Bruce Narramore (Carter & Narramore, 1979), Larry Crabb (Crabb, 1977), Kirk Farnsworth (1982), Gary Collins (1977, 1981), and a few others proposed new models of integration. We were all young, psychologically trained, charged with energy, ignored by the professional psychology establishment, but convinced that our faith and our psychology could be combined in ways that would help emotionally hurting people, stimulate psychological and spiritual maturity, and enable the church to be a more sensitive, caring institution. When Jay

Adams (1970) led the first wave of vehement attacks on psychology, we read (and sometimes unfairly criticized) his works and the writings of other critics who followed. But the opposition inspired us to keep going with our integration efforts.

Worthington suggests that since 1982 the development of integration models has slowed to a trickle. Most of us who worked on such models have turned to other issues. We were (and are) still interested in integration, but even as model development became rarer in mainstream psychology, Christians also moved away from theory and focused more on practical issues such as Christian counseling, recovery, and spiritual development. We all had discovered—to our distress—that Christian theologians were like our secular psychological colleagues in that both had minimal interest in the integration of theology and psychology. As a result, some of the earlier leaders in the integration field began the formal study of theology. One product of this effort is my introduction to theology, written specifically for psychologists and other counselors (Collins, 1993).

Today we still talk about integration and read books such as this one, but as Faw (1998) notes, the term remains confusing and is used in a variety of ways. *Integration* has become a word shrouded in mystery, a slogan, a buzzword that gives us warm feelings but is used more as a gimmick to attract students than as a genuine scholarly achievement or a practical methodology. In addition to the confusion about what integration means, there are different opinions about what we are attempting to integrate. Do we integrate psychology and theology, psychology and Christianity, psychology and the Bible, counseling and Christianity, faith and learning, faith and practice, or all of the above? And what is our goal? Is it to relate one field of study to another, to harmonize two approaches to understanding and changing behavior, to reach some kind of unification, to develop a coherent and competent theory of counseling? Would words such as *synthesis, interface, interconnection,* or *interaction* add any clarity? Would it be even better if Christians abandoned psychology and gave up on the integration process altogether?

Perhaps we have now entered a fourth phase of integration history, a phase of reevaluation and renewed interest. Several thought-provoking and helpful articles have attempted to bring order to this field (Clinton,

1990a; Eck, 1996; Faw, 1998; Foster & Bolsinger, 1990; Narramore, 1992; Worthington, 1994). The authors have critiqued the integration efforts of a decade or more ago, evaluated present-day efforts to integrate, and attempted to clarify or redefine terms, methods, and goals. Some, like Clinton (1990b), Ellens (1997), and Heard (1993), have proposed new integration models. Bouma-Prediger (1990) has suggested that we need to distinguish four different kinds of integration: *interdisciplinary integration* that compares and combines two unique disciplines—such as psychology and theology—in some fruitful way, *intradisciplinary integration* that attempts to align theoretical perspective and professional practice within a discipline, *faith-praxis integration* that aims to bring consistency between one's faith and way of life, and *experiential integration* that refers to an inner harmony within oneself or between oneself and God.

Personal Perspectives on Integration

It was exciting for me to be among those who first entered the evangelical field of integration, but in reviewing the literature and preparing to write this chapter I have pondered why my focus changed over the years. The technical academic articles and debates about the fine points of integration are still stimulating for me to read. They are challenging for students entering the field of psychology, and they keep professors on the cutting edge of scholarly debate. But I wonder if all of the discussions are needed, if the hundreds of integration courses and articles have real and lasting practical relevance for impacting lives. And what about the psychophobic but sometimes insightful critics of psychology and integration? Are they worth taking seriously?

Issues like these have led me to several observations about the current field of integration. Discussed in no intended order of priority, these observations in the following paragraphs suggest that integration is worthwhile, undefinable, personal, and hermeneutically based. To have maximum impact in the years ahead, integration must be eschatological, culturally sensitive, outreach oriented, and Spirit led.

Integration Is Worthwhile

A student entering the fields of psychology or counseling might learn about the complex issues surrounding integration and wonder why anyone should even bother to relate his or her faith to psychology. I, however, believe integration is worthwhile for at least three reasons.

First, integration efforts are worthwhile because *Christians have a responsibility to care for the world, including its people.* Among other reasons, we human beings were created to protect, cultivate, and have dominion over the planet where we live (Gen 1:26-28). Earlier generations may have abdicated this responsibility, but we have an ongoing duty to subdue and replenish the earth, as thousands of modern environmentalists proclaim. I believe this is a duty given by God to all human beings, including but not limited to Christians. We are God's stewards of the world.

But the world is more than an environmentally polluted planet. It is a planet populated by confused, troubled people steeped in interpersonal, internal, and spiritual turmoil. We all are people who have sinned against God and tried to live according to our own efforts. But in the midst of this ever increasing population, God has rescued and redeemed a community of Christ followers, people transformed solely because of God's incredible grace and mercy. We who call ourselves Christians live in the midst of people—believers as well as nonbelievers—who need hope and healing. Jesus was acutely alert to the suffering people in his day, active in healing, and intent on changing lives. He was a model of compassion and caring whose followers are called to be the same, using every resource at our disposal to relieve suffering and bring comfort.

Christ followers believe that he is sufficient to meet every human need in this world (2 Pet 1:3). Sometimes he does this through direct intervention, but more often he accomplishes his perfect will by working through imperfect people. He uses preachers to proclaim, physicians to heal, writers and teachers to teach, psychologists or counselors to restore and promote stability, and many others to minister with their abilities and God-given gifts (Rom 12:3-8; 1 Cor 12). We who are psychologists and counselors submit our lives and our training to the Holy Spirit's control, determined to live out our Christian convictions in the practice of our professions. We use our specialized training, our Bible knowledge, and our sensitivity to the Holy Spirit's guidance to strengthen marriages, restore broken relationships, resolve inner conflicts, and encourage personal and spiritual enrichment. In a world steeped in sin's darkness, we seek to be lights shining through acts of caregiving so that people will see Christ, some will become his disciples, and many will give praise to the Father (Mt 5:16; 28:19-20). When we learn of people traumatized by violence, abuse, war, or natural disaster, we determine to use our training and knowledge—psychological and biblical—to minister in the name of Christ, even if this means no more than giving a cup of cold water (Mt 10:42). In these actions, we are members of the body of Christ, moving away from the church building, using our psychological training to minister to people who otherwise might never have contact with true Christ followers.

When we meet or work alongside non-Christian professional colleagues, we do not merge into their worldviews and hide our Christian perspectives under a cover of psychojargon and heady theorizing. Neither do we disrespect our secular colleagues by insensitively bombarding them with theologies and catchy evangelism efforts. Instead, we are like Paul in Athens. He reasoned with the religious leaders, including his potential critics, dialogued in the marketplace, made the effort to understand the culture, talked about his beliefs as he went about his activities, and earned enough respect from his pagan associates to be given a hearing. As a result, some sneered but many believed (see Acts 17:16-23, 32-33).

For years I have traveled to other countries to give lectures and lead workshops. Very early I learned that every speaker who goes abroad, even invited speakers, must earn the right to be heard. Audiences will listen politely to our speeches, but we will not connect on an emotional level or make the maximum impact unless we take the time to study the culture, learn about its values and mores, and demonstrate our respect for others with different beliefs and ways. In a similar way, the psychological community is unimpressed and untouched by colleagues who have not made the effort to learn and understand the psychological field. Trained and knowledgeable Christian counselors and psychologists can be salt and light, gently but not abrasively penetrating and influencing their professions, reaching people who would not be reached otherwise (Mt 5:13). Knowledgeable about psychology and Scripture, Christians can gently and respectfully be prepared to give reasons for their beliefs and their hope (1 Pet 3:15). This is a worthy calling.

Second, integration efforts are worthwhile because *Christians have the challenge of understanding the world, including its people.* Of course, we are finite creatures whose minds are distorted by sin and whose capacities to comprehend are limited. Nevertheless, since "God has revealed himself in both his world and his Word, one's grasp of his truth, finite and faltering though it is, will be enhanced by bringing these sources of truth together" (Faw, 1998, p. 151). People who study psychology join with Christians in physics, biology, history, the arts, sociology, and many other fields to gain a deeper and clearer comprehension of this complex universe that God created and sustains.

Introductory textbooks give various definitions of psychology, most describing it as the scientific study of human behavior. I view psychology as the study of human behavior and human nature, including overt actions that others can see, as well as less observable or unobservable variables such as motivations, inner conflicts, mental processes, perceptions, personal struggles, spirituality, and basic genetic and biological makeup. For decades students have taken psychology courses with the desire to "understand and help people," only to be disappointed when they find that most of the field has an entirely different focus. Clinging tenaciously to a rapidly disappearing, Enlightenment-based logical positivism, mainstream psychology (the kind students read about in introductory textbooks) has kept itself rigidly planted in scientific methodology. Unaware or unwilling to acknowledge that scientific psychology is fading fast, they continue to look for presumably objective, value-free, statistically analyzable data. Often that data comes filtered through selective perception and gives answers to irrelevant and obtuse questions that only a few researchers care about. Students want guidance about significant issues such as the meaning of life, the reasons for our existence, the causes of our inner struggles, or where we are going. They discover, instead, that a scientific understanding of human behavior does not answer any of these questions. It can't. Why then don't these students and their professors abandon the field, forget about integration, if they are Christians, and move on to more fulfilling pursuits? Wouldn't it be better to study the Bible to get all the information possible about people? Why is psychology still one of the most popular courses even on Christian college campuses?

Psychology is popular and worth studying because more than any other discipline it is committed to understanding people. While many in the field cleave to an outdated methodology that has limited value, numerous others view psychology as a broader and richer study of people in all of their complexity. These psychologists systematically and carefully use science, clinical observation, interviews, analysis of written materials including diaries and novels, case histories, and various other methods to know about people. As a result of all these investigations, including what has come through the scientific methods that many have criticized, psychology has accumulated and continues to gather a mountain of useful information about how people live, think, struggle, interact, and act.

Christians in psychology are able to go further than their secular colleagues. Through the influence and inner witness of the Holy Spirit, we have "inside information" about the universe, the origin and ultimate future of human life, and our purposes for living. Such understanding grows and our explanations become clearer when we grasp the truths of the Bible. Despite its wealth of information about human beings, their universe, and their God, the Bible is not intended to be a psychology textbook. But it supplies crucial background assumptions by which we can shape and judge psychological theories and conclusions (Van Leeuwen, 1996). For example, Scripture alerts us to the place of sin in shaping human behavior, the role of God in bringing healing, the reasons for temptations that can disrupt our lives, and the principles for living in harmony with others.

The Bible gives us all we need to know about God, human depravity, salvation, amazing grace, and many other issues that psychologists never touch or try to comprehend. Of course, the Bible does not tell us about issues such as the biological basis of depression, the effect of accurate empathy, the lifelong devastation of emotional or physical abuse, the means by which people learn, the developmental stages of infancy, the fine points of conflict resolution, or the ways to treat dyslexia or paranoia. Psychology focuses on issues like these. But even as the psychologist is limited in understanding if he or she is ignorant of the truths of Scripture and the systematic study of theologians, so the Christian is also limited in understanding people if there is little awareness of the field of psychology with its proven insights into the complexities of human behavior. The study of integration helps us to understand both fields and ultimately to engage in the Christian psychology that Evans defines as "psychology which is done to further the kingdom of God, carried out by citizens of that kingdom whose character and convictions reflect their citizenship, and whose work as psychologists is informed and illuminated by Christian character, convictions, and understanding" (1989, p. 132).

Third, integration efforts are worthwhile because *Christians must allow their commitment to Christ to penetrate every part of their lives.* The Christian faith is not an "add on" religion, tacked on as an appendage to life. As a Christ follower, my whole life exists to know him, to obey him, to submit to his lordship. I cannot prove that he called me to be a psychologist, but this is my profession, and I seek to live out that profession led by his Spirit and in a way that is pleasing and honoring to God. This is a type of integration in which I seek to live with an internal harmony between my faith commitment and my way of life. This is an integrated way of living that affects my thinking, my morals, my integrity, my relationships with people, my duties as a citizen. It guides the ways in which I interact with my family, friends, clients, and students. My faith commitment must have a bearing on how I deal with my finances, write my articles, teach my classes, and counsel with people whom I seek to encourage and help. My goal is to live a faith-saturated life. On this side of heaven only Jesus lived a perfect life. Today some Christians are more committed to this task than others, and some are more successful. But all are called to follow in the steps of the Master (1 Pet 2:21).

This is the type of integration that Bouma-Prediger (1990) termed faith-praxis integration. It is not limited to scholars or professional psychologists; neither is it solely a concern for Christians. Even people who have no explicit religious commitment tend to live their lives in accordance with the clusters of values, beliefs, and worldviews that form the core of their lives. One mark of the emerging postmodern era is a tendency for people to live in accordance with shifting value clusters. Disillusioned with institutionalized religion, these mostly young people build a virtual faith that has no rules, absolutes, rituals, or permanent core values (Beaudoin, 1998). As a result, their moral choices and behaviors in one situation may be radically different from what they believe and value in another situation. And they see nothing wrong with the inconsistency.

Christians are different. We may join with our postmodern colleagues in shunning some of the rigid Enlightenment embrace of scientific methodology, rationalism, and linear thinking. But we do not jettison the scriptural foundation upon which we must build our lives, worldviews, and psychologies. That biblical core of truth is the only sure rock of stability amidst the shifting sands of the contemporary world. Scripture is the foundation from which we integrate Christianity into psychology and into every nook and cranny of our lives.

Integration Is Undefinable

As we have seen, even after several decades we still cannot define integration in a way that is generally accepted. There are several reasons for this. First, there is no agreement about what we are integrating. To this point I have written mostly about psychology and *Christianity*, but in earlier writings I have discussed the integration of psychology and *the Bible*, and the integration of psychology and *theology* as if these are the same. They are not.

Christianity, for example, is a religion claimed by a vast number of people, many of whom have no conception of what it means to be a Christ follower. These people differ broadly in their perspectives and beliefs about Christ, ways of worship, theologies, and understanding of basic Christian doctrines.

The Bible, in contrast, is God's Word, a written document that many Christians believe to be inerrant and that most believers consider to be a trustworthy guide for faith and living. It is a guide that gives us glimpses into the nature and works of an infinite God. But Bibles differ from language to language and from one version to another.

Theology is a human system of thought. Evangelical theologians build their theological systems on God's revelation as found in the Bible and as interpreted by each theologian. Others build their theologies on experience, on the teachings of church fathers and other leaders, on contemporary scholarship, or on some other foundation. Even as psychology is diverse and complex, so are definitions of Christianity, interpretations of the Bible, and Christian theologies. All of this adds to the complexity of trying to define integration.

A second issue that confuses integration is the fact that all of these fields are in transition. They keep changing. It is futile to think that we can compile a stack of core, never-changing psychological facts and another pile of biblical or theological facts, and then nail them together to give us a stable structure that is integrated, merged, unified, and useful for understanding and changing people. Because of these transitions, I am beginning to think that instead of integration, we should think about the *joining* of psychology and theology (or psychology and Christianity, or psychology and the Bible).

When a person joins a partnership, a church, or a college faculty, neither side merges with the other, and there is no effort to obliterate the identities of those joined in order to make a third entity. When I became a full-time professor, I joined an academic institution that was changing and growing. I was doing the same. Two years after I signed my contract, both the institution and I had changed; the same is true of everybody involved with the school. But we are together, working as an ever-evolving team to accomplish some common purposes.

Psychology and the various aspects of the Christian religion are like that. Currently, for example, psychology is undergoing a cataclysmic paradigm shift as naturalism and Enlightenment thinking fade and postmodern perspectives take over and open up new directions in the field (Grace & Poelstra, 1995; Ingram, 1995). The church and the Christian religion are also changing as baby boomers grow older, the impact of Generation X is felt, and more contemporary forms of worship become accepted. Theology is also changing, as it always has. New movements and ways of thinking appear and affect theological thinking. New translations of Scripture, new archaeological findings, and new perspectives on the biblical languages bring changes to our understanding of the Bible. Our world is not static. Joining psychology and theology or psychology and the Bible helps us understand human beings better, and we learn how to better help people who are in psychological-spiritual need. But all of these fields will look different after another decade passes. This is exciting for people who thrive on change; it is distressing for others. It brings me to an observation about the personal nature of psychology, theology, and integration.

Integration Is Personal

For many years I taught a course in personality theory. My students read about Freud, Jung, Rogers, and others. At some point, usually near the end of the course, I would ask them to tell me their favorites. Most of the students resonated with one or two theorists and largely rejected the rest. I was the same. Regardless of my efforts to be neutral and fair in treating the theorists in my lectures, I liked some better than others.

Why do we have these differences? Like snowflakes that fall in winter, each human being is unique. We have similarities, of course, but we have different tastes, background experiences, physical features, perceptions, opinions, interests, and abilities. When I first studied personality theory, it quickly became apparent that the theories were more a reflection of the theorists than anything else. Consider Carl Rogers, for example. He was an American steeped in optimism, a man who began his career in a liberal seminary where the innate potential of human beings was emphasized. He developed his theories in university settings, often working with highly capable students and other intellectual and articulate individuals. Apparently Rogers's personality was warm and accepting; he was not inclined to confront or to challenge his clients aggressively. All of this was reflected in his writings and his approaches to understanding and counseling others.

I most clearly saw this impact of personality when I spent a year in Europe, writing a book about Paul Tournier. He called himself an old, country doctor who was not a professor or psychiatrist. His counseling reflected his life experiences—living on the outskirts of Calvinistic Geneva, molded by his personal loneliness as an orphan, affected by people who shared their experiences together in something called the Oxford Movement, influenced by living through World War II, changed by the experiences of his medical patients, never able to shake a pervasive insecurity. Unlike some of his more academically oriented peers, he never even tried to hide the fact that his writings came from his own experiences and reflected his own struggles. Tournier's theories were a reflection of Tournier.

The same is true of any person, Christian or non-Christian, who goes into the fields of psychology, counseling, or theology. Each of us is shaped by our Christian experiences, personalities, backgrounds, families, relationships, successes and failures, cultures, circle of friends, self-perceptions, denominational or church experiences, work histories, training, theological beliefs, and many others. This is so obvious that it tends to be overlooked. We talk about psychology and theology as if these were two neutral and objective hunks of information that we will somehow, someday, put together. In reality, every effort at integration is a reflection of the integrators. Every approach to counseling is the same—a reflection of the counselor's uniqueness, including his or her perspectives on Scripture.

I have not thought much about this, but surely there is a Gary Collins approach to counseling, writing, and teaching. I might try to tell others about my approach if I could. I might even write books urging others to follow my approach. I could even claim, arrogantly and confidently, that my approach is *the* biblical approach. Instead it is at best *one* biblical approach, guided by the Holy Spirit who knows me intimately and uses my distinctiveness to touch other lives. The same is true for all of us.

When we integrate and counsel, we need to remember that we are dealing with individuals. Even this conclusion had some of its roots, so far as I can remember, in a graduate school paper I wrote about Gordon Allport, who believed in individual uniqueness. My belief that integration is personal reflects a part of my personality.

Integration Is Hermeneutically Based

Until I enrolled in seminary (after I had my degree in psychology), I had never even heard the word *hermeneutics*. The word is thought to have come from Hermes, the Greek god who served as a messenger for the other gods, bringing and interpreting their messages to human beings (Virkler, 1981). As used by Christians, hermeneutics involves the art and methodology of interpreting the Bible. According to Heard (1993), however, the word has a much broader meaning and covers at least three distinct but related enterprises. First, there is hermeneutics that deals with the interpretation of religious and sacred texts such as the Bible. The second type is the interpretation of legal and literary texts—the kind of interpretation that high school English teachers give in their descriptions of what Chaucer, Shakespeare, or Hemingway meant when they wrote. The third hermeneutical enterprise involves understanding the natural and social sciences, including psychology.

Bible scholars agree on a number of hermeneutical principles that enable us to interpret Scripture accurately. It is widely accepted, for example, that interpreters should consider the type of literature that is being interpreted (e.g., poetry or history), the person to whom a text is addressed, the context of a specific verse, and whether or not there are parallel passages in other parts of the Bible that add clarification. Applying this to psychology and counseling, Cranmer and Eck (1994) demonstrate convincingly that both the therapist and client must develop an accurate understanding of how to read and apply the Scriptures correctly. Whenever a person approaches the Bible, he or she must be aware of both the text and the reader. Christians believe that the biblical *text* is objective, unchanging truth, but our interpretations will be in error if we fail to recognize the customs, rules, historical contexts, and ways of thinking of the biblical writers. Even when we genuinely seek the guidance of the Holy Spirit, no human interpretation of God's Word is infallible. The *reader's* own assumptions, opinions, and expectations also influence interpretation, including the passages we choose to study or the versions of the Bible we consult. For example, feminist, racist, prodivorce, antipsychology, progay, or antigay readers each bring a set of assumptions and often find in the text what each seeks.

It is well known that something similar happens with the interpretation of psychological data. Within recent years there have been heated debates about the etiology of homosexuality. Is it learned or biologically innate? Can it be changed through counseling or willpower, or is it implanted in one's genetic makeup like skin color? The answers to these questions often are based on selectively chosen research data or on the same data interpreted in different ways.

When someone comes to a counselor to discuss a problem, hermeneutics plays a key role in how the problem is understood. As a Christian psychologist I take it for granted that the Bible, God's special revelation, is an infallible source of information about human behavior, pathology, attitudes, spirituality, sin, guilt, and forgiveness. I believe that all human problems result from the Fall of Adam and Eve, when sin polluted the world and the human race. Every problem is the result of that sin, and sometimes problems come from an individual's direct disobedience. But

I do not believe that every psychological problem comes directly from the sinful behavior of the one having the problem. Psalm 73 is a sobering reminder that some people sin freely and appear to have no problems while they live in prosperity on this earth, yet others live lives of faithfulness and obedience but still struggle with multiple difficulties.

I have a friend who walks slowly, with difficulty, relying on the assistance of a walker. Many years ago he was riding his bicycle on a Sunday afternoon when an eight-year-old came careening around the corner and knocked him to the ground; he hit his head and almost didn't survive. In the early days of his rehabilitation my friend went through periods of depression, anxiety, frustration, and loneliness; he struggled to understand why God had allowed the accident to happen. Were these psychological and spiritual problems the result of sin in my friend's life? Did they come from the sin of the unthinking child who collided with my friend? Wouldn't it be more accurate to say that they came because we live in a fallen world where things like this happen? Some of my friend's problems came because of his physiological reactions to the accident, his need to readjust his lifestyle, and his difficulties in relearning some basic motor skills. If I had been his counselor, I would have prayed for him and prayed with him. We might have read the Bible together. But we also would have tried to understand the various causes of his problems and the best psychological, physiological, and theological ways to bring healing. My knowledge of special revelation—the Bible—would have been combined with my knowledge of general revelation—what God has taught me about his world through my study of psychology, physiology, counseling, rehabilitation, and other fields.

In what has been the major writing project of my life thus far, I wrote a book that grappled with about thirty problem issues, looked at each from a biblical and psychological perspective, drew on my experiences as a counselor, then gave guidelines for helping others deal with these problems (Collins, 1988). In writing the book I drew material primarily from two fields, tried to be as fair and as objective as possible in my hermeneutical interpretation of the data, and reached conclusions that I hoped others would find to be helpful. The method of sifting through the data was prolonged and difficult, but the result was a text that gave my best shot at understanding the causes and treatment of different problems. This was an exercise in both hermeneutics and integration.

Integration (Including Treatment) Must Be Eschatological

Thus far my observations about integration have concerned ongoing issues relating psychology and Christian theology. The remaining four observations take a more futuristic perspective and consider what the future integration or joining of psychology and biblical theology could be or even must be.

I am grateful to Warren Heard (1993) for introducing me to the idea of eschatologically oriented psychology. *Eschatology* is a theological term referring to the study of future things. Probably I am not the only one who has shied away from this branch of theology because of the proclamations of a few vocal and overzealous theologians who delight in linking obscure Bible verses with contemporary issues and making fanciful declarations about the future. Heard takes a very different view. He notes that eschatology has been overlooked in discussions on the integration of psychology and theology. Then he argues that with its focus on the future, eschatology could be the key to development of a truly Christian psychology.

For all of this century psychotherapy and much of Christian counseling has concentrated on the past. We have assumed that past experiences produce most present problems, so the best way to help is to take "archaeological expeditions" into the backgrounds of our clients in order to dig out and deal with the real causes of their current distresses. Once the past is cleaned up and the impact of harmful previous experiences has been removed or neutralized, we assume that the counselee gets better automatically. This is a nice theory (although I cannot recall Jesus ever using this approach), but we know that it does not always work. Most of us have known people who have spent thousands of dollars at the encouragement of their counselors to rummage around in the past, but they have never seemed to move beyond the historical explorations, so their present circumstances have not changed much. There can be no doubt that the past does affect the present and the future. In many cases there needs to be an exploration of the lingering impact of past trauma, rejection, abuse, or other negative experiences. But maybe we have put too much emphasis on the past and not nearly enough on the future.

Heard (1993) argues that Jesus and the New Testament writers were more focused on the future than on the past. To the Philippians, for example, Paul wrote about "forgetting what is behind and straining toward what is ahead" (Phil 3:13-14). He was not writing about therapy, of course, but he was expressing a mindset that needs to characterize Christians. Paul did not imply that the Philippians should completely forget everything in the past. In his writings the apostle often mentioned events in the past that were worth remembering (e.g., Eph 2:11-12; 1 Thess 1:3; 2:9; 2 Tim 2:8), and every counselor knows that there are things in our clients' pasts that need to be reviewed. But Paul recommends that we dwell less on the past and more on what lies ahead.

This is a paradigm shift, a new way of thinking that will take time to learn. Heard suggests that it is a unique position through which the Christian community can move psychology forward as leaders, instead of being followers of the latest psychological fads and theories. The development of this eschatological perspective is

> a *process* and takes place over a period of time. To be able to view events, past and present, from the standpoint of the future is not a product of repeated assertions, either by the therapist or by the client; it is a work of the Spirit, as the Spirit renews the client's mind. . . . Once this eschatological perspective is achieved, the client is able to pass through those painful events (as well as the present ones), not as one whose identity is that of an abused child, as one who conceives of herself as damaged goods, but as one who is healed and whole in Christ. (p. 129)

I remember the first few months after I left graduate school. I felt like a caged bird that had been freed. Free from the critical gaze of my secular supervisors, I no longer needed to pretend that God did not exist in the counseling room, that sin could not be at the basis of client problems, that religion was more harmful than helpful. But what I remember most was my discovery of the writings of William Glasser (1965). Unlike my former professors, Glasser did not seem to care much about the past; he was more interested in the present and the client's thoughts, hopes, and visions about the future. It was an early form of eschatologically oriented therapy, written by a nonbeliever and published long before the current fascination with the more future-focused brief, strategic therapies.

As we move into a new century, perhaps we need new, creative minds committed to developing new, more future-oriented approaches to helping and to integration. Such approaches will neither ignore the past nor downplay the present. That would be therapeutically irresponsible. But Christians, more than any others, are believers in hope and dispensers of hope. That hope is future oriented.

Integration Must Be Culturally Sensitive

When I gave the Finch Lectures at Fuller Theological Seminary in 1978, one of the invited respondents pointed out that I had forgotten the impact of culture. My lectures had overlooked how the social forces of a culture influence one's psychology, theology, therapy, and integration.

My thought turned almost immediately to the former Soviet Union, which at that time was at the apex of communism. To the extent that psychology was allowed to develop, it was highly controlled and Pavlovian. Treatment of emotional disorders was repressive and never permitted to be fashioned by Christian love. The integration of psychology and theology probably never entered anybody's mind, not even the minds of Christians. After the fall of communism, our eyes were opened to a major part of the world where there were almost no trained professional counselors and there was little awareness of the possibilities of joining psychology and Christianity to bring hope and healing to troubled souls. The Soviet psychology had been shaped by the Soviet culture and ideology.

I saw something similar years later when I began to pay regular visits to Asia. Counselors there were aware of the popularity of client-centered therapy in America, and many tried to introduce it in their countries. In doing so, they failed to realize that this was a product of our Western individualistic culture. It was doomed to fail in Asia, where loyalty to the family and respect for the wisdom and advice of one's elders is far more important than any individualistic, client-centered, nondirective approach to helping.

Reading the integration literature that has accumulated over the past few years, I have been struck with the cultural sterility of what I read. There is almost no awareness of society, no sensitivity to multicultural or crosscultural issues, no recognition that approaches to psychology and theology are both greatly influenced by the cultures in which we live. Some writers have begun dealing with the growing emergence of post-modern thought since this threatens to undermine much of what Enlightenment-molded psychologists and theologians have done for the past century, but I look in vain for references to technology, to ways in which the media are shaping our lives and our theories, or to the impact of galloping change.

Worthington (1994) may be right when he places me in both the first and second waves of integration. To the extent that I am in the current wave, I want to focus my attention and creative energies on something other than writing theoretical articles—important as this is. I prefer to devote my efforts to finding ways to bring my Christianity and my knowledge of psychology and theology to bear on the unique challenges of a rapidly changing, early-twenty-first-century world.

As one example, let us consider the emergence of the post-baby-boom generation. Most of them dislike the label, but they are commonly known as Generation X. Jimmy Long is a campus minister who has spent years working with members of this age group. Long (1997) believes that we are at a turning point in history, in the midst of a category five (the most intense) societal hurricane that already is changing the society. The strong winds of change have been blowing more gently for years, but today they are borne in full by Generation X, the first purely postmodern generation. It never is fair or accurate to characterize an entire generation within a few sentences, but some trends are commonly accepted. Instead of objective, universal truth, they prefer tolerance and personal choice. They value community rather than individual autonomy, virtual reality instead of facts arising from scientific discovery. They are more concerned about getting along than about getting ahead. They are more interested in building relationships than in building careers. In a discussion of leadership, Long (1997, pp. 152-153) contrasts the types of leadership that were spawned by the Enlightenment versus those of Generation X.

Enlightenment (Boomer) Leadership	Postmodern (Xer) Leadership
Positional	Earned
Perfect	Wounded healer
Supervisory	Mentoring
Product-oriented	Process-oriented
Individual	Team
Dictatorial	Participatory
Aspiring	Inspiring
Controlling	Empowering

When I first read this list, my mind turned from leadership to counseling. The emerging adult generation wants helpers who are willing to be mentors, counselors who admit that they are wounded healers, helpers who earn the respect of their clients and participate with them in the process of healing. Degrees, titles, theories, reputations, and methods mean little to this group. They want authentic relationships with counselors who care.

"I don't want to be somebody's project," a young man said to me recently over lunch. We had taken over a year to build a friendship, a year for me to earn his trust, for him to understand that I really believed in him. I don't think he has ever been to a counselor, and neither of us sees me in that role. But he wants a relationship with a caring friend. I want the same.

Will attitudes like this have a bearing on how we do counseling in the future? Our counseling, church ministries, and integration activities will be increasingly irrelevant if we ignore issues such as the thinking of postmodern Generation Xers, the unique perspectives of those who are members of minority groups, the feminist concerns of many women, including Christians, or the ways in which individuals are shaped by technology, including the Internet. Psychology, theology, integration, counseling, counselor education, Christian ministry—if they are to be relevant, none of these can be done in a cultural vacuum.

Integration Must Be Outreach Oriented
In 1991 I agreed, reluctantly, to get involved with an organization known

as the American Association of Christian Counselors (AACC). Through the very hard work of a small group of people, but mostly because of the grace of God, the organization exploded from a little collection of less than a thousand members to over fifteen thousand. Almost overnight my busy life got busier as I found myself involved in marketing, publications, member services, recruitment, financial reports, strategic planning, and conferences. In my capacity as president of the AACC, I began traveling around the country, meeting Christian counselors from various settings. I heard about their struggles with managed care, declining incomes, legal concerns, and ethical dilemmas. Some counselors were doing very well, but others were overworked, underpaid, and wondering if they could survive. The integration of psychology and theology was of little interest to these practitioners; they were more interested in meeting the needs of their hurting clients, maintaining their practices, and providing for their families.

I am a strong believer in theory, solid scholarship, and quality research. We need more of all three in the Christian community, especially the evangelical Christian community. In time there may be institutes or private foundations to support such activities, but at present, most of the intellectual work in the area of integration comes from academic environments. In contrast, most of the practical work of integration takes place away from campus. Whereas the professors, scholars, and students read, write, and lead us in the cognitive aspects of integration, practitioners like those in AACC are the frontline leaders of applied integration. The academics who write and read books like this one must never forget the practitioners who have limited time or leisure to read because of their never-ending caseloads. The practitioner needs guidance from the scholar-leader, but the academic also needs guidance from the therapeutic trenches. And all of us need to be aware of how our efforts can affect the world.

When Martin Seligman became president of the American Psychological Association, he announced a "new initiative" to create a "whole new profession" that would study ethnopolitical issues. Seligman concluded that "ninety-nine percent of what APA does is about domestic problems" (Seligman, 1998), but he wanted to broaden that narrow emphasis. He noted that all around the world there are people oppressed by ethnopolitical conflicts—Cambodian refugees separated from their families, Rwandan victims of a genocide that claimed 850,000 lives *after* a peace treaty was signed, Bosnian Muslims and Croats dodging Serbian sniper fire while running to the market for bread, individuals scattered around the world who live in constant fear of terrorist attack. Rescue organizations come into these dangerous areas with food, blankets, and tents for housing, but where are the psychologists? Who is helping traumatized civilians cope? Who is meeting the emotional needs of abandoned children or poor people in American cities who are immobilized by fear of violence? Seligman and his colleagues determined that their new discipline will encourage psychologists to research ethnopolitical conflicts, find ways to meet the psychological needs of the victims, make direct interventions to resolve such warfare and perhaps even develop ways to intervene before such conflict begins (McGuire, 1998).

When I first read about Seligman's proposal I felt a surge of excitement, but then I began to reflect. For centuries Christians have been at the forefront of social action. We are still there, especially through organizations such as Compassion International, World Vision, and Food for the Hungry. Why then have we who are Christian psychologists been so slow to find ways to get involved with the emotional needs of traumatized, suffering, often hopeless people who will never enter counseling offices or never know about integration? I was excited to learn that secular psychologists are taking a new initiative in this area, but it angered me to think that Christians in psychology are standing on the sidelines watching. "I believe psychology has always attracted the most idealistic of young people, but we've offered a more narrow outlet for their idealism—clinical practice," Seligman told an interviewer. "Now, that's all tied up in all kinds of financial issues, like managed care. But we see this [new] line of study as a profession that will speak to their idealism and their talent" (Sleek, 1998).

"Are Christian counselors going to leave this to secular psychology?" I asked an AACC audience in one of my talks at a regional meeting. Finding ways to get out of our offices, our classrooms, and even our communities is a challenge for psychologists who understand the basics of theology and who are committed to integration. This is practical integration, one example of many. No discussion of integration is complete if this emphasis on outreach is overlooked.

Integration Must Be Spirit Led

When Mark McMinn wrote his important book *Psychology, Theology and Spirituality in Christian Counseling* (McMinn, 1996), he boldly tackled issues that concern all who are interested in integration. He discussed the practice of prayer and confession, the use of Scripture, and the role of sin, forgiveness, and the psychological impact of redemption. His book is a model of the approach that I have tried to represent in this chapter.

Like McMinn's book, this chapter could have included useful case histories, practical methods, guidelines for integration and counseling, or more philosophical-psychological discussions of specific theological issues. Instead I have taken a different approach. I have tried to be alert to the prior publications in the area even while I have drawn on many of my own observations as a more seasoned but still active trooper in the integration journey.

I wish I could give a formula for integration. It might be convenient if we could approach integration armed with some currently nonexistent integration tools. A good integration manual, for example, might help us decide how to join psychology and theology or psychology and biblical Christianity into some kind of whole. A scale might let us weigh the ingredients and determine what is heavy in the different fields and what is lightweight. A good integration cookbook might tell us how to mix up a cure for depression, an antidote to anxiety, or a potion that could help our critics (or maybe us) see psychology more clearly. But there are no tools like this, and there never will be.

But we have something better, far better. We have the Holy Spirit who dwells within, guiding, sustaining, teaching, confronting, challenging, and convicting us. Like counseling, theory building, or any other human activity, the true integration of faith with psychology can never be a solely human enterprise. Integration has to start within—within you and within me. As the Holy Spirit is allowed to control our lives, he guides us. As we seek to become more familiar with Scripture, we learn the ways of God. As we worship in private devotional times and in consistent fellowship with the body of Christ, we become more Christ-infused, and this in turn affects our work as psychologists. When we realize that intimacy with Christ is more important than making an impact for Christ, he begins to transform our lives. As we submit ourselves to accountability relationships and determine to serve Christ in and through community, our lives become walking examples of integration. As he is integrated into our lives, we in turn can penetrate our professions and influence our world.

Henri Nouwen was a priest and writer who influenced my life through his many books. Trained as a psychologist and theologian, Nouwen never gave rules for integrating faith with practice, probably because he realized there are none. Instead he showed us what integration is like. He demonstrated that integration is not a noun but a verb. It is a way of life, an overt expression of caring that flows from an inner experience of communion with God. Sometimes I think we have systematized and intellectually conceptualized psychology and theology so much that we have squeezed out the spiritual. Our counseling becomes routine and dead. There is no place for the Holy Spirit's direction and effect. We fail to realize that practical integration involves humbling ourselves before God and trusting that his Spirit will work through our committed lives to touch and impact others.

Nouwen demonstrated this in his own life. Earlier in his career, he taught at Harvard, Yale, and Notre Dame. He had a hectic schedule and wide acceptance as a conference speaker. But he knew that all of this activity was suffocating his own spiritual life. To the surprise of many, he withdrew from the pressured pace and became a priest at Daybreak, a community for mentally disabled adults in Toronto. There he lived in a simple room and took care of a young man named Adam who could not walk, talk, dress himself, or care for his own bodily needs. Nouwen wanted to be like Christ to that young man who did not even realize how much he was in need (Nouwen, 1997).

Integration involves theory and research. I have argued that integration is worthwhile, undefinable, personal, and hermeneutically based. To have maximum impact in the years ahead, it also should be eschatological, culturally sensitive, and outreach oriented. But at its core, integration is a Spirit-led activity and a way of life that starts and ultimately takes place in the mind and soul of the integrator.

References

Adams, J. E. (1970). *Competent to counsel*. Nutley, NJ: Presbyterian and Reformed.

Allport, G. W. (1950). *The individual and his religion: A psychological interpretation*. New York: Macmillan.

Beaudoin, T. (1998). *Virtual faith: The irreverent spiritual quest of Generation X*. San Francisco: Jossey-Bass.

Bouma-Prediger, S. (1990). The task of integration: A modest proposal. *Journal of Psychology and Theology, 18*, 21-31.

Bube, R. J. (1971). *The human quest: A new look at science and the Christian faith*. Waco, TX: Word.

Carter, J. D., & Mohline, R. J. (1976). The nature and scope of integration: A proposal. *Journal of Psychology and Theology, 4*, 3-14.

Carter, J. D., & Narramore, B. (1979). *The integration of psychology and theology: An introduction*. Grand Rapids, MI: Zondervan.

Clinton, S. M. (1990a). A critique of integration models. *Journal of Psychology and Theology, 18*, 13-20.

Clinton, S. M. (1990b). The foundation integration model. *Journal of Psychology and Theology, 18*, 115-122.

Collins, G. R. (1973). Psychology on a new foundation: A proposal for the future. *Journal of Psychology and Theology, 1*, 19-27.

Collins, G. R. (1977). *The rebuilding of psychology: An integration of psychology and Christianity*. Wheaton, IL: Tyndale House.

Collins, G. R. (1981). *Psychology and theology: Prospects for integration*. Nashville: Abingdon.

Collins, G. R. (1988). *Christian counseling: A comprehensive guide* (Rev. ed.). Dallas: Word.

Collins, G. R. (1993). *The biblical basis of Christian counseling for people helpers*. Colorado Springs, CO: NavPress.

Crabb, L. J., Jr. (1977). *Effective biblical counseling*. Grand Rapids, MI: Zondervan.

Cranmer, D., & Eck, B. E. (1994). God said it: Psychology and biblical interpretation, how text and reader interact through the glass darkly. *Journal of Psychology and Theology, 22*, 207-214.

Eck, B. E. (1996). Integrating the integrators: An organizing framework for a multifaceted process of integration. *Journal of Psychology and Christianity, 15*, 101-115.

Ellens, J. H. (1997). The interface of psychology and theology. *Journal of Psychology and Christianity, 16*, 5-17.

Evans, C. S. (1989). *Wisdom and humanness in psychology: Prospects for a Christian approach.* Grand Rapids, MI: Baker.

Farnsworth, K. E. (1982). The conduct of integration. *Journal of Psychology and Theology, 10,* 308-319.

Faw, H. W. (1998). Wilderness wanderings and promised integration: The quest for clarity. *Journal of Psychology and Theology, 26,* 147-158.

Foster, J. D., & Bolsinger, S. A. (1990). Prominent themes in evangelical integration literature. *Journal of Psychology and Theology, 18,* 3-12.

Glasser, W. (1965). *Reality therapy.* New York: Harper & Row.

Grace, C. R., & Poelstra, P. L. (1995). Excellence in pedagogy: Some obstacles to integration for the Christian psychology professor. *Journal of Psychology and Theology, 23,* 237-243.

Heard, W. J., Jr. (1993). Eschatologically oriented psychology: A new paradigm for the integration of psychology and Christianity. In D. A. Carson & J. D. Woodbridge (Eds.), *God and culture: Essays in honor of Carl F. H. Henry* (pp. 106-133). Grand Rapids, MI: Eerdmans.

Ingram, J. A. (1995). Contemporary issues and Christian models of integration: Into the modern/postmodern age. *Journal of Psychology and Theology 23,* 3-14.

Long, J. (1997). *Generating hope: A strategy for reaching the postmodern generation.* Downers Grove, IL: InterVarsity Press.

Maslow, A. H. (1964). *Religions, values and peak-experiences.* Columbus: Ohio State University Press.

McGuire, P. A. (1998, August 1). Historic conference focuses on creating a new division. *APA Monitor,* 15.

McMinn, M. R. (1996). *Psychology, theology and spirituality in Christian counseling.* Wheaton, IL: Tyndale House.

Meehl, P. (1958). *What, then, is man?* St. Louis: Concordia.

Menninger, K. (1973). *Whatever became of sin?* New York: Hawthorn.

Mowrer, O. H. (1961). *The crisis in psychiatry and religion.* Princeton, NJ: Van Nostrand.

Narramore, B. (1992). Barriers to the integration of faith and learning in Christian graduate training programs in psychology. *Journal of Psychology and Theology, 20,* 119-126.

Narramore, C. M. (1960). *The psychology of counseling.* Grand Rapids, MI: Zondervan.

Nouwen, H. J. M. (1997). *Adam: God's beloved.* Mary Knoll, NJ: Orbis Books.

Seligman, M. E. P. (1998, spring). Individual profile. *Psychology International,* 6-7.

Sleek, S. (1998, March). Quelling ethnopolitical strife is the goal of a new initiative. *APA Monitor*, 14.

Tournier, P. (1964). *The whole person in a broken world*. New York: Harper & Row.

Van Leeuwen, M. S. (1996). Five uneasy questions, or will success spoil Christian psychologists? *Journal of Psychology and Christianity, 15*, 150-160.

Virkler, H. A. (1981). *Hermeneutics: Principles and processes of biblical interpretation*. Grand Rapids, MI: Baker.

Worthington, E. L., Jr. (1994). A blueprint for interdisciplinary integration. *Journal of Psychology and Theology, 22*, 79-86.

A Levels-of-Explanation Response

David G. Myers

Gary Collins says many things wisely and well. He is a compassionate conservative who cares for God's world and its people, and who has devoted his life to assisting caregivers worldwide.

At several points while reading Collins's chapter I found myself saying Amen! Some examples:

☐ *Engaging psychology.* "The psychological community is unimpressed and untouched by colleagues who have not made the effort to learn and understand the psychological field. Trained and knowledgeable Christian counselors and psychologists can be salt and light, gently but not abrasively penetrating and impacting their professions."

☐ *The call to understand the human creation and to worship God with our inquiring minds.* "Christians have the challenge of understanding the world, including its people. . . . Since 'God has revealed himself in both his world and his Word, one's grasp of his truth, finite and faltering though it is, will be enhanced by bringing these sources of truth together' (Faw, 1998, p. 151)."

☐ *The definition of psychology.* "I view psychology as the study of human behavior and human nature." (Although Collins is from the mental health end of psychology and I am from the research end, our definitions are on the same page.)

Nevertheless, our differences loom large enough to offer readers, in Barry Goldwater's words, "a choice, not an echo."

First, we differ sharply on whether "scientific psychology is fading fast." It is fading, thinks Gary Collins, because mainstream psychology still clings "tenaciously to a rapidly disappearing, Enlightenment-based logical positivism." Mainstream psychology "(the kind students read about in introductory textbooks) has kept itself rigidly planted in scientific methodology." Rather than dismissing mainstream psychology as dehumanizing and providing mere commonsense findings (Powlison's view) or as uninformative compared to the wisdom of the ages (Roberts's view), Collins dismisses it for giving "answers to irrelevant and obtuse questions that only a few researchers care about." He also faults psychology for not offering students guidance on "the meaning of life, the reasons for our existence . . . or where we are going" (which is like criticizing bowling for not being aerobic exercise or like criticizing biology for not being internal medicine). Should we not credit rather than fault psychologists who resist pontificating on questions beyond their competence?

My opposite impression is that scientific psychology is *rising fast* and has provided answers to all sorts of humanly significant questions that students find *fascinating*.

Consider first the growth in psychological science. The science-oriented American Psychological Society has enjoyed explosive growth, from five thousand members in 1988 to sixteen thousand in 1999. The expanding research literature published in the increasing number of journals is harder than ever to keep up with. Government funding of psychological science has rebounded from its Reagan-era lull and is now steadily rising. Private foundations also are expanding their support of mainstream psychology. These include the Pew Charitable Trust, which now funds the graduate educations of students aspiring to become intellectual contributors in mainstream disciplines, and the Templeton Foundation, which recently awarded $5 million for scientific research on forgiveness and has more such initiatives in the works. Psychology enrollments are expanding and now spreading into high schools, where the number of students taking the AP psychology exam (which tests mainstream scientific psychology) increased from 3,914 in 1992 to 21,974 in 1998 to 28,340 in 1999.

Strict behaviorism and its associated logical positivism are now dead horses in scientific psychology (as are Freud and humanistic psychology). Taking the place of these three dead horses (which some Christians in the antipsychology movement continue to flog as if they still represented psychology) are cognitive science, neuroscience, cognitive neuroscience and—at the turn of the millennium—behavior genetics, molecular genetics, and evolutionary psychology.

I don't fault those in the mental health professions for seeming oblivious to much of this (it's their primary job to be helping-professionals). But I do sense some wishful thinking about the demise of psychological science. One of social psychology's intriguing phenomena is the false consensus effect, which includes a tendency to overestimate the commonality of one's opinions. We mistakenly extrapolate from our own views and those of the mostly like-minded people around us to the world at large—who often turn out to share our views less than we had supposed. Are those who don't see or support the growth in psychological science perhaps falsely presuming a consensus for their disdain?

Ergo, in the world at large, scientific psychology is *not* fading fast. What *is* fading is its nonscientific alternatives, notably psychoanalytic and humanistic psychology, whose offerings history has not judged kindly. But is psychology "undergoing a cataclysmic paradigm shift as naturalism and Enlightenment thinking fade and postmodern perspectives take over"? Except for a reminder of psychology's biases and value-ladenness—lessons taught earlier by psychology's Marxist, feminist, and conservative Christian critics—postmodernism has so far taken us nowhere. What has it taught us? What insights from postmodern psychology would Gary Collins pose as questions for future psychology AP and GRE exams? Those in psychological science can offer a very long list of mind-expanding insights into human nature (regarding sleep and sex, perception and persuasion, motives and memories, and much else).

And do we not address questions of interest to almost any student who lives and breathes? Here are some that I promise answers to in the introduction to my *Psychology*, 5th edition:

> For most people whose exposure to psychology comes from popular books, magazines and TV, psychologists analyze personality, offer counseling, and dispense child-rearing advice.
>
> Do they? Yes, and much more. Consider some of psychology's ques-

tions, questions that from time to time you may wonder about:
- Have you ever found yourself reacting to something just as one of your parents would—perhaps in a way you vowed you never would—and then wondered how much of your personality you inherited? To what degree are you really like your mother or your father? *To what extent is your parents' influence transmitted through their genes? To what extent through the home and neighborhood environments they gave you?*
- Have you ever played peekaboo with a six-month-old infant and wondered why the baby finds the game so delightful? When you momentarily move behind a door, the baby reacts as though you actually disappear—only to reappear later out of thin air. *What do babies actually perceive and think?*
- Have you ever awakened from a nightmare and, with a wave of relief, wondered why we have such crazy dreams? *How often, and why, do we dream?*
- Have you ever wondered what makes for school and work success? Are some people just born smarter? *Does sheer intelligence explain why some people get richer, think more creatively or relate more sensitively?*
- Do you ever get depressed or anxious and wonder whether you'll ever feel "normal"? *What triggers our bad moods—and our good ones?*
- Have you ever worried about how to act among people of a different culture, race or sex? *In what ways are we alike as members of the human family? How do we differ?*

Finally, one smaller issue. Collins's list of contributors to the waves of integration includes the contributions of American conservative evangelicals but notably excludes the more science-friendly contributions of British evangelicals such as the late Donald MacKay and the still-active Malcolm Jeeves. MacKay was a brilliant neurophysiologist, artificial-intelligence expert, and philosopher of science. Jeeves has been a cognitive neuroscience researcher, editor-in-chief of *Neuropsychologica*, chair of one of Britain's three top-rated psychology departments, and president of the Royal Society of Edinburgh. Both have earned their evangelical colors as authors of several InterVarsity Press books and as speakers at many Christian gatherings and on many Christian college campuses. My good friend Jeeves met his wife while both were doing beach evangelism, and to this day gives active witness to his faith in conversation with leading intellectuals.

Both MacKay and Jeeves would find the antiscience views of their American evangelical counterparts puzzling if not dismaying. Their conviction has been that science—psychological science included—offers, at its own levels of explanation, a limited but wonderfully useful perspective on human nature. Like the architectural plan and elevation drawings of a house, different perspectives can each give us useful information.

Better yet, says Jeeves (1997), consider how the brain manages to take in visual information, process its component features separately, and, after combining these information streams with previously stored knowledge, recognize and act on it. As Christian scholars, should we not likewise welcome all sorts of "bottom up" input and process it "top down" as we draw on our stored knowledge? Bottom up and top down processing are complementary and mutually enriching. We may therefore think of scientific information, on the one hand, and the insights of past sages and biblical revelation, on the other, "as coming together for each of us to enrich our overall understanding of the mystery of human nature" (pp. 232-233).

While mindful of the significant questions that psychology cannot address (and which are the domains of other important disciplines), MacKay and Jeeves therefore celebrate psychology for what it offers us. Their perspective on psychology, and my own, is like that declared by Agnes Clerke in *A Popular History of Astronomy* (1893):

> What has been done is little—scarcely a beginning; yet it is much in comparison with the total blank of a century past. And our knowledge will, we are easily persuaded, appear in turn the merest ignorance to those who come after us. Yet it is not to be despised, since by it we reach up groping to touch the hem of the garment of the Most High.

Resources

Clerke, A. (1893). *A popular history of astronomy.* Edingburgh: A & C Black.
Jeeves, M. (1997). *Human nature at the millennium.* Grand Rapids, MI: Baker.
Myers, D. G. (1999). *Psychology* (5th ed.). New York: W. H. Freeman.

A Christian Psychology Response
Robert C. Roberts

Gary Collins has written a moving personal meditation based in his experiences as one of the key figures in the integration movement of the past three or four decades. His essay ranges widely and uses the word *integration* in a variety of references. One of his remarks is that integration is indefinable. As the token philosopher in this book, perhaps I will be pardoned for making one more effort to get to the heart of the term as it is used—or should be used—in connection with Christians' interaction with psychology. My "definition" will not be one that would occur in a dictionary (unless it was a dictionary of Christian psychology). And the real substance of my definition will be in the discussion that leads up to it. With such a definition in hand, I will then comment briefly on some things that Collins says. We meet variants of the basic idea and phenomenon of integration in many different contexts. Let us think about three integration words: *graft* (horticulture), *introduce* (ecology), and *adopt* (into a family).

When my brother-in-law grafts a branch of one kind of apple tree onto another kind of apple tree, he binds the two so they will grow together, integrating into a single tree. If the grafting succeeds, it creates organic continuity between the old branch and the new; the sap flows from the roots and trunk of the tree into the new branch more or less the same way it does into the original branches, and the new branch lives and grows and produces fruit. But it produces its own kind of fruit, which is similar but not identical to the fruit that grows on the rest of the tree. The new branch becomes part of the organic unity of the old tree, but it also retains its own special character, so that the whole tree has been changed to some extent.

When Chinese ring-necked pheasants were introduced into the American Midwest, they were quickly integrated into the ecological system. They ate the local grains and insects, thus affecting those populations. The coyotes, weasels, and other predators ate the pheasants, thus being affected by the introduction of this new food source. In turn (I don't know the details) the new pheasant foods and pheasant predators no doubt changed the habits and physical condition of the pheasants at least slightly from what they had been in the Chinese habitats. Thus the pheasants, initially foreigners, became an integral part of Nebraska plains ecology. In the process, both the pheasants and the original system underwent some change, while remaining recognizably similar to what they were before the integration.

When a child, especially a somewhat older one, is adopted into a family, we see similar dynamics, but they are even more revealing about the nature of the kind of integration that Collins is discussing. Here I am not talking about mere legal adoption but what we might call spiritual or moral adoption. A family, like a fruit tree or an ecological niche, is a system of patterns of relation and interaction of its parts. An adopted child has its own character, derived in part from whatever previous "family" it belonged to, and of course the new family has *its* character. If the adoption is successful as a moral and spiritual matter, then the child who is not born a member of the family is integrated into the family—becoming an "integral" part of the family. He or she begins to think and behave and react in ways that are more characteristic of the family. Also the character of the family will undergo subtle or not-so-subtle changes in virtue of the adoption, thinking and behaving and reacting in somewhat different ways than they did before the integration.

We could look at other cases of integration—for example, integration of a racial or ethnic minority into a community, or the introduction of a new paragraph into an already existing text. But let our three examples suffice as instructive analogies to the kind of integration that is central to Collins's concerns. In each case, integration is a *process* leading to a relatively stable *state* of integration. The process begins when an *element* (a branch, a species, a child) originally *foreign* to a *system* (a tree, an ecological niche, a family) is introduced into the system. (The foreign element cannot, however, be *too* foreign or integration will be impossible. One cannot graft a spruce branch onto an apple tree; pheasants would never adapt to a marine or arctic environment; a severely disturbed child might destroy the family into which he or she was adopted. It is an interesting question whether there are ideas and practices in twentieth-century psychology that are so foreign to Christianity that they cannot be adapted to it.) The process continues as the element and the system, originally foreign to one another, *adjust* to one another through their interaction, each changing somewhat to accommodate the other. A state of integration is reached when the element and the system have adjusted to one another sufficiently to produce a new version of the old system, in which the integrated element functions harmoniously as a part.

The element and system involved for Collins clearly come from psychology and Christianity. But which is the system and which supplies the element? At one point Collins speaks of integrating Christianity into psychology. That would suggest that psychology is the system and Christianity supplies some elements (prayer, a doctrine of grace, public worship?) that would be adapted for use in psychology. This might mean that our primary allegiance is to a psychological system—say, Freudian theory and practice—and integration would be the process of introducing some Christian elements. This suggestion would be very problematic and is not, I think, what Collins intends. Clearly his primary allegiance is to Christianity. He thinks that integration cannot be defined because it is unclear whether psychology is to be integrated into Christianity, the Bible, or theology. I suggest that we speak of integrating elements from psychology into *Christian thought and practice*. The Bible is our standard for Christian thought and practice, and theology is careful Christian thought about God and human beings and the church and such topics. When Christians differ in their theologies (that is, their understanding of the Bible), somewhat different integrative *proposals* are made, but this does not affect the *definition* of integration.

So I propose that Christian thought and practice be the relevant system into which elements of psychologies may be integrated. These elements might be data, theoretical claims or practices. The process of integration will result in a state of integration that will be the psychologically informed Christian thought and practice of a given community at a given time. In accordance with our previous reflections we can expect that after integration neither the Christian system of thought and practice nor the psychological elements will be quite the same as before. Here then is a formulated definition of integration for the present context: *Integration is a process by which elements of psychologies and a Christian system of thought and practice are adapted to one another to form a somewhat new system of Christian thought and practice; the resulting system can also be called an integration.*

Now let us return to the things that Collins calls (or seems to call) integration in his essay. When he says that "integration efforts are worthwhile *because Christians have a responsibility to care for the world, including its people,*" integration seems to refer to Christian action that supplies the means of grace to people who need help. The same applies to his plea that "integration must be outreach oriented" and "integration must be Spirit led." It would be odd to refer to such Christian action as integration, except that Collins has in mind action that makes use of techniques and theories from secular psychology. This then is the practice of that new system of Christian thought and practice that is the result of the process of integration, according to the definition. When Collins speaks of integration as intelligent witness to secular colleagues in psychology, it is the same system in action, except that now the emphasis is perhaps on the thought involved. At that point Collins also speaks of integration as the activity of studying and understanding both psychology (presumably secular psychology) and the Bible. So here he is referring to the process by which the new system of thought and practice develops.

When Collins says that "integration is personal," he seems to mean that the process of adapting elements of psychologies and Christian thought and practice so that they form a whole is influenced by the personal tastes and background experiences of those pursuing the process. To say that integration is hermeneutically based is to say that the process involves interpreting and understanding the Bible and interpreting and understanding psychological data and peoples' problems, all of which is no doubt correct and consistent with our definition. When he recommends that integration be culturally sensitive, he is saying that as we adapt elements of psychologies for use in our Christian thought and practice, we should be sensitive to the cultural origins of the psychologies and to our own cultural biases, as well as to the ways in which culture affects the persons to whom we minister. This point might have been subsumed under his discussion of hermeneutics.

When Collins says that integration must be eschatological, integration again refers to the system of Christian thought and practice that results from the process of adapting Christianity and elements of secular psychologies, and he is proposing that such a system be characterized by the future orientation that is often found in the Bible. (But I should point out that he errs in thinking that eschatology is the study of future things; it is the study of *last* things. Since William Glasser's psychology had nothing to do with the second coming of Christ, the resurrection of the dead, the final judgment, or even the secular counterpart of any such thing, it is wrong to say Glasser's psychotherapy "was an early form of eschatologically oriented therapy.")

Collins uses the word *integration* to refer to living "a faith-saturated life." He rightly points out that such integration "is not limited to scholars or professional psychologists," so we need not concern ourselves whether this kind of integration fits our definition (it does not), since our definition is designed for that special context. Here *integration* is a somewhat unusual word for *really taking Christian teachings and practice to heart.* This is, of course, just as important for psychologists as for any other Christians.

So we see that except for the last mentioned usage, which makes a general point about the Christian life quite independent of psychology in the sense germane to this book, Collins's discussion does have a conceptual focus and is not the meandering fantasia of themes that he takes it to be. This is a result that we might well expect in the writing of a man who has given his whole adult life to thinking about integration themes and has been a leader in the field.

My hermeneutical exercise will perhaps seem to some the height of vain fastidiousness, but to psychologists with a penchant for ideas it may give the comfort of firmer conceptual orientation and clarity. In this response I have merely clarified the concept of integration; I have neither endorsed integration nor criticized it. In my chapter (this volume) I have stressed the importance of nonintegrative Christian psychology both as a discipline worth pursuing in itself and as a preparation for responsible integration. I mentioned that I do endorse integration as an activity for Christian psychologists. In my response to Powlison I have defended the possibility of integration while agreeing with some of Powlison's worries about its present-day practice.

A Biblical Counseling Response

David Powlison

Gary Collins tells the story of his experience, commitments, and hopes, how one professional psychologist seeks to live as a faithful Christian. I greatly respect his effort to live faithfully—a difficult enough walk for any of us, whatever our working philosophy of counseling. Many of the things Collins does and aspires to are admirable Christian virtues and wisdoms. With all my heart I hope that every disciple of Jesus who happens to be a mental health professional does much that Gary Collins suggests positively.

Be an evangelist for Jesus Christ. Use your degree, credentials, and network of relationships to make disciples of one of the most skeptical, committedly self-sufficient people groups on earth: secular mental health professionals and academic psychologists. They have rarely been intelligently evangelized. Don't bring a message limited to change in personal faith and morals. Touch them at their core theoretical and professional assumptions, bringing God's radical view of persons, change, and change agents. Christianity 101 turns the field upside down: every human being is exhaustively dependent on and accountable to the only God; the human psyche operates vis-à-vis God, whether actors and observers know it or not; neither biology nor social experience casts the deciding vote on how a life is lived; all psychotherapies perform a ther-

apy of the word, discipling devotees into either Christ's image or an idol-
atrous image; and so forth.[1]

Similarly, bring Christ relevantly to those you counsel. To the degree
you truly understand them—gifts, sins, sufferings, blessings, opportunities—you will see how the grace and peace of Christ is their pervading
need. Don't teach anxious man-fearers and self-trusters either to trust in
you or to trust in themselves more effectively. Don't teach headstrong,
desire-driven people to redirect, temper, or exchange their fallen desires.
Christ utterly reorients people to himself.

Be a learner about people. Study your own life in the light of the Searcher
of hearts, the Friend of sinners and sufferers. Study other people with a
tender heart and that same redemptive gaze and intentions. Always see
how you are essentially like others. Never fall into the world's diagnostic
judgmentalism. Subject every one of the world's diagnostic and theoretical categories to a radical paradigm shift. Don't think that secular psychologies are the best or even a reliable source of supple, penetrating,
relevant, life-renovating truth.

Think hermeneutically. To walk in Christ is to continually perform a
threefold interpretation: exegete Scripture, exegete people (including
yourself), exegete the situations that people face. All of human life is an
interpretive activity, and the counseling process is a particularly intensi-
fied version. You dare not be naive, thinking either that there is "neutral,
scientific" truth regarding people or that truth is subjective. There *is*
objective truth—God's point of view. And there are countless partial
truths, half-truths, distortions, and lies. Various "fields" of human study
and activity are like human beings themselves: strewn with slivers of
truth but subject to systematic distortions, needing corrective reinterpre-
tation by the redemptive Word.

Live, think, and practice eschatologically. The future tells all. The secrets
of all hearts will be revealed; every knee will bow. Your dissertation advi-
sor, your supervisor, your colleagues, and every man, woman, and child
you counsel are included in "all" and "every." The drama of every life
turns on fidelity or infidelity unto a day of reckoning. To gaze eschatologically is one of many keys to the truly Christian psychology, to sound

---

[1]See Welch (1995) for an exemplar.

pastoral theology. The twentieth-century church has been rather poor at relating its faith and practice to the issues of counseling. It has tended instead toward either "religious" quick fixes or "being followers of the latest psychological fads and theories." Become part of the solution, not a perpetuation of the problem.

Live, think, and practice in ways that are culturally sensitive. The Faith's psychology is for every nation, tribe, tongue, and people. Which of the other psychologies truly bridges cultures? The unadulterated Freud, Jung, Adler, and Frankl plausibly "work" for Europeans casting about for a post-Christian meaning system. But to diffuse, even into the American context, they had to be rejigged. Soviet psychology plausibly "worked" under that politicized eschatology. Rogers, Skinner, biopsychiatry, and psychotherapy plausibly "work" in America because they are products of an optimistic, pragmatic, "can do" culture of the expert. But all the Western psychologies are implausible in other cultural contexts for various reasons. The Faith's psychology rings true everywhere. Gen-Xers, most world cultures, and the living God delight in authentic relationships between caring friends and devalue the legitimating badges of professional psychotherapy. Wise, truth-filled love is *the* credential for counseling others.

Be outreach-oriented. Christ would have us touch the variously afflicted in a mercy ministry of both Word and deed. While American mental health professions obsess over managed care, how to build a profitable practice, and how to maintain professional perquisites and privileges, true Christian ministry rolls up its sleeves.

Be led by the Holy Spirit. The Spirit produces "faith working through love," creating Christ-infused people who get about the business of being disciples and doing ministry.

These wisdoms are about being a Christian. But what do they have to do with "integration"? They say nothing particular regarding "the integration of x and y." Indeed, I know plumbers who understand their calling in these same terms: "Plumbing is worthwhile. I share Christ with peers and customers. I really get an education in human nature from my customers—and from my own reactions as I pursue integrity. My vision of Christ's return helps me keep perspective in troubles. I do work gratis or cut-rate for those who are poor. I seek to walk in the Spirit." Plumbing has a distinctive knowledge base and sphere of practice. But personality theories and psychotherapies overlap at every point with sound theology and sound Christian practice.

The *debate* turns on how the Faith should interact with the ideas and practices of the modern secular psychologies. According to Collins, we need to join, blend, or copractice two different things, Christianity and psychology. Each makes an essential and constitutive contribution. Historically, this has been termed "integration." The other point of view (per Robert Roberts and myself) is that the Faith itself teaches a distinctive psychology, decidedly subordinating competing theories and competing professional structures. Evangelical psychotherapists' distinctive knowledge is vulnerable both to good pastoral theology and to the chaos and indeterminacy in their field of particular expertise. Their distinctive sphere of practice is vulnerable to wise, effective disciple-making by pastoral and peer ministry.

Collins perplexed me with his definition(s) of *integration*. With one hand he rendered the term semantically useless. "Waves of integration," "integration is undefinable," and "integration is personal" describe all as flux and idiosyncratic opinion. Collins puts a brave face on it—this is "exciting for people who thrive on change." But he provides no anchors. This is distressing not only for those who find change distressing but also for those who love change, discontinuity, spontaneity, flexibility, a proper relativism, a fresh perspective. *God* anchors the dazzling variety of the many in the glorious continuities of the One. All is not flux, however chaotic the state of scholarship, fields, disciplines, and personal proclivities.

With the other hand Collins resuscitates the term *integration*—ambiguously, evocatively—as the definitive noun for his positive program: "Integration is . . ." His bottom line is an extended defense of this notion: "The role of professional clinical psychologist is a valid and decidedly Christian ministerial calling. The verb *to integrate* is synonymous with 'to be a Christian.' Walking in the Holy Spirit, the practitioner of 'integration' does evangelism, mercy ministry, personal cure of souls, one-anothering friendship, and sound theology in a ministry of Word and deed to every nation, tribe, tongue, and people."

This should trouble both integrationists and critics. It will dismay colleagues whose professional and departmental existence depends on "integration" being an activity and agenda that is definable, theologically defensible, intellectually productive, and practically helpful. If integration is in a state of intellectual confusion, if the term signifies a mystery, a slogan, a buzzword that elicits warm feelings, a recruiting gimmick more than a genuine scholarly achievement or practical methodology, then what? One of the fathers of the faith doubts the intellectual program and instead bends his efforts into transmuting Christian psychologists into pastors, deacons, theologians, one-anothering friends, and everyday walkers in the Spirit. I cannot imagine that the board of Fuller, Wheaton, Reformed, or Trinity will find that this commends the need for a psychology department or legitimizes an integrationist philosophy within the counseling department. Why should something so uncertain be crucial to intellectual integrity and practical efficacy? It does not take "integration" to say, "Be a Christian. Think theologically. Know and love people. Do ministry."

Collins may be agnostic about integration's viability as an intellectual program, but he earnestly advocates the validation of psychologists as distinctively Christian workers. This thrusts crucial questions out into the open. Should professedly Christian psychotherapists be defined as freelance ministers of the Word of Christ? Do their education and credentials equip them to engage in cure of souls as designated experts? If the evangelical psychotherapy movement no longer bases its identity on claims to distinctive knowledge and a distinctive sphere of practice, will it subordinate itself to vigorous theological and ecclesiastical oversight? No evangelical should object if the guiding intention of evangelical psychologists were to infiltrate the secular mental health system. There the credentials mean something. But to create an evangelical mental health establishment, to set themselves up as the church's experts on human nature and curing souls, to cultivate a Christian clientele, these things are deeply troubling. However credible, even admirable, the personal faith of individuals involved, such a program co-opts the church's essential ministry by an alien profession—and the track record bears witness that essentially alien ideas attend the profession.

To the degree that Collins's practitioners of "integration" really walk in the Holy Spirit by doing evangelism, mercy ministry, personal cure of souls, friendship-based one-anothering, and sound theology, they cease to be psychologists in any technical, twentieth-century definition. They become pastoral theologians, biblical counselors, and mere Christians, "psychologists" in the old sense. They become less and less "integrationists," attempting to marry incompatible paradigms. I know many Christians with advanced education, experience, and credentials in psychology who no longer think that the modern psychologies contribute anything constitutive for wisdom and effectiveness in counseling.

On the other hand, to the degree that practitioners of "integration" continue to tout their identity as mental health professionals, claiming affiliation or evidencing affinity with one or more of the modern personality theories and psychotherapies, they fail to do Christian ministry. Collins's attempt to turn psychotherapists into Christian workers and mere Christians, while continuing to validate them as professional psychologists, cannot work. The more they remain distinctively clinical psychologists, the more they will work largely at cross purposes to the Faith's psychology.

Finally, let me propose a guiding resolution to the flux so evident within "fields," "disciplines," and "professions." Our primary need is not to "integrate" fields, whether as bodies of knowledge or as spheres of professional activity. The goal is much simpler: accurately understand people and help them. The Faith has anchors in Scripture and subsequent Christian culture. Our Father's word is truth; death awaits all and all hearts are steeped in evil; Jesus Christ remains the same, full of effective compassion; speaking the truth in love, we grow up. Augustine still speaks truth about our disordered loves and Christ's past, present, and future grace. Francis of Assisi's prayer overturns the "psychological needs" theory that dominates recent Christian psychology. We need these and other understandings that express the mind of God our merciful Father, who made, knows, judges, and changes people. We need to comfort the disturbed, disturb the comfortable, and change all into Jesus' likeness. Whether or not such forms of understanding, skill, and love are reflected in the current status of fields and professions is significant but secondary. Contemporary psychologies may be godless; theologies may be scholastic; psychotherapies may nurture human autonomy; pastoral theologies may extol the pulpit and ignore counseling; medicine may medicalize moral issues; literature may glorify evil. What exists may or may not be true and helpful. We are not playing an intellectual game: God's glory and human lives are at stake. Let's get to work, producing requisite pastoral wisdoms where they are absent that we may serve the call of God and the needs of humankind.

References
Welch, E. (1995). A discussion among clergy: Pastoral counseling talks with secular psychology. *Journal of Biblical Counseling, 13*(2), 23-34.

4 A Christian Psychology View

Robert C. Roberts

Integration and Two Alternatives

At Wheaton College, where I taught, the watchword is "the integration of faith and learning."* The contrasting case is that of Christian schools in which the academic curriculum in economics, history, psychology, philosophy, chemistry, mathematics, and so forth is pretty much what you would expect in a purely secular school, but the teachers and students are mostly Christians. They pray before classes, belong to small group Bible studies, organize evangelistic projects for the weekends and regularly attend the chapel that dominates the center of campus. At Wheaton a person does all the above, but also tries to bring faith into closer involvement with the subject matter of the lectures and discussions in the academic program. We try to see how psychology itself, for example, looks when brought under the lordship of Jesus Christ, how philosophical theories will be different and more powerful if we assume that God exists, how biological explanations will not be the same if we assume the doctrine of divine creation. If the Wheaton model is the *integration* of faith and learning, the other model might be called the *juxtaposition* of

*This essay stems from work that I started in 1992-1995, when I was supported by a generous grant from the Pew Charitable Trusts for research in Christian psychology.

faith and learning. The supposition of either of these models seems to be that faith is one thing and learning another, and that they are sufficiently alien to one another that they can *either* be juxtaposed but allowed otherwise to be autonomous from one another, *or* they can, by effort, be brought together so that they interpenetrate and influence one another. Both models suppose an initial alienness of faith and learning.

This supposition is more plausible in some disciplines than in others. The strongest case for my thesis that sometimes neither integration nor juxtaposition is the appropriate model is that of theology. Theology is a branch of learning, but no one is much inclined to speak of the integration of faith and theology. The two are already, by their nature, too intimately and naturally involved with one another for it to make sense to propose integrating them. To do so is a bit like proposing intimate intertwining of the lives of Sarah and Bill, who are happily surrounded by their seventeen grandchildren and five great-grandchildren on the occasion of their fiftieth wedding anniversary. The case is less obvious for psychology, but I shall argue that the integration model is not always the best way to think about the relation between psychology and faith.

To think it is the best model is to accept a certain view of psychology, which the psychological "establishment"—represented by psychology departments in major universities and the American Psychological Association—has socialized us into accepting implicitly. At Wheaton College, for example, all the psychology faculty have credentials and a theoretical orientation that is sanctioned by the psychological establishment. In the clinical program they come trained in, and to some extent committed to, one of the major psychotherapeutic models—cognitive-behavioral, psychoanalytic, family systems, or humanistic—and in the broader department they have sanctioned skills and areas of expertise such as personality, developmental psychology, assessment, experimental design, statistics, neuropsychology, and so forth. These models, disciplines, and skills do not have a very long history, by historical standards, so if one accepts this picture as the picture of *psychology as such*, it makes a lot of sense to think that if Christians are going to practice psychology with integrity, we had better figure out how to integrate it with our faith. That is, psychology and faith are clearly coming from very different directions; the one originates in various strands of the Enlightenment and Romantic individualism or science or scientism, the other in a blend of ancient Hebrew theocracy and classic Hellenism. Faith and psychology are thus originally alien entities, not related in anything like the basically united way that faith and theology are.

What Is Psychology?

The integration model is compelling if we accept the establishment view of what psychology is. But if we take a broader historical perspective, it is clear that what the psychological establishment calls psychology is not the only thing that might justifiably go by that name (Van Leeuwen, 1985). If we look closely at the alternatives, it is almost as clear that what the establishment calls psychology, while it has made significant contributions to our understanding of human nature and functioning, is not always superior to other kinds of psychology that have been offered from time to time in history. It seems clear to me, for example, that while the twentieth-century behaviorist school and its softer, more "mind"-friendly successors have taught us some important things about human susceptibility to conditioning, the account of human action offered in Aristotle's *Nicomachean Ethics* (fourth century B.C.) is superior to anything that that twentieth-century style of inquiry has produced. (For a brief history of the concept of human agency in that twentieth-century psychology, see Johnson, 1997b, pp. 144-151.) Similarly, I would agree with Martha Nussbaum's high opinion of the theory of emotion developed by the Stoic Chrysippus (third century B.C.; see Nussbaum, 1994), a broadly cognitive theory that is the equal or superior of anything analogous produced by the psychological establishment. A very sophisticated theory of emotion, from which twentieth-century theorists could profit, is the account in Thomas Aquinas's *Summa Theologiæ* (thirteenth century A.D.; see Roberts, 1992), the first part of the second part, questions 22 to 48. In a very different style, English and Russian novels of the nineteenth century, by such authors as Jane Austen, Charles Dickens, George Eliot, Fyodor Dostoyevsky, and Leo Tolstoy are sources of tremendous psychological insight into issues of human motivation, basic psychological needs, forms and sources of pathology, and much more. Aristotle, Chrysippus, Tolstoy, and the rest are not regarded by the psychological establishment as bona fide psychologists because of their lack of connection with "scientific" procedures of inquiry, scientific medicine, and an established profession of psychology, the three major sources of prestige and authority for what the psychological establishment more or less exclusively calls psychology.

Of the above mentioned sources, Aquinas and Dostoyevsky belong clearly within the Christian tradition, and several of the novelists are heavily influenced by Christianity. Let me mention some other sources of distinctively Christian psychology. The desert fathers (see Ward, 1975; Stewart, 1991) were remarkably insightful Christian counselors. Evagrius Ponticus (1981) and John Cassian (1955; see Stewart, 1998) systematize some of the teachings of the desert fathers that began the long Christian tradition of analyzing and offering therapeutic strategies against the "thoughts" or "passions" known as the "seven deadly sins." Saint Augustine's *Confessions* and other works embody a psychology that makes the love and service of God essential to human nature and human well being. I mentioned Thomas Aquinas's account of the emotions, but his *Summa Theologiæ* contains rich and deep discussions of many other psychological topics—for example, habits, actions, basic human nature, sin, the process of sanctification, and virtues, which are states of properly functioning character or personality. Richard Baxter's *Christian Directory* (1673) is an enormous collection of pastoral advice, much of which is psychological and which is virtually untapped by contemporary Christian psychologists. Two major works of psychological relevance by Jonathan Edwards are *A Treatise Concerning Religious Affections* (1746) and *Charity and Its Fruits* (1852). Perhaps the greatest and most profound of Christian psychologists is Søren Kierkegaard. Virtually everything he wrote touched on psychology, but I will mention especially his books *The Concept of Anxiety* (1844), *Concluding Unscientific Postscript* (1846), *The Sickness unto Death* (1849), *Christian Discourses* (1848), *Works of Love* (1847), and *Upbuilding Discourses in Various Spirits* (1847).

The psychological establishment's conception of psychology, insofar as it excludes the kind of thing I have been mentioning, is *one* possible conception and a rather narrow one at that. Furthermore, not everything that passes as psychology in the establishment is strongly connected to either science or scientific medicine; some of it is connected to these things only by association. For example, much of "classic" personality theory is based not in any strict way on empirical data but rather on contestable premises that seem to have more a philosophical than a scientific character (see Griffiths, 1997; Vitz, 1997). And the kind of constructs that typically arise out of clinical experience—contestable again—are made on the basis of the kind of careful but not statistically worked up observations that informed an Aristotle, a Chrysippus, a Thomas Aquinas. That conceptions basic to the kind of constructs that distinguish one therapeutic school from another or one personality theory from another are contestable is shown by the diversity and rivalry of those theories displayed in such books as Raymond J. Corsini's *Current Psychotherapies* (1979) and Salvatore Maddi's *Personality Theories: A Comparative Analysis* (1980). I have also explored this diversity and rivalry (Roberts, 1993).

I propose a broader conception of psychology. A psychology is *a coherent body of thought and practice (a system), at least partially articulate, for understanding, measuring, assessing, and possibly changing people's emotions, thoughts, perceptions, and behaviors, and their dispositions to these. It will typically posit or assume some conception of the goal or purpose of human life, or the basic drives and problems of human life, or at least the proper functioning of some special part of the person (such as the perceptual organs), and it will have some conception of how a person develops, properly or improperly, toward the achievement of that goal, the satisfaction of those drives, the solution of those problems or that proper functioning. It will accordingly also have some conception of the obstacles to a successful development and of the configurations of emotion-, thought-, perception-, and behavior-dispositions that result from an unsuccessful development.* It seems to me that this definition covers the activities of psychologists who specialize in the functioning of the brain or perceptual organs, of child psychologists, gerontologists, developmental psychologists, industrial psychologists, personality theorists, clinicians of various stripes, educational psychologists, and social psychologists. It also covers Evagrius, Augustine, Aquinas, Baxter, Kierkegaard, and Dostoyevsky. By this definition, then, Christian psychology, as embodied in their works, is a branch or type of psychology. And if these people are psychologists, then the integration model of relating faith and psychology is not the only or primary one. These are people in whom faith and psychology have an *original union* as tight as that between faith and theology. In them, psychological thought and practice is simply an aspect of faith.

Some Projects in Christian Psychology

The fact that at schools such as Wheaton integration of psychology and theology is the model of relationship between the two suggests that we have bought the establishment view of psychology. If we think of Augustine, Evagrius, and Kierkegaard as psychologists at all, we think of them as peripheral to the *main* enterprise, perhaps as mainly philosophers or theologians who had a few psychological insights that may help us integrate our faith with *real* psychology. I want to suggest that we think of them, instead, as primary psychologists, of equal or superior status with Freud, Erikson, Kohut, Kagan, Sullivan, Vygotsky, Piaget, Minuchin, Perls, Rogers, Beck, Lazarus, and the rest.

Our task as Christian psychologists, as I see it, is in large part to retrieve the Christian psychology of the past, understand what these writers have to say, sift it for what has enduring Christian importance and present it to our contemporaries in a form that can be understood and used. No doubt some "integration" will occur in the very process of retrieval and presentation because it will be useful, from time to time, to compare Christian psychology with one or another of the psychologies of the establishment and because the form in which we will work up the insights of these Christian psychologists will no doubt be suggested by psychology as the establishment writes and practices it. To take an extreme example, Dostoyevsky's mode of presenting his psychology—namely, writing novels that are now classics—is not very likely to be *our* mode of presenting his ideas. Our presentation will probably look much more like the books and essays that establishment psychologists tend to write. But our endeavor will not be primarily to integrate but to retrieve, evaluate, and communicate something originally Christian.

Now I want to report briefly on a few efforts I know of in Christian psychology, and then, in a later section, to do a bit of it before your eyes, to give you a better idea of what I am talking about. The writings of the desert fathers, especially Evagrius Ponticus and John Cassian, who are best known for their diagnosis and therapy of human problems in terms of the "seven deadly sins," have been the subject of work by Diogenes Allen (1997), Dennis Okholm (1997), and Columba Stewart (1991, 1998). In a somewhat more integrative mode, see also Mangis (in press). Thomas Oden (1984), alarmed that since about 1920 Christian writers on pastoral care have let modern psychotherapies inform their work far more than the classic Christian tradition, has expounded Pope Gregory the Great's treatise *Pastoral Care* in a proposal to retrieve the pastoral psychology of this resource for present-day clergy. Benedict Groeschel (1983) has mined part of the Catholic mystical tradition, especially John of the Cross and Teresa of Ávila, for insights about psychological development. Eric Johnson (1998) has explored the history of the Christian concept of the soul. Walter Sundberg (1997) has written about the relationship between suffering and therapy in the thought of such Reformation and Counter Reformation figures as Martin Luther and Ignatius of Loyola. C. Stephen Evans (1990) has written on Kierkegaard's psychological method: his claim that "a human being is spirit," his concepts of sin, anxiety, despair, and self-deception, his treatment of human psychological development, and Kierkegaard as a therapist. Eric Johnson (1996a, 1996b, 1999) has developed some ideas, based on Scripture, about the Christian notion of human cognitive maturity. I have recently written a couple of things on Kierkegaard's moral psychology, especially his concepts of emotion, passion, and virtue (Roberts, 1997c, 1998a). Historically wide-ranging sources, with discussion, can be found in Oden (1986, 1987, 1989a, 1989b). In the winter 1998 issue of the *Journal of Psychology and Christianity* 17(4), articles exploring psychology and counseling within the Christian tradition include studies of Augustine (Eric L. Johnson), Thomas Aquinas (Richard W. Cross), Richard Baxter (Kenneth L. Roth), Joseph Butler (Mark R. Talbot), George Berkeley (James S. Spiegel), John Wesley (H. Newton Malony), and Kierkegaard (Julia Watkin).

The following are some less historically oriented efforts in Christian psychology. The first book to argue for an explicitly Christian psychology was C. Stephen Evans's *Wisdom and Humanness in Psychology: Prospects for a Christian Approach* (1989). Paul Vitz (1997) has sketched a Christian theory of personality in the classic style (see the critique of Vitz by Paul J. Griffiths [1997], who resists the whole notion of a Christian psychology). A. A. Howsepian (1997) has proposed a revision of the psychological establishment's current definition of psychosis in light of the Christian tradition's concept of sin. I have suggested some of the salient features of a Christian psychology in its relation to science and theology, its concept of human sociality, its concept of human agency, and its relation to the concept of sin (Roberts, 1997d). Also in a somewhat programmatic vein, see Johnson (1997a). Cornelius Plantinga (1994) has written a very fine book on sin that bristles with Christian psychological insights. C. S. Lewis's *The Screwtape Letters* (1943) is a wonderful piece of Christian psychology. Several of my own efforts in Christian psychology have taken the form of exploring the psychology of the Bible. One is an attempt to discern the parameters of a personality theory that might be derivable from the Bible as a whole (Roberts, 1997a), and I have explored one of those parameters—the human disposition and need for attachment—in the New Testament and compared this biblical conception with John Bowlby's (Roberts, 1997b). I have also outlined a form of psychotherapy that might be elicited almost directly from the letters of the apostle Paul (Roberts, in press). I will continue my efforts in biblical psychology later in this essay.

Two Aspects of Method

A primary aim of Christian psychology is to make available the distinctive psychology of the Christian tradition to the intellect and practice of persons in our time. It is a different enterprise from integration, whose aim is to produce a happy blend of one or another of the twentieth-century psychologies with the thought and practice of the church. The goal of Christian psychology, then, is two-dimensional: to read the tradition *pure*, and yet to read it for what we and our contemporaries can recognize as *psychology*.

Thus in one dimension the method of Christian psychology must prevent the psychologies of the twentieth century from contaminating the substance of what we say about the nature of persons, the goals and mechanisms of psychological development, the forms of psychopathology, and our approaches to correcting dysfunction and facilitating psychological growth. I say "contaminate the substance" because, as I have argued elsewhere (Roberts, 1993), the psychologies of the twentieth century are all, in one way or another, rivals and alternatives to the Christian psychology. That is, they are incompatible with it in a variety of ways, so that an integration of them always runs the risk of contamination. In some of them (e.g., that of Sigmund Freud or Heinz Kohut) the personality ideal is intrinsically atheistic. In others the self is conceived too individualistically and so compromises Christian sociality (e.g., that of Carl Rogers or Albert Ellis). In others the assumed structure of motivation is egoistic, thus undermining the Christian ideal of love (e.g., certain forms of assertiveness training). In others responsibility for pathology is undermined in therapy, eroding the concept of sin (e.g., some forms of family therapy). In others, the historical, which is essential to the Christian concept of salvation, is systematically undercut by symbolic interpretation (notably Carl Jung). Such potential contaminations are substantive. If they are taken up into the thought and practice of the church, Christianity itself will be poisoned and the character and form of life to which Christ calls us will be compromised (see Vitz, 1994). Thus one aspect of the method of Christian psychology is prophylactic: It is to bracket the *substance* of twentieth-century psychologies so that we can put the Christian tradition in the psychological driver's seat.

But our task is also to retrieve the Christian psychology in a *form* that is recognizable to twenty-first-century people as psychology. We want not only to avoid contamination of our way of life but also to commend it to others, both those outside the Christian community and those inside who have already been more or less contaminated (that is, all of us). We want to present Christian psychology as a discussion partner with twentieth-century psychologies and as offering viable alternatives to what is unacceptable to us in those psychologies. But, I have been arguing, to make the Christian tradition "speak the language of psychology" is not as much of a stretch as it may seem at first, since many of the general questions that contemporary psychology asks are in large part questions that the church has always had the resources to answer in its own way. The Christian psychologist will want to ask of the Christian tradition the broad formal questions that contemporary psychologies answer (especially personality psychology and psychotherapy): What are the basic directions, tendencies, needs, teleologies, of human psychic nature? What are the fundamental mechanisms or psychic strategies by which those directions, tendencies, needs, and so on are pursued and satisfied? What environmental conditions are needed to facilitate such growth? What is the personality profile of a mature, psychologically well-developed person? What are some of the typical and not so typical dysfunctional or improper patterns of behavior, emotion, thought, and perception, and how do these develop? What are some strategies by which the immature or dysfunctional can be helped to mature and to overcome their distortions? The Christian tradition naturally answers these questions, but I think that readers of contemporary expositions of Christianity will rarely feel that answers to questions in the discipline of psychology are being offered.

The line we must toe between perverting the substance of *our* psychology and failing to attain the form of *a* psychology is a fine one. Many of the studies that I identified in the previous section as efforts in Christian psychology are imperfect in one of these two directions: some tend to read back into the older authors a substantive psychology that really comes from the twentieth century, so that the result borders on a sort of sloppy integration; others are so perfectly scholarly and historical or theological that they do not strongly commend themselves to modern readers as the sort of thing that we have come to know and love as psychology.

A nice example of a judicious and clear treatment of a source for Christian psychology is Columba Stewart's piece on radical self-honesty in the desert fathers (1991). Not only does Stewart give plenty of well-illustrated information about the therapeutic practice of these ancient Christians, but he is careful to distinguish what they are doing from some possible twentieth-century look-alikes. Thus he exemplifies an important methodological principle of Christian psychology: to be especially attentive to *differences* between the Christian tradition and twentieth-century psychologies.

If we are well versed in a modern psychological outlook, it tends to become a grid by which we divide up the psychobehavioral world. Under such conditions it is much more difficult to distinguish Christianity from a psychology than it is to see the similarities between them, because we tend to "read" Christianity in terms of the easier, more contemporary framework. Most writers on psychology and Christianity are, in my opinion, far too quick to assimilate the Christian tradition to the more familiar contemporary models. Much discussion of religion and psychology consists in pointing out parallels and similarities between

Christianity and one psychology or another, or simply reading into Christian texts the insights and beliefs of twentieth-century psychologists. For example Alan Jones (1985), in a book whose subtitle *(The Desert Way of Spirituality)* would lead us to expect the Christian psychology of the desert fathers to be its fundamental orientation, is eager to see parallels with psychoanalysis. So we repeatedly read phrases such as "The goal of psychoanalysis, like that of spiritual formation, is to aid in the integration of the emotional with the intellectual life" (p. 42), "Where psychoanalysis talks of neuroses, the Christian tradition . . . talks of the appetites or the passions" (p. 43), "The concern of both psychoanalysis and the desert tradition is precisely 'clear-sighted vision and critical contemplation' of what life has to offer" (p. 47), "A good analyst, like a wise father or mother of the desert, is committed to a path of detachment" (p. 48), "The way of both psychoanalysis and the desert tradition is one of interiority" (p. 50), and so forth. At some level of generality such parallels no doubt exist, but if the desert fathers are to inform our psychology in any serious way, these parallels need to be pursued in the context of a careful critical discussion of differences.

Similarly, Thomas Oden, in a book that is useful in some ways, seems too quick to read the psychology of Carl Rogers into that of Gregory the Great. Purporting to expound Gregory, Oden comments, "The pastor therefore becomes an agent of realism on behalf of the parishioner to clarify prevailing self-deceptions. This occurs through deeply empathic interior participation in the other's consciousness, deeply respecting the person" (1984, p. 56). Oden does not cite any text of Gregory's in support of this attribution, and one searches in vain for references in *Pastoral Care* to such vintage Rogerian ideas as "deeply empathic interior participation" and its supposed power to release from the bondage of self-deception. This is ironic; given that Oden wishes to rescue pastoral work from the dominance of modern therapies and return it to the classical tradition, one would expect him aggressively to distinguish Gregory's thought from these other approaches.

The other side of the method I am commending—to construe psychology-rich items from the Christian tradition in terms of the *form* (broad questions) of twentieth-century psychology—is just about as rarely exemplified as the requirement to let the psychologists of the Christian tradition speak substantively for themselves. Careful scholarly works like the one I mentioned from Columba Stewart on the desert fathers are an important help to the person pursuing Christian psychology, but they are not the thing itself.

Psychology in the Sermon on the Mount

I have written about the importance of Christian psychologists retrieving psychological ideas from our tradition, which is already psychologically rich. But in that tradition the Bible has a very special and authoritative place (Johnson, 1992; Talbot, 1997). It is the fountainhead of Christian ideas, including psychological ones. Much of the foundational work in Christian psychology will therefore be the careful reading of Scripture by people who know what psychology in the twentieth century was and can therefore sniff out the biblical psychology. As I envision this endeavor, it is the business of psychologically informed Bible scholars, philosophers, and theologians as well as biblically informed professional psychologists. I shall now offer a somewhat extended illustration of Christian psychology, focusing on a central part of Scripture. After a few introductory comments I will give an overview of the psychology in the Sermon on the Mount, and then will focus more narrowly with a sequential psychological commentary on Matthew 5.

The Sermon is usually classified as ethics, but it is a special kind of ethics that is closer to what we know as psychology than what we have come to think of as ethics. We think of ethics as rules for action and social policies that promote certain actions and discourage others. The Sermon does have much to say about actions, but it is also, and more deeply, about character—about the form of persons. It is about how to live, by being a person of a certain kind of character who acts well as a part of living well. And it is about the transformation of persons from being one kind of character and living less well to being another kind who live well. But the study of character, the aspects of its well-being, and the change of character for the better seem to be a sort of psychology and psychotherapy in a broad sense of these words. To further the assimilation of the Sermon to psychology, we might also point out that modern psychologies are ethical systems. Don Browning (1987) has argued this point, even though he thinks of ethics as a matter of act-injunctions. I have made the point (Roberts, 1993) in a way that conceives ethics more classically, as reflection about the virtues and vices.

One reason we might be surprised by the suggestion that the Sermon contains psychology is that we have come to expect a certain vocabulary to be present wherever psychology is, and most if not all this expected vocabulary is absent from the Sermon. We do not find any of the following terms: *stimulus, environment, behavior, personality, dysfunction, unconscious, motivation, emotion, therapy, fee, self object, drive, defense mechanism, empathy, congruence, selfhood.* But these items (and many more) are parts of systems of thought and practice in which human nature is characterized, in which human actions, thoughts, and emotions are explained and evaluated, and in which a change from negatively evaluated ones to positively evaluated ones is commended and facilitated. The Sermon certainly does not have the same conception of human nature, nor the same pattern of explanations and evaluations of actions, thoughts, and emotions, nor the same recommendations or strategies for change as the psychologies that are structured by words such as the ones listed above. But in its own vocabulary—in terms such as blessed *(makarios)*, poor in spirit *(ptōchoi tō pneumati)*, to sorrow *(pentheō)*, humble or gentle *(praÿs)*, to comfort *(parakaleō)*, pure in heart *(katharoi tē kardia)*, peacemaker *(eirēnopoios)*, righteousness *(dikaiosynē)*, to get angry *(orgizomai)*, to commit adultery *(moicheuō)*, to lust *(epithymeō)*, love *(agapē)*, pray *(proseuchomai)*, to forgive *(aphiēmi)*, trespass *(paraptōma)*, treasure *(thēsauros)*, heart *(kardia)*, hypocrite *(hypokritēs)*, reward *(misthos)*, and others—it certainly does offer its own conception of human nature; an ideal of personality functioning; explanations and evaluations of actions, thoughts, and emotions; and recommendations or strategies for change.

Overview of the Sermon as Psychology

The Sermon conceptualizes *personal well-being* as comprised of the following traits of character with their implied actions and attitudes: gentleness, desire for righteousness, mercy, purity of heart, being a peacemaker, being a lover of enemies, being disposed to forgive offenses, poverty of spirit, being persecuted for Jesus' sake, mourning, penitence, humility, respect for great things, self-unawareness (the opposite of private ostentation), treasuring the kingdom of God, expecting good things from God, endurance through difficulties. A person who had these traits or was disposed to these actions and emotions would, according to the psychology of the Sermon, be "mature," "perfect" *(teleios)* or "blessed," "happy" *(makarios)*, or solidly founded like a house built on a rock (Mt 7:24).

. The Sermon conceptualizes *personal pathology* as a disposition to anger, grudge-bearing, and revenge; to lust, adultery, and divorce; to hatred of enemies; as greed, acquisitiveness, or being mastered by Mammon; as hypocrisy and ostentation (both public and private); as arrogance and disrespect for what is great; as anxiety about necessities; as judgmentalism and blindness to one's own faults. A person who is given to or mired in such dispositions to action and attitude will be functioning poorly as a human being, will not be mature, happy, or solidly founded. Were we to elaborate the psychology of the Sermon, we could infer more traits of health from some of the traits of dysfunction and more traits of dysfunction from some of the traits of health, simply by inferring to the contrary of each. (Throughout we are assuming that the psychology of the Sermon is a consistent system of thought and practice.)

While *psychological explanation* is not as patent in the Sermon as the pictures of personal well-being and pathology, some patterns of explanation are explicit and others can be inferred. Inwardness (e.g., lust, anger) explains actions (adultery, revenge). Certain blindnesses are explained by perverse patterns of "treasuring." Shapes of personality ("hearts") are explained by "treasurings." Seeing God is explained by purity of heart. Hatred of God is explained by reference to being mastered by Mammon. An elaborated biblical psychology would multiply patterns of explanation by exploring the system of concepts that operate in the Sermon and elsewhere in the Bible.

A number of *therapeutic interventions* (or avenues by which a person might move from pathological to healthy patterns of thought, passion, and action) are rather explicit in the Sermon: be poor in spirit, mourn, behave gently, hunger for righteousness, be merciful, be pure in heart, make peace, allow yourself to be persecuted for the sake of Jesus, let your light shine before people, keep the commandments, take responsibility for your own anger, take responsibility for other people's anger, control your lustful eye, do not seek revenge on those who offend you, do not be ostentatious in your piety, do not fret about daily needs but seek the kingdom, focus chiefly on your own shortcomings rather than on those of others, do not hold others in contempt because of their shortcomings.

For a couple of reasons these interventions might not sound very therapeutic or very much like psychology to a person of our historical location. One reason is that some of them seem to go against the recommendations of some well-established psychotherapies of our own day. To this we can simply reply, Too bad; the Christian psychology is a different psychology. A more interesting objection would be that these "interventions" all seem to have the form of bald commandments: Just do this, or, Just don't do that. But some people may be at a loss as to *how* to do what is commanded. What is needed, and what contemporary psychotherapies tend to provide, is some facilitation of the therapeutic action, some discipline by which, perhaps stepwise, a person can implement the commanded change. Here the postbiblical psychological tradition—the desert fathers, Gregory the Great, the sixteenth-century mystics, and others—have responded by devising disciplines and helps that can be provided by advisors.

Comments on Matthew 5

It is obvious that in the rather short compass of this illustration of Christian psychology I cannot give a full discussion of the psychology of the Sermon, even of chapter five. My comments will thus often take the form of suggesting directions of further thought and research.

5:1-12. Verses 3-11 all call some group or kind of person "blessed" *(makarioi),* that is, "happy" or "well off," thus establishing an immediate connection with contemporary therapeutic psychology. The word *happy* is a somewhat misleading translation for modern readers if it suggests to us a simple state of "feeling good." To be *makarios* is to be well and to be doing well, but it is compatible with suffering tribulations and obstacles. Thus the concept of well-being that drives the psychology of the Sermon is quite different from its counterpart in some of the modern psychologies. The groups that Jesus describes are certainly not "well adjusted" to their social and physical setting, nor are they contented and enjoying life, though they are free from a certain kind of anxiety (see Mt 6:25-33). Of the groups that Jesus describes as *makarioi,* the mourners and the persecuted are both obviously suffering; the rest are grouped according to their virtues: the poor in spirit, the gentle, those who hunger and thirst for righteousness, the merciful, the pure in heart, and the peacemakers.

Nevertheless, the concept of *makarios* does make a connection with psychology in our sense of the word: well-being is certainly the *form* of any goal of psychotherapy, however much the different therapies may differ in their particular conceptions of this goal (see Roberts, 1993, part one). Is Jesus offering a conception of therapy that differs from any of the ones being offered today? I don't think we see very many therapists commending gentleness, and mercy, and purity of heart, and hunger and thirst for righteousness as strategies for psychological well-being. They tend, instead, to try to facilitate high self-esteem, contentment, individual satisfaction, individuation, a sense of empowerment.

Jesus suggests how each suffering or trait is a blessing: because of its connection with possessing the kingdom of God, being comforted, inheriting the earth, having one's desire for righteousness satisfied, obtaining mercy, seeing God, being called children of God. But these are explanations that the Christian psychologist will want to elaborate on. From the point of view of the gospel of Jesus Christ, happiness is certainly grounded in the new creation that comes in Jesus. The new order is one that supports people of these sorts; it is an order in which they can function so as to be "happy." But people live at least partially in the old order, so it is instructive for them to be reminded of their happiness and the other context (the kingdom) in which their virtues constitute a more obvious well-being. Jesus may be engaging in some "reframing" here. People who are being persecuted will not be immediately inclined to see themselves as happy, and there can be something therapeutic in having Jesus remind them that they are actually functioning better than may outwardly appear.

The Christian psychologist will want to investigate the various categories so as to know what traits are actually being commended. It is not obvious what poverty of spirit is, and it could well be that some of the other categories such as purity of heart or being a peacemaker are not immediately obvious either. The Christian psychologist will also want to know how one becomes poor in spirit, a peacemaker, and so on. What is the therapy for those who are not? How can people be helped in this undertaking? And what are the consequences of not having these traits? Are there particular kinds of things that tend to go wrong in the lives of people who lack the traits? If we knew this, we would have material for some diagnostic explanations as well. The way to answer these questions may be a combination of conceptual-historical and empirical research.

5:13-16. The disciples, says Jesus, are "salt" and "light." Each of these metaphors describes some personal orientation or set of traits or state of life that is good and healthy. But it is good for someone other than its possessor. The salt is good, not for the salt but for those who are eating. The light is good, not for the light but for those who are making their way through the world. The disciples are expected to permeate the world, as salt does the food and as light does the landscape. We might say that for Jesus personal or psychic well-being is never abstractly or privately for the person in whom it resides. This too seems to mark a difference between the psychology of the Sermon and many of the psychologies of our day. To be *makarios*, it seems, is to possess a kind of well-being whose "wellness" belongs to others whom one affects, as well as to oneself.

Here Jesus tells his disciples to let their good works be seen by people, but later he will condemn the religious who are ostentatious in their piety. Is there tension between these teachings? The concept of inwardness that is prominent in the Sermon (Mt 5:21-30) is at least part of the solution to this puzzle. Jesus' point is really not that we should be careful not to be seen giving alms, for example; his point is that being seen should not be our motive in giving the alms. If that is our motive (and if we succeed in being seen and honored), then we "have our reward" because that is the satisfaction that we were seeking in the action. We will not have the reward of being in the will of God and in the style of his kingdom, which is what the righteous seek in such actions.

5:17-20. Jesus is not here to relax the law but to fulfill it. The Jews were very positive about the law, in part because they thought of it as a blessing to them, a guide for their life, a guide for happiness and well-being (see Ps 1). One might say that for the Jew the law was God's psychotherapy. Jesus is claiming the same for his own teaching, and claiming a kind of continuity between the two.

5:21-26. Jesus is quite insistent that anger itself, and not just its unto-ward consequences such as murder, is a problem, a barrier to well-being. Most psychologists will agree that anger can be a problem, but not all of them will give the kind of explanation of anger's dysfunctionality that is suggested by the Sermon. They may suggest that it is bad for the sub-ject's physical health, that it tends to prevent the subject from getting what he or she wants from people, that in excess it is not good for mar-riages and partnerships. These are all acceptable points, no doubt, but they are not the heart of the matter in Jesus' psychology. There we might say that anger (when it is improper) is a disruption of the spirit of the kingdom, which is one of loving fellowship with God and fellow people.

In verse 23 Jesus makes a switch that can be confusing. In the first two verses he has been warning against *our* anger, but in verse 23 he starts talking about what we should do if *somebody else* is angry (or at any rate has cause to be angry) *at us.* The upshot seems to be that we are not only to take responsibility for mitigating our own anger at others, but we are also to take responsibility for mitigating others' anger at us. The well-functioning person, in Jesus' conception, is one whose general policy and demeanor is to minimize anger, both in oneself and in those with whom one has to do. I say "general" because Jesus himself sometimes displays anger (Mk 3:1-6), and the apostle Paul seems to have understood anger among disciples as not always inappropriate (Eph 4:26-27). Thus discern-ment is needed. Jesus' stress both on the spiritual significance of anger and on each person's responsibility for anger, whether her own or some-body else's, should be of guiding interest in our psychological work.

5:27-32. Adultery and divorce are topics that often come up in coun-seling, and a psychologist's treatment (theoretical and practical) of these is an expression of his or her more general views about human nature, sexuality, and the family.

In Jesus' discussion of adultery, as in that of anger, he stresses the inwardness that constitutes the relationship. A person whose serious sex-ual desires are directed to someone other than his or her spouse has already adulterated the marriage bond, because it is a spiritual thing and not just a matter of outward behavior. Christian psychologists will want to know how to manage lust. Since the therapy that Jesus seems, on a lit-eral reading, to commend—an operation we might call auto-ophthalmectomy—will not be encouraged by most Christian psychologists, we must look for some nonliteral counterpart. To know how to help the sufferer "pluck out the lustful eye," it will be essential to know what lust is (how it differs from an ordinary, normal, and acceptable attraction to members of the opposite sex, and how it compares with what our contemporaries call a sex "addiction"). We will want to know what choices, habits of life, and environmental influences tend to promote it and which ones tend to mitigate it. We will want to distinguish the lust of the married from that of the unmarried. We will want to explore how it is that lust has the alienating effect that Jesus seems to ascribe to it. And we will want to know whether and how it is connected with other sins such as greed, selfishness, pride, and anger. If it is so connected, it may need to be treated in connection with other pathologies or they in connection with it. Such a conception of lust will be distinctive of Christian psychology, since in most psychologies current today lust is not treated as a pathology or as the source of pathologies.

If the marriage bond is not to be compromised even in thought, it is certainly a great evil to break it formally and outwardly by divorce. Behind this teaching about divorce that sounds so "inhumane" to modern therapeutic ears is the Judeo-Christian concept of the marriage "self"—a psychology of marriage, if you will—that the two are "one flesh." This thought is behind Paul's statement in 1 Corinthians 6:18 that sexual sins are unique in being against the sinner's own body (read "self"). Jesus seems to be saying that the marriage bond—the self of the one flesh—is indestructible by the formality of divorce, so that postdivorce sexual activity with a person other than the original spouse is adultery. Jesus does not proscribe divorce, though on the present reading he denies the efficacy of any such formal procedure to dismantle the marriage, so perhaps he would allow that sometimes permanent separation is an option (see 1 Cor 7:11). In the clause "except on the ground of unchastity" he seems to allow that adultery itself can destroy the bond, so that the "innocent" party's postdivorce sexual activity with a new partner can be *treated* as not amounting to adultery. Perhaps the thought is that it is as though the original partner were dead (see Rom 7:2-3). But it seems that on the "one flesh" view, remarriage even by the "innocent" party is a compromise involving "self"-damage. I think it is safe to say that no modern psychological theory about sex and marriage duplicates the biblical psychology on this point.

5:33-37. Why would it be evil to swear by something as opposed to just saying yes or no and keeping one's word? In verses 34-36 Jesus explains his prohibition by referring to the qualities of the things that people were inclined to swear by, thus suggesting that to swear by them was to slight their greatness. In other words, it is a failure of respect. It is as if one says, "If I don't keep this oath, then Jerusalem be damned. If I go back on my word, you can have my hair." On this reading, the dysfunction would be a kind of arrogance in acting as though one is lord of one's own hair or that one is in a position to say, "Let Jerusalem be damned." Or the thought might be that in swearing by these things, one casts the responsibility onto the thing and away from oneself. "If I default on my word, take Jerusalem and we'll be even." Perhaps plain swearing expresses both responsibility and respectful humility. These virtues might be a psychological theme: There is something healthy about "healthy respect"—for the earth, for the great king and his city, for human achievements, for one's own body. People who lack such respect do seem to us to be shallow or immature and likely to make bad decisions in life. This is perhaps a characteristic of people who think very instrumentally about cities, paintings, forests, and their own work. And there is something deep about a person who intelligently but steadfastly keeps his word. No doubt there are pathologies, or at least problems in living, that result from lack of respect and lack of responsibility for one's word. A Christian psychology will trace these out.

5:38-42. Retaliation is basically dysfunctional and immature behavior. The contrasting actions that Jesus commends—turning the other cheek, giving more than is extorted, going the second mile—are calculated to stop cyclical retaliation and thus cyclical anger and hatred, which destroy or prevent mutual love and cooperation. These are illustrations of a style of response to offenses, and the Christian psychologist working with someone who has a problem with vengefulness will want to facilitate in him or her a disposition to respond creatively within the Christian style. Accordingly, the phrase "do not resist one who is evil" needs to be applied discriminately. Jesus himself certainly resisted the "evil" scribes and Pharisees, though he did not retaliate. He was sometimes angry at them and did not hesitate to criticize them, even in rather colorful terms, and no doubt he made them angry. Jesus is not commending doormat-hood or passivity.

The Christian psychologist will be interested in finding ways to help people make the needed discriminations here and to develop the required creativity. He or she will also be interested in helping people to recognize subtle retaliations that otherwise might go unnoticed, yet that may be a chief cause of poor functioning in relationships. The founda-tional commitment of Jesus' psychology is to love. The psychological premise is that psychic and relational well-being will paradigmatically be love, a beneficent and benevolent relating in which the other is seen and treated as a brother or sister, a respected and valued fellow human being. Deviations from the paradigm such as anger are justified only as arising from a motivational background of love.

5:43-48. As if we needed any more convincing that in the Sermon Jesus is doing, in part, the kind of thing that modern psychologists do (though admittedly in substantively different and largely rival terms), Jesus ends this pericope on loving one's enemies by exhorting the disciples to be *teleioi* as their father in heaven is *teleios.* My dictionary gives the follow-ing as translations of this word: complete, perfect, whole, full-grown, mature. So *teleios* has intimate connections to developmental and thera-peutic psychology. The suggestion is that to love one's enemies is to exemplify the behavior and attitude of a mature, grown-up, properly functioning human being, and that to hate one's enemies is childish, an example of stunted growth. A person who hates his enemies is "incom-plete"; a person who loves his enemies is in the likeness of his perfect heavenly Father—a complete human person.

Empirical Research

Most of what I have been commending in this essay is a fine-grained retrieval of psychological concepts from the Christian tradition and above all from the Bible. In a number of my remarks on the Sermon I also commended the fine-grained exploration of connections among concepts within the Christian view of persons, their well-being and pathology. But contemporary psychologists are not just constructors of conceptual sys-tems; one of their main activities is empirical research. Is there room for empirical research in Christian psychology? Certainly there is. I mentioned that in the Sermon some patterns of explanation are suggested. Seeing God is explained by purity of heart. Hatred of God is explained by being mastered by Mammon. These explanations are testable by the methods of empirical psychology. But it is worth noting that in tandem with setting up empirical studies that would test these explanatory claims, it will be crucial to pursue the conceptual analysis that I have been commending. It will have to be determined, for example, what seeing God and being pure in heart amount to if it is to be established that the one does or does not cause the other, and this can only be established historically and conceptually. I also mentioned earlier that Jesus seems to claim that certain activities will tend to change people in certain ways; such claims could also be tested. As the Christian psychology is retrieved through conceptual and historical research, many questions that are fit for empirical testing emerge. And such research has in turn an effect on the conceptual work, for if we find that the claims of Christian psychology (as we understand them) seem to be disconfirmed by empirical research, we have reason for thinking that we have misconstructed the Christian psychology, and we return to the Bible and the tradition to read it again for a better interpretation.

Some empirical research is already being done that will count as research in Christian psychology. Much of it falls under the traditional rubric of "psychology of religion," and the people doing it may not endorse the project that I am calling Christian psychology, even if they are Christians. They may, for example, have an Enlightenment understanding of social science and believe that ideologically "neutral" scientific research is capable of giving us a complete psychology. They may think that it is epistemologically perverse to start with traditional beliefs about God and sin and a set of contestable virtues that are supposed to constitute psychological well-being; they may think that such positions are legitimate only as the *outcomes* of objective research. Still, if their research is about Christian psychological beliefs, it will be of interest to the Christian psychologist. And, of course, empirical research done by Christian psychologists will similarly be of interest to psychologists of religion. Accordingly, in the next paragraph I will not distinguish between researchers who believe in Christian psychology and those who do not.

I offer here a few examples from one scholarly journal (and make no pretense of being exhaustive). While the Christian tradition does not have a canonical statement on the causes of homosexual orientation and behavior, the question is certainly relevant to the Christian psychology of sex; on this see Jones and Workman (1989) and Cole (1995). One psychological belief that Christians are likely to hold is that prayer and meditative communion with God can have beneficial effects. For some empirical research on this question, see Carlson, Bacaseta, and Simanton (1988), Finney and Malony (1985b), and Poloma and Pendleton (1991); see Finney and Malony (1985a) for a review of empirical studies of Christian prayer. A related question is about the impact of religious commitment on the healthiness or unhealthiness of mental and social functioning (Gartner, Larson & Allen, 1991; Watson, Hood & Morris, 1985). P. J. Watson and associates (Watson, Morris & Hood, 1988a, 1988b, 1988c, 1989a, 1989b) examined several questions concerned with the effect of belief in sin and belief in God's forgiveness on such negative measures of mental health as depression, social anxiety, hopelessness, neuroticism, and irrational beliefs; and such positive measures as empathic concern, assertiveness, self-awareness, and a sense of self-efficacy. While the results of their empirical studies do not unambiguously support the healthiness of religious beliefs (and the authors note weaknesses in their measurement instruments that make their results somewhat less than fully compelling), the general force of their research is to show that the supposed unhealthiness of believing in sin (posited by such psychologists as Sigmund Freud, Nathaniel Branden, and Albert Ellis) is greatly overestimated and rather crudely conceived. On the contrary, their research suggests that a consciousness of sin as part of intrinsic (that is, genuine and mature) religiousness, especially when combined with a sense of God's grace, tends to promote a number of marks of mental health.

These are just a few examples. Some other questions that could be subjected to empirical investigations are the following: How effective are the spiritual disciplines (prayer, meditation, Bible reading, fasting, solitude, etc.) in forming such Christian virtues as humility, compassion, forbearance, and longsuffering? Under what conditions are such disciplines maximally formative? How do patterns of early attachment to caretakers affect Christian faith during adulthood? What styles of parenting are most likely to produce Christian character traits in our children? How does the regular practice of prayer affect mental health? How does membership in a Christian community affect Christian character? How does it affect mental health? What empirical backing can be given for the biblical "one flesh" view of marriage? What is the causal role of respect in the formation of a healthy personality? What are the causal connections (if any) among such "works of the flesh" as greed, lust, anger, sloth, selfishness, and envy?

The Promise of Christian Psychology

Why should we pursue Christian psychology, the psychology of our faith, and not be satisfied integrating faith with one or another of the psychologies of the establishment, or even be satisfied juxtaposing our faith with one of these psychologies? The basic answer to this question is that psychology is native to Christianity; it is already fundamental to our faith. It is not something we can ignore and then with impunity replace with something more up-to-date, somewhat in the way Rudolf Bultmann and his demythologizers thought that we could replace the "worldview" of the New Testament with an existentialist ontology while still retaining the essential faith of the apostles (for a critique of Bultmann's project, see Roberts, 1976).

If the experience of the churches in the twentieth century is any indication for the future, we can expect that in the measure that we lose touch with our own psychology and replace it with one of the psychologies of the establishment or some conglomeration of them, we will also lose touch with the apostolic faith. Ours is a psychological age, an age in which people hunger and thirst for psychology as an orientation to life, buy by the millions self-help books that induct them into psychological ways of thinking about themselves that are in many ways alien and contrary to the faith, and become formed in the image of this advice and theory. Our experience has been that the juxtaposition model does not work very well, precisely because of the enormous seductiveness of the establishment psychologies and the equally impressive impoverishment of our Christian thought about persons if we have no psychology but that of the establishment. The insight that we cannot, in faith, simply leave our psychological thinking to be done by non-Christians, or even to be done by Christians according to the canons and methods of the establishment, is the chief impetus to adopt the integration model.

On the integration model we start from a Christian standpoint and attempt to assess various pieces of establishment psychology so as to discriminate what is consistent with our faith from what is not, to adopt what is consistent with it, and to adapt what has potential but is not originally consistent with the faith. I think that establishment psychology has much to teach us, and so I advocate the enterprise of integration. But a crux in the process is indicated by the phrase "from a Christian standpoint." Integration will be poorly executed to the extent that psychologists who are Christian are ignorant of the great tradition of Christian psychology that stretches from the Bible through the desert fathers and medieval church, through the Reformation and Counter Reformation to Richard Baxter and Søren Kierkegaard and Fyodor Dostoyevsky. It seems clear to me that many if not most Christians who are psychologists teaching in colleges and universities and working in clinical settings are far better versed in the establishment psychologies than they are in the psychology of their own religious tradition. Many are not even aware that their tradition *has* a psychology of its own; for them psychology is the psychology of the establishment. The promise of Christian psychology is that this situation can change.

In some disciplines the task of integration is not particularly momentous. Wheaton College does not have special courses in the integration of faith and algebra or faith and chemistry. And I suppose the reason for this is that the church has had very little of a distinctively Christian nature to say about algebra and chemistry. There is no tradition of Christian algebra or of Christian chemistry. These disciplines can be safely left to the best practitioners, whether or not these are persons of faith. There are, however, specially designed courses in the integration of faith and psychology. The reason is that from the beginning the church has had a considerable stake in certain claims about human nature, human motivation, human relationships, human development, healthy and unhealthy formations of character, and about how change from bad to good functioning can be facilitated—in other words, in claims about the kinds of things that the modern psychologies are about. Consequently it seems to me that all Christians who work as professionals in psychology departments or clinical settings should be at least as well versed in the thought of some great Christian psychologist as they are in their own corner of establishment psychology.

References

Allen, D. (1997). Ascetic theology and psychology. In R. C. Roberts & M. R. Talbot (Eds.), *Limning the psyche: Explorations in Christian psychology* (pp. 297-316). Grand Rapids, MI: Eerdmans.

Baxter, R. (1673/1990). *A Christian directory.* Foreword by J. I. Packer. Ligonier, PA: Soli Deo Gloria.

Browning, D. S. (1987). *Religious thought and the modern psychologies: A critical conversation in the theology of culture.* Philadelphia: Fortress Press.

Carlson, C. R., Bacaseta, P. E., & Simanton, D. A. (1988). A controlled evaluation of devotional meditation and progressive relaxation. *Journal of Psychology and Theology, 16,* 362-368.

Cassian, J. (1955). *The conferences* and *The twelve books of the institutes of the Coenobium* (E. C. S. Gibson, Trans.). In P. Schaff and H. Wace (Eds.), *The Nicene and post-Nicene fathers* (2nd series. Vol. 11). Grand Rapids, MI: Eerdmans.

Cole, S. O. (1995). The biological basis of homosexuality: A Christian assessment. *Journal of Psychology and Theology, 23,* 89-100.

Corsini, R. J. (1979). *Current psychotherapies.* Itasca, IL: F. E. Peacock.

Edwards, J. (1746/1959). *A treatise concerning religious affections.* New Haven, CT: Yale University Press.

Edwards, J. (1852/1969). *Charity and its fruits.* Edinburgh: Banner of Truth.

Evagrius Ponticus. (1981). *Praktikos* and *Chapters on prayer.* (J. E. Bamberger, Trans.). Kalamazoo, MI: Cistercian Publications.

Evans, C. S. (1989). *Wisdom and humanness in psychology: Prospects for a Christian approach.* Grand Rapids, MI: Baker.

Evans, C. S. (1990). *Søren Kierkegaard's Christian psychology: Insight for counseling and pastoral care.* Grand Rapids, MI: Zondervan.

Finney, J. R., & Malony, H. N., Jr. (1985a). Empirical studies of Christian prayer: A review of the literature. *Journal of Psychology and Theology, 13,* 104-115.

Finney, J. R., & Malony, H. N., Jr. (1985b). An empirical study of contemplative prayer as an adjunct to psychotherapy. *Journal of Psychology and Theology, 13,* 273-284.

Gartner, J., Larson, D. B., & Allen, G. D. (1991). Religious commitment and mental health: A review of the empirical literature. *Journal of Psychology and Theology, 19,* 6-25.

Griffiths, P. (1997). Metaphysics and personality theory. In R. C. Roberts & M. R. Talbot (Eds.), *Limning the psyche: Explorations in Christian psychology* (pp. 41-57). Grand Rapids, MI: Eerdmans.

Groeschel, B. (1983). *Spiritual passages: The psychology of spiritual development.* New York: Crossroad.

Howsepian, A. A. (1997). Sin and psychosis. In R. C. Roberts & M. R. Talbot (Eds.), *Limning the psyche: Explorations in Christian psychology* (pp. 264-281). Grand Rapids, MI: Eerdmans.

Johnson, E. L. (1992). A place for the Bible within psychological science. *Journal of Psychology and Theology, 20,* 346-355.

Johnson, E. L. (1996a). The call of wisdom: Adult development within Christian community. Part 1, The crisis of modern theories of post-formal development. *Journal of Psychology and Theology, 24,* 83-92.

Johnson, E. L. (1996b). The call of wisdom: Adult development within Christian community. Part 2, Towards a covenantal constructivist model of post-formal development. *Journal of Psychology and Theology, 24,* 93-103.

Johnson, E. L. (1997a). Christ the lord of psychology. *Journal of Psychology and Theology, 25,* 11-27.

Johnson, E. L. (1997b). Human agency and its social formation. In R. C. Roberts & M. R. Talbot (Eds.), *Limning the psyche: Explorations in Christian psychology* (pp. 138-164). Grand Rapids, MI: Eerdmans.

Johnson, E. L. (1998). Whatever happened to the human soul? A brief Christian genealogy of a psychological term. *Journal of Psychology and Theology, 26,* 16-28.

Johnson, E. L. (1999). Growing in wisdom in Christian community: Toward measures of Christian postformal development. *Journal of Psychology and Theology, 27.*

Jones, A. W. (1985). *Soul making: The desert way of spirituality.* San Francisco: Harper & Row.

Jones, S. L., & Workman, D. E. (1989). Homosexuality: The behavioral sciences and the church. *Journal of Psychology and Theology, 17,* 213-225.

Kierkegaard, S. (1844/1980). *The concept of anxiety* (R. Thomte, Trans.). Princeton, NJ: Princeton University Press.

Kierkegaard, S. (1846/1992) *Concluding unscientific postscript to philosophical fragments* (H. Hong & E. Hong, Trans.). Princeton, NJ: Princeton University Press.

Kierkegaard, S. (1847/1993). *Upbuilding discourses in various spirits* (H. Hong

& E. Hong, Trans.). Princeton, NJ: Princeton University Press.

Kierkegaard, S. (1847/1995). *Works of love* (H. Hong and E. Hong, Trans.). Princeton, NJ: Princeton University Press.

Kierkegaard, S. (1848/1997). *Christian discourses* and *The crisis and a crisis in the life of an actress* (H. Hong & E. Hong, Trans.). Princeton, NJ: Princeton University Press.

Kierkeaard, S. (1849/1980). *Sickness unto death* (H. Hong & E. Hong, Trans.). Princeton, NJ: Princeton University Press.

Lewis, C. S. (1943). *The Screwtape letters*. New York: Macmillan.

Maddi, S. (1980). *Personality theories: A comparative analysis*. Homewood, IL: Dorsey.

Mangis, M. (in press). The integration of psychoanalytic psychology and contemplative theology: Lessons from the history of spiritual direction. In M. McMinn & T. Phillips (Eds.), *Care for the soul: Exploring the intersection of theology and psychology*. Downers Grove, IL: InterVarsity Press.

Nussbaum, M. (1994). *The therapy of desire*. New York: Cambridge University Press.

Oden, T. (1984). *Care of souls in the classic tradition*. Philadelphia: Fortress.

Oden, T. (1986). *Crisis ministries*. New York: Crossroad.

Oden, T. (1987). *Becoming a minister*. New York: Crossroad.

Oden, T. (1989a). *Pastoral counsel*. New York: Crossroad.

Oden, T. (1989b). *Ministry through word and sacrament*. New York: Crossroad.

Okholm, D. (1997). Being stuffed and being fulfilled. In R. C. Roberts & M. R. Talbot (Eds.), *Limning the Psyche: Explorations in Christian psychology* (pp. 317-338). Grand Rapids, MI: Eerdmans.

Plantinga, C. (1994). *Not the way it's supposed to be: A breviary of sin*. Grand Rapids, MI: Eerdmans.

Poloma, M. M., & Pendleton, B. F. (1991). The effects of prayer and prayer experiences on measures of general well-being. *Journal of Psychology and Theology, 19*, 71-83.

Roberts, R. (1976). *Rudolf Bultmann's theology: A critical interpretation*. Grand Rapids, MI: Eerdmans.

Roberts, R. (1992). Thomas Aquinas on the morality of emotions. *History of Philosophy Quarterly, 9*, 287-305.

Roberts, R. (1993). *Taking the word to heart: Self and other in an age of therapies*. Grand Rapids, MI: Eerdmans.

Roberts, R. (1997a). Parameters of a Christian psychology. In R. C. Roberts & M. R. Talbot (Eds.), *Limning the psyche: Explorations in Christian psychology* (pp. 74-101). Grand Rapids, MI: Eerdmans.

Roberts, R. (1997b). Attachment: Bowlby and the Bible. In R. C. Roberts & M. R. Talbot (Eds.), *Limning the psyche: Explorations in Christian psychology* (pp. 206-228). Grand Rapids, MI: Eerdmans.

Roberts, R. (1997c). Dialectical emotions and the virtue of faith. In R. L. Perkins (Ed.), *International Kierkegaard commentary: Concluding unscientific postscript* (pp. 73-93). Macon, GA: Mercer University Press.

Roberts, R. (1997d). Christian psychology? In R. C. Roberts & M. R. Talbot (Eds.), *Limning the psyche: Explorations in Christian psychology* (pp. 1-19). Grand Rapids, MI: Eerdmans.

Roberts, R. (in press). Existence, emotion and virtue: Classical themes in Kierkegaard. In A. Hannay & G. D. Marino (Eds.), *The Cambridge companion to Kierkegaard* (pp. 177-206). Cambridge: Cambridge University Press.

Roberts, R. (in press). Outline of Pauline psychotherapy. In M. McMinn & T. Phillips (Eds.), *Care for the soul: Exploring the intersection of theology and psychology.* Downers Grove, IL: InterVarsity Press.

Stewart, C. (1991). The desert fathers on radical self-honesty. *Vox Benedictina, 8,* 6-53.

Stewart, C. (1998). *Cassian the monk.* Oxford: Oxford University Press.

Sundberg, W. (1997). The therapy of adversity and penitence. In R. C. Roberts & M. R. Talbot (Eds.), *Limning the psyche: Explorations in Christian psychology* (pp. 282-296). Grand Rapids, MI: Eerdmans.

Talbot, M. R. (1997). Starting from scripture. In R. C. Roberts & M. R. Talbot (Eds.), *Limning the psyche: Explorations in Christian psychology* (pp. 102-122). Grand Rapids, MI: Eerdmans.

Van Leeuwen, M. S. (1985). *The person in psychology: A contemporary Christian appraisal.* Grand Rapids, MI: Eerdmans.

Vitz, P. C. (1994). *Psychology as religion: The cult of self-worship* (2nd ed.). Grand Rapids, MI: Eerdmans.

Vitz, P. C. (1997). A Christian theory of personality. In R. C. Roberts & M. R. Talbot (Eds.), *Limning the psyche: Explorations in Christian psychology* (pp. 20-40). Grand Rapids, MI: Eerdmans.

Ward, B. (Ed.). (1975). *The sayings of the desert fathers.* Kalamazoo, MI: Cisterian Publications.

Watson, P. J., Hood, J. W., & Morris, R. J. (1985). Religiosity, sin and self-esteem. *Journal of Psychology and Theology, 13,* 116-126.

Watson, P. J., Morris, R. J., & Hood, J. W. (1988a). Sin and self-functioning. Part 1, Grace, guilt and self-consciousness. *Journal of Psychology and Theology, 16,* 254-269.

Watson, P. J., Morris, R. J., & Hood, J. W. (1988b). Sin and self-functioning.

Part 2, Grace, guilt and psychological adjustment. *Journal of Psychology and Theology, 16,* 270-281.

Watson, P. J., Morris, R. J., & Hood, J. W. (1988c). Sin and self-functioning. Part 3, The psychology and ideology of irrational beliefs. *Journal of Psychology and Theology, 16,* 348-361.

Watson, P. J., Morris, R. J., & Hood, J. W. (1989a). Sin and self-functioning. Part 4, Depression, assertiveness and religious commitments. *Journal of Psychology and Theology, 17,* 44-58.

Watson, P. J., Morris, R. J., & Hood, J. W. (1989b). Sin and self-functioning. Part 5, Antireligious humanistic values, individualism and the community. *Journal of Psychology and Theology, 17,* 157-172.

A Levels-of-Explanation Response

David G. Myers

What a wise and wonderful experiment the Wheaton College psychology department undertook when it welcomed to its staff a Christian philosopher. Almost alone among Christian philosophers, Robert Roberts has related his knowledge of intellectual history to psychology. He helps not only the Wheaton psychologists but all of us to step back from our focused work in psychology and see the bigger picture. Some ideas that we take to be new, he finds germinating in the intellectual history of the past twenty-five hundred years. He also finds in the teachings of Jesus, notably the Sermon on the Mount, "psychologically rich" insights relevant to our day and our work.

What is true of David Powlison and Gary Collins is also true of Robert Roberts, however. All three represent the antiscience view. All three discuss a "psychology" that is a great distance from the psychological science that I spend my days reading and distilling in my psychology texts. None of the three chapters mention a smidgen of research. None describe and critique the psychology that is published in most journals of the American Psychological Association and American Psychological Society, written up in introductory psychology textbooks, taught in colleges and universities, and tested in the Advanced Placement and Graduate Record psychology exams. Take their critiques of psychology to any top-rated psychology graduate program and the likely response would be: "you've got the wrong department. These chapters do not describe or engage what we do."

Ah, but that is "establishment psychology," Roberts correctly observes. Instead, he prefers "a broader conception of psychology. A psychology is a coherent body of thought and practice . . . for understanding, measuring, assessing, and possibly changing people's emotions, thoughts, perceptions, and behaviors, and their dispositions to these." This more theoretical, philosophical definition of psychology covers not only contemporary psychology but "Evagrius, Augustine, Aquinas, Baxter, Kierkegaard, and Dostoyevsky." And why not? Aristotle's understanding of conditioning he finds "superior to anything that the twentieth-century style of inquiry has produced." The Stoics of the same era gave us a cognitive theory of emotion "that is the equal or superior of anything analogous produced by the psychological establishment." The novels of Austen, Dickens, Eliot, Tolstoy, and Dostoyevsky are "sources of tremendous psychological insight into issues of human motivation, basic psychological needs, forms, and sources of pathology, and much more." And we haven't even gotten to the Sermon on the Mount and the other teachings of Jesus and the biblical literature.

Roberts gets no quarrel from me on the rich insights of these wisdom literatures. In fact, I will add my three favorites to his list: La Rochefoucauld's *Maxims,* Blaise Pascal's *Pensées,* and Francis Bacon's *Novum Organum.* All three of these authors, writing in the 1600s, have stunned and awed me with their anticipation of big ideas in late twentieth-century psychology.

"Humility is often but a trick whereby pride abases itself only to exalt itself later," wrote La Rochefoucauld, whose maxims anticipated recent work on self-serving bias, self-disparagement, and self-handicapping.

"The heart has its reasons which reason does not know," observed Pascal in one of his many perceptive thoughts. Three centuries later, scientists have proved Pascal correct. We know more than we know we know. Our thinking is partly *controlled* (deliberate and conscious) and— more than most of us once supposed—partly *automatic* (effortless and without our awareness). Automatic thinking occurs not "on screen" but off screen, out of sight, where reason does not know.

And consider some of the "idols" or fallacies of the mind identified by Bacon, a Christian statesman and philosopher who popularized the idea that science explored God's "book of nature."

☐ *Finding order in random events.* "The human understanding, from its peculiar nature, easily supposes a greater degree of order and equality in things that it really find." Experiment after experiment has confirmed Bacon's hunch. People readily see correlations or cause-effect links where none exist (a phenomenon that fuels astrology, gambling, and superstitious good-luck rituals).

☐ *Overconfident judgments.* "Cognitive conceit" describes our tendency to be more confident than correct. "Which is longer, the Panama or the Suez Canal?" If you feel 75 percent sure of your answer, the odds are about 60 percent that you're right (a phenomenon that inflates scientists' assessments of their theories, clinicians' assessments of their diagnoses, and likely theologians' assessments of their doctrines). Bacon's take on this rings true: "Some men become attached to particular sciences and contemplations, either from supposing themselves the authors and inventors of them or from having bestowed the greatest pains upon such subjects, and thus become most habituated to them."

☐ *The confirmation bias.* Many experiments find that we also are more disposed to search for and recall instances that confirm our beliefs than to search for contrary instances. Bacon foresaw how confirmation bias could sustain superstitions: "All superstition is much the same whether it be that of astrology, dreams, omens, retributive judgments, or the like, in all of which the deluded believers observe events which are fulfilled, but neglect and pass over their failure, though it be much more common."

☐ *The biasing power of preconceptions.* "The human understanding," said Bacon, "when any proposition has been once laid down . . . forces everything else to add fresh support and confirmation." Indeed, with both visual perceptions and everyday opinions, experiments show that to believe is often to see. It's true as we read Scripture too. "The Bible always comes interpreted," Martin Marty has said. "Oppressors and the oppressed . . . read the book differently." And that is one reason for our being wary of Christians who want to impose *their* understanding of Scripture on all psychology.

☐ *The persuasive power of vivid information.* In experiments, vivid experiences and anecdotes tend to overwhelm statistical information. A potent story of welfare fraud may make a more lasting and persuasive impression than facts about welfare use and abuse. Many people fear air travel (with vivid crash images coming readily to mind) more than getting in a car—despite their being, during the 1980s, *seventy-six times* safer mile per mile in a commercial aircraft than on America's roads. "The human understanding is most excited by that which strikes and enters the mind at once and suddenly and by which the imagination is immediately filled and inflated," Bacon understood. "It then begins almost imperceptibly to conceive and suppose that everything is similar to the few objects which have taken possession of the mind, while it is very slow and unfit for the transition to the remote and heterogeneous instances by which axioms and tried as by fire."

So, if it's all been said before better than it's said now, why bother with "establishment" psychology? First, not only has today's wisdom been said before but often its opposite also. Roberts finds Aristotle's wisdom superior to our own—but he selects only that part of Aristotle's wisdom which he now recognizes as correct by the light of today's knowledge. Aristotle was also wrong about some things. He believed the mind was in the heart, which pumps warmth and vitality to the body. The heart remains our Valentine symbol for love, but science has long overtaken philosophy on this issue. It's your brain, not your heart, that falls in love.

In hindsight Bacon looks brilliant. But few hit the jackpot as he did. So until we do the research, how are we to know whether "the pen is mightier than the sword" or "actions speak louder than words"? From the sages of the ages we can get a similarly conflicting portrayal of human nature. We know from Roman satirist Juvenal that people "hate those who have been condemned" and from Ralph Waldo Emerson that "the martyr cannot be dishonored." We can base our persuasive appeals on the assumption of Shakespeare's Lysander that "the will of man is by his reason sway'd," or we can follow the advice of Lord Chesterfield: "Address yourself generally to the senses, to the heart, and to the weaknesses of mankind, but rarely to their reason." Such contradictory propositions suggest the need for careful studies that will winnow fact from falsehood.

Second, Bacon's sensitivity to cognitive bias, which I believe Roberts, Powlison, and Collins will join me in resonating with, drove him *toward* science rather than away from it. Knowing our vulnerability to error beckons us not to disparage the human sciences but to restrain our unchecked speculations. Aware that we can conceive and defend almost any theory, we must be candid about our own presuppositions and check our theories against the data of God's creation. "Our method and that of the sceptics agree in some respects at first setting out," said Bacon, "but differ most widely, and are completely opposed to each other in their conclusion; for they roundly assert that nothing can be known; we that but a small part of nature can be known, by the present method; their next step, however, is to destroy the authority of the senses and understanding, whilst we invent and supply them with assistance."

The third reason we should engage rather than dismiss establishment psychology is because it's where one finds the action—the most exciting discourse and discovery. (The NFL may represent "establishment" football and the American Medical Association and National Institutes of Health may represent "establishment" medicine, but if you want to be a leader in football or medicine, you'd best not scorn them.) Roberts is unimpressed with the action in psychology. He'd rather put his money on the sages of the ages. And rather than respect literature and philosophy as distinct and valuable disciplines that ask their own questions with their own methods, he would broaden psychology to incorporate them (as if psychology isn't already sufficiently diverse and inclusive).

My own enthusiasm for psychological science lies at the other end of the continuum. I *am* impressed. I spend my days reading psychological science and struggle to choose from the rich buffet what to include in my introductory psychology text. Are these antipsychology folks really reading the same discipline, I wonder? How could someone not be intrigued by findings that few if any sages anticipated:

☐ the functions of our two brain hemispheres

☐ the quantified heritability of a multitude of traits

☐ the remarkable cognitive abilities of newborns

☐ the extent to which peer influences trump parental nurture in shaping children's language, smoking habits, and lifestyle

☐ the effects of experience at different ages on the brain's neural networks

☐ the nature of intellective changes with aging

☐ how eyewitnesses construct and reconstruct memories
☐ the powers and limits of intuition
☐ the components of intelligence
☐ the effect of stress on the body's immune system
☐ the ways in which our self-concept guides our information processing
☐ the effect of aerobic exercise on mild depression and anxiety
☐ the things that do and don't predict human happiness

My sympathies are with John Calvin. Rather than dismiss the scholarship of his day, Calvin (1559) reflected that we cannot read the best minds of our time "without great admiration. We marvel at them because we are compelled to recognize how preeminent they are. But shall we count anything praiseworthy or noble without recognizing at the same time that it comes from God?" (p. 274).

Psychological science is barely more than a century old. What we have learned is only a beginning and will seem as relative ignorance to our great grandchildren. As I emphasized in my chapter, the scope of its questions and answers are limited. It's only one perspective on life. Yet what we have learned—and my list only scratches the surface—is, methinks, worth celebrating.

If establishment psychology is indeed where the action is, do we really want to run off into the corner to create our own little Christian psychology? By doing so do we not risk irrelevance? Are we not called to be in the world if not of it? to be leaven in the loaf? salt and light to the world? Therefore we need more Christian scholars not in the stands but down on the playing field. With an intellectual super bowl being played out, don't we want Christians called into the game and not just playing touch football with one another behind the bleachers?

We benefit from having some in the stands, of whom Roberts is an able example as he surveys and reflects on the game below and its larger context. (As a philosopher it's not his job to get in the game.) But let there also be Christians who will prepare themselves to play the game. As C. S. Lewis once declared, "We do not need more Christian books; we need more books by Christians about everything with Christian values built in." Reformed philosopher Nicholas Wolterstorff (1984) said it well in urging the Christian psychologist to occupy the academy as a Christian who sees the world in the light of the gospel, but occupy it also as a psychologist, not as one who surveys the scene from outside and now and then makes some clucking noises, but as one who participates in the nitty-gritty of actual psychological explorations. Do not just be a critic. Be a creative initiator, faithful in your thinking as in your doing the gospel of Jesus Christ.

I was delighted, therefore, by Roberts's conclusion: granting "room" for empirical research in his vision for psychology. He goes on to offer a wonderful list of questions for exploration: Do certain activities change people in ways that Jesus seems to claim? Does religion or prayer boost health? How effective are spiritual disciplines in forming Christian virtues? What are the causes of homosexual orientation and behavior? "If we find that the claims of Christian psychology (as we understand them) seem to be disconfirmed by empirical research, we have reason for thinking that we have misconstructed the Christian psychology, and we return to the Bible and the tradition to read it again for a better interpretation." Despite my misgivings about creating a separatist Christian psychology, I can only applaud.

Why not go a step further? In addition to encouraging Christians to engage issues of special interest to Christians, why not also engage the big intellectual issues of our day? Rather than conceding the main intellectual playing field to secularists, why not ponder, for example, what the explosion of new research on mind-brain connections, behavioral and molecular genetics, and human origins means for our self-understanding? (This, in fact, is the thrust of a recent collaborative exploration led by Christian scholars at Fuller Seminary and published as *Whatever Happened to the Soul?*) And why not encourage our bright and aspiring Wheaton undergraduate students to apply to Stanford, Michigan, or Ohio State in preparation for becoming part of the future intellectual leadership of psychology?

References

Bacon, F. (1620). *Novum Organum.*

Calvin, J. (1559/1975). *Institutes of the Christian religion,* 2.2.15-16 (J. T. McNeill, Ed., F. L. Battles, Trans.). Philadelphia: Westminster.

La Rochefoucauld, F. (1678). *Maxims.*

Pascal, B. (1660). *Pensées.*

Wolterstorff, N. (1984). Integration of faith and science—the very idea. *Journal of Psychology and Christianity, 3,* 12-19.

Brown, W. S., Malony, H. N., & Murphy, N. C. (1998). *Whatever happened to the soul?* Minneapolis: Fortress.

An Integration Response

Gary R. Collins

As I read his chapter, I appreciated Dr. Roberts's respect for Scripture, awareness of history and efforts to put contemporary psychology into a broader philosophical-theological perspective. Like others before him, he points out that writers from centuries ago dealt perceptively with behaviors, emotions, thoughts, and motivations that too many contemporary psychologists think are only now being discovered and analyzed. As Roberts so correctly asserts, psychological education is narrow if it focuses mainly on twentieth-century research reports and ignores some of the classical works that this chapter cites.

The chapter left me with several concerns, however. First, I felt uncomfortable with some of Roberts's views of integration. In reading and rereading his "broader conception of psychology," I was not sure what made this broader or different from what we might read in contemporary introduction to psychology textbooks. My guess is that most psychologists would agree with Roberts's definition but wonder (as I did) how this is unique and how it covers Evagrius, Augustine, Aquinas, and the others. A few paragraphs later I questioned the author's statement that the aim of integration is "to produce a happy blend of one or another of the twentieth-century psychologies with the thought and practice of the church." I agree that there have been a few—some advocates of transactional analysis, integrity theory, or logotherapy, for example—who have sought to link one of the twentieth-century psychologies with

Christian thought, but these are rare efforts and do not represent the aim of integration. I was surprised, as well, that a man with an impressive knowledge of history would cite a 1989 book by C. Stephen Evans as "the first book to argue for an explicitly Christian psychology." What about my own little book *The Rebuilding of Psychology* (Collins, 1977), the Carter and Narramore *Introduction to Psychology and Theology* (1979), Cosgrove's *Psychology Gone Awry* (1979), or writings by the early leaders in the Pastoral Psychology movement?

In reading the chapter I sensed that Roberts was arguing so strongly for the inclusion of psychologically oriented writings from the far past that he was throwing out much of the psychology of the past hundred years. He writes that he simply wants to "bracket the substance of twentieth-century psychologies so that we can put the Christian tradition in the driver's seat," but before and after that statement he argues strongly that modern psychologies "contaminate the substance" of our efforts to understand and help people with psychological needs. Surely Roberts is right in his view that the worldviews of people like Rogers, Ellis, Freud, and Jung are at odds with the core teachings of Scripture. I agree that uncritical efforts to absorb and integrate these into our Christian psychologies will be contaminating. But few who believe in the integration of faith and learning would absorb and integrate these secular worldviews without weeding out the values, assumptions and methods that are at odds with biblical truth. Even as we learn from the ancient writers, Christian and non-Christian, surely we can learn from more contemporary writers and integrate some of their insights into our Christian psychologies. But the insights of psychological and theological writers, both ancient and modern, must be tested against the Word of God. This is the standard against which all psychological insights must be evaluated.

Robert's commentary on the Sermon on the Mount shows how biblical teaching is relevant to the issues that concern psychologists and their clients. We need more of this biblical analysis, especially by writers who can avoid what Roberts points out as the tendency to "read back into the older authors [presumably including the biblical writers] a substantive psychology that really comes from the twentieth century."

I appreciated Roberts's affirmation of research. Certainly there is no inconsistency between drawing from the insights of the past and learning from contemporary empirical investigations. We must be careful not to elevate research too highly, however. He writes that "if we find that the claims of Christian psychology (as we understand them) seem to be disconfirmed by empirical research, we have reason for thinking that we have misconstructed the Christian psychology, and we return to the Bible and the tradition to read it again for a better interpretation." That is one valuable approach. Another is to look again at the research. I'm sure Roberts would agree that research is not infallible. It is not the only standard against which we test our psychologies. Sometimes our Christian psychology and our biblical interpretations are right on target and the "disconfirming" research is flawed.

Perhaps my three final comments are more picky. First, I wish Roberts had not been so inclined to talk about "establishment psychology" as if there is one "rather narrow" psychological approach out there that represents all that he resists. This gives an "us versus them" tone that seems to pit the "good guys against the bad guys." I'm not so sure that the establishment is nearly as unified as the author suggests. Second, I was surprised to read that faith and theology are "already, by their nature, too intimately and naturally involved with one another for it to make sense to propose integrating them." I see theology as a human system of thought, just as psychology is a human system of thought. Biblical theology (like biblically sensitive psychology) is tied closely to the Christian's faith, but from my perspective a lot of theology (like a lot of psychology) is anything but "intimately and naturally involved" with or "tight" in its tie to personal faith. Instead, a lot of theology is diametrically opposed to my faith and to the faith of numerous other Christians. Third, it may be unfair to expect a historical essay to look ahead. But I wish the author had commented about the impact of postmodernism on modern psychology, including Christian psychology. He writes that it is "very unlikely" that establishment psychologists would present ideas through novels, but the emergence of narrative therapy would suggest that this is *very likely* to become an increasing possibility. Roberts raises some existential questions that psychology has been unable to answer, but current fascination with spirituality in psychology suggests that at least some in the field are more open to ancient wisdom and existential issues than they have been in the past. The field is evolving and moving forward in interesting ways that cannot be overlooked.

Overall, I appreciated Roberts's essay. Like Thomas Oden, Richard Foster, and others, he challenged me to look more carefully at traditional Christian literature. It is true, no doubt, that many of the issues that psychologists address today were being dealt with long before the science of psychology appeared. It could be argued that psychology imposed itself on the Christian terrain, then tried to exclude anything Christian. To now limit our understanding of people to what psychology has discovered empirically is to restrict our vision greatly. I appreciate Roberts's call to a broader, much more Christian psychology than what we see in the general psychology books.

References

Carter, J. D., and Narramore, B. (1979). *The integration of psychology and theology: An introduction.* Grand Rapids, MI: Zondervan.

Collins, G. R. (1977). *The rebuilding of psychology.* Wheaton, IL: Tyndale House.

Cosgrove, M. P. (1979). *Psychology gone awry: An analysis of psychological world.* Grand Rapids, MI: Zondervan.

A Biblical Counseling Response

David Powlison

I much appreciate the fundamental direction of Robert Roberts's thought: wise Christians are "people in whom faith and psychology have an *original union* as tight as that between faith and theology. In them, psychological thought and practice is simply an aspect of faith." By taking the "broader historical perspective," he debunks the "establishment" definition of psychology and establishes a broader, more humane, more Christian conception of the kinds of knowledge and counseling efficacy we need, attending particularly to wisdom from ignored sources. He makes the case that Christianity possesses and sets forth a distinctive psychology. I agree with all my heart.

Roberts's article and mine complement and supplement each other. I am intrigued to see how similar our paths are: a desire to tap the Scripture afresh in the light of contemporary questions, attending to historical theology, the relativizing of scientistic truth claims by history and philosophy of science, even the quirk of stumbling upon Martha Nussbaum's intriguing work. It is perhaps no accident that neither of us is socialized into the intellectual and professional habits of professional psychologists. He is a philosopher with psychological interests. I was rerouted out of psychology and resocialized. As a non-Christian, I majored in psychology, worked four years in psychiatric hospitals, underwent extensive psychotherapy, and planned to go on to graduate school in clinical psychology. My three best friends in college became a psychiatrist, a psychoanalyst, and a clinical psychologist. I became a Christian when on the brink of joining them.

It would be redundant to list our many points of agreement. But I will critique Roberts gently on six points, hoping to supplement and balance his argument and to strengthen its consistency.

First, his approach needs to be guarded against an antiquarian tendency, as if the Christian psychology were something chiefly to be recovered from the past, not something also forged afresh in the present. What John Murray said of theology is also true of our psychology: "A theology that does not build on the past ignores our debt to history and naively overlooks the fact that the present is conditioned by history. A theology that relies on the past evades the demands of the present" (Murray, 1982, p. 9). Our task is never less than recovering old truth; our task can never be merely that. To *develop* the Faith's psychology will result in fresh truths. Old truths will pulse with new life when seen from novel perspectives, with previously unimagined applications. New skills, altered forms of church life, and redefinitions of ministry will arise.

As Roberts says, the rediscovery of long lost wisdoms helps deliver the church from subjection to various contemporary psychologies and reasserts positive Christian wisdom. But we also need fresh pastoral theology in order to draw from the past discerningly. Not all earlier practical theologies were created equal. Not all are equally worth recovering. We must appropriate some and leave others behind. To discern the difference demands criteria for judgment.

Second, Roberts's project is largely a literary project with a literary product. He explores sources contained in libraries and converses with voices inhabiting academia. His scholarly gifts can greatly serve the health of Christ's body politic. For someone with his credentials even to say, "There *is* a truly Christian psychology, and the others are rivals and alternatives," nourishes the morale of God's people. But Roberts's intellectual project runs the danger of becoming bookish. He does not portray the significance of engagement with the living documents: real people, with real needs to be comprehended, converted, consoled, protected, provided for, and changed. He demonstrates how conceptual-historical research and empirical research provide two ways to develop the Faith's psychology. I would not subtract these but would add that examining and ordering one's own life in the light of the Christ of Scripture and seeking to help others similarly examine and order their lives are prime sources of learning our psychology by heart.

Third, Roberts rightly critiques "juxtaposing" faith and psychology (approximately David Myers's approach) and "integrating" faith and psychology (approximately Gary Collins's approach). Both views tend to treat biblical thinking as a screen, filter, or boundary through which a Christian sifts psychology's claims to knowledge and efficacy, attempting to weed out the bad from the good. In contrast, Roberts and I think Christianity exerts systemic effects when it comes to psychology, not occasional effects. The Faith teaches the "Christian standpoint": corrective eyeglasses, a comprehensively altered gaze, a fundamentally reoriented practice.

But Roberts's argument also needs to be differentiated from "biblicism," the tendency among evangelicals to box ourselves up in the Bible and to box up the Bible. Biblicism addresses contemporary questions only by citing proof texts. It treats Scripture as a collection of timeless "verses," an exhaustive but scrambled encyclopedia whose topics can be accessed using a concordance. It honors the text superstitiously, enshrining the Word of God, rather than working with and from the Scripture to hammer out extensive and intensive practical theological wisdom.

Interestingly, evangelicals on *both* sides of the psychology question— both critics of psychology and integrationist psychologists—treat the Bible this way. Critics and advocates of psychology often share the same view of the *kind* of thing Scripture is, though they differ widely in their assessment of the scope and relevancy of its contents. One side says Scripture contains everything: "Here are the proof texts for anorexia." The other side says Scripture doesn't contain everything: because there are no proof texts on anorexia, the Bible is not about anorexia, therefore we must turn to psychology for understanding. Sound pastoral theology, contrary to both, says the Bible *is* about the phenomena our culture labels anorexia, but it offers something better and richer than an anorexia verse. As we learn to think thematically and systematically, we might even say the Bible is all about anorexia.

For example, anorexia is one particular extension of Paul's statement that "the works of the flesh are obvious." Though the condition we call anorexia is not specifically named, Christ teaches us to identify the *kind of thing* it is. We are further challenged, then, to tease out the constellation of "lusts of the flesh" driving the syndrome. We have the inexpressible privilege of speaking and embodying timely, finely tailored grace to recapture those whose hearts have been kidnapped by lies. I have often witnessed the process by which the power of Christ's grace penetrates such a self-absorbed, loveless, unbelieving way of life. The lights come on, usually slowly, inviting, and compelling faith-working-through-love (Gal 5:6; 5:13—6:10). We would be fools to turn to other paradigms for systematic understanding and aid. However informative their descriptions of phenomena, they misinterpret and mishandle what they describe.

To successfully argue that there is a Christian psychology demands that we accurately define the nature of the Bible and the need for practical theological development and application. In shorthand, Scripture is a compendium of all wisdom (eyeglasses) and an exemplar of many specific wisdoms; it is not an encyclopedia of all specific wisdoms. The church always has work to do, cultivating the Faith's gaze, attitude, voice, and hands.[1]

Fourth, I heartily agree with Roberts that the Christian psychology should guide empirical research. The alternative is to let a fundamentally false theory—usually some form of social or biological determinism—control research. But I think that Roberts lapsed a bit toward the "establishment" view when he illustrated the impact of the Christian psychology only with respect to a fairly narrow band of explicitly "religious" topics: prayer, the effect of particular religious beliefs, and factors influencing Christian virtue. Our psychology should affect research into *anything*—at minimum affecting our presuppositions and interpretive categories, the criteria by which we weigh the significance of findings, and the implications we draw. The more important the topic studied, the more the Christian psychology will exert overt influence. For example, without God's realigning Word, it is *impossible* for human beings to accurately observe and interpret such things as human motivation: conflict-

---

[1]See Frame (1997, pp. 272-280) and Powlison (1999) for further discussion of the nature of Scripture and theology. For recent examples of the sort of practical theological writing I have in mind, see the *Journal of Biblical Counseling*.

ing instincts? primary and secondary drives? sociobiological hard-wiring? compensation for low self-esteem? unmet needs from the hierarchy of needs? lusts of the flesh? Describing an earlier generation of rationalistic psychologists, John Calvin noted astutely that when it comes to making sense of human desires, "The natural man refuses to be led to recognize the diseases of his lusts. The light of nature is extinguished before he even enters upon this abyss. The philosophers . . . take no account of the evil desires that gently tickle the mind" (Calvin, 1960, p. 284). Secular theories grope in the dark and don't know over what they stumble; Christians alone know what we are researching.

Fifth, Roberts's discussion of "Jesus' psychology" in the Sermon on the Mount is filled with gems. I would only add that the Lord's "psychology" is not simply a point of view and set of propositions substantively different from rival psychologies in its conceptual structure. Jesus *lived* the true psychology. He is the only human who has *done* the Christian psychology: incarnation. He has done it *for* us: substitution. He has done and does the Christian psychology *to* us: ministry of Word and deed. Our faith trusts, loves, and needs Jesus. The Faith's psychology is brighter, deeper, sweeter, and higher than the alternatives because it sees and lives "with respect to Another." Obedience—our ability to think and practice the Christian psychology—is not a collection of virtues and propositions in abstraction from reliance on and loyalty to our Redeemer.

Finally, Roberts seems to assume that "professionals in psychology departments or clinical settings" will be the chief knowers and agents of the Christian psychology he proposes. Here he seems a bit colored by the "establishment" definition of the designated experts in psychological knowledge and practice. He fails to affirm countless "Christian psychologists" who may actually be much more on his wavelength: pastors, plumbers, English teachers, pastors' spouses, disciplers, Bible professors at Christian colleges, prison chaplains, growing new believers, wise friends, pastoral theologians, teenagers learning to love God, missionaries, and so forth. At times I wished Roberts had put the term "Christian psychologist" in quotes, so readers would be reminded that he argues for a countercultural definition. Most Christian *professional* psychologists integrate or juxtapose and don't really believe or practice as if there were a fully-orbed, distinctively Christian psychology to be generated out of the Faith's internal resources. But countless other Christians do believe and practice as if God has given us exactly such a splendid, relevant, fully-orbed creature.

I thought Roberts pulled his punches in his closing charge to professional psychologists. Though they might lack time and inclination, few would object in principle to becoming "at least as well versed in the thought of some great Christian psychologist as they are in their own corner of establishment psychology." That statement leaves too much room to assimilate the faith to alien psychologies, to syncretize or to disconnect intellectual curiosity from the functional faith and practice that drives professional life. It invites mental health professionals to become well versed in two things; it does not bid them to critique seriously "their own corner of establishment psychology," and so to live out the logic of Roberts's core argument. Those professionals should *adopt* the explicitly Christian psychology of seminal psychologists such as David and Paul, and keep learning from any subsequent psychologists who come close to replicating and extending the model. It's the only *true* psychology, because it's the way the Psychologist of psychologists thinks, gazes, and practices.

References

Calvin, J. (1960). *Institutes of the Christian religion* (Ford Lewis Battles, Trans.). Philadelphia: Westminster Press.

Frame, J. (1997). In defense of something close to biblicism: Reflections on sola scriptura and history in theological method. *Westminster Theological Journal, 59,* 269-291.

Murray, J. (1982). *Collected writings*. Edinburgh, U.K.: Banner of Truth Trust.

Powlison, D. (1999). Counsel Ephesians. *Journal of Biblical Counseling, 17*(2), 2-11.

5   A Biblical Counseling View

David Powlison

The Christian faith makes distinctive claims about God and presses those claims on all human beings. But none of the Bible's assertions about God exist abstracted from equally distinctive and pressing claims about humanity. The once-for-all faith is for and about real people in every situation of real life. It is not about folk tinctured with a particular religiosity, or about a religious sector of life in which only those so inclined participate. Human beings are creatures of the Bible's God, made for loyalty but gone wild: "God made man upright, but they have sought out many devices" (Eccles 7:29 RSV). These realities play out down to the slightest nuance of our psyches. Human beings are salvageable and transformable through the Word made flesh: "He who believes in the Son has eternal life; he who does not obey the Son shall not see life, but the wrath of God rests upon him" (Jn 3:36 RSV). That choice and its ramifications define the drama playing out every day in every soul. This is what a person *is* and *does*, willy-nilly. The entirety of human "psychology" takes place God-referentially whether or not we are aware of it, whether or not our theories and therapies comprehend it. A person cannot be truly understood or truly aided if this lifeblood of humanness is drained away, leaving a figment, a beast, an automaton, a humanoid, a counterfeit, a corpse to be studied and assisted.

How does the Bible's point of view on humanness relate to the modern social and behavioral sciences, and to those diverse activities, institutions, professions, and causes that have nestled under the moral and intellectual authority of "objective, scientific" psychology? We Christians have a distinctive and comprehensive point of view about our souls and the cure for what ails us. God's view of our psychology and his call to psychotherapeutic intervention differ essentially and pervasively from both the theories and therapies that have dominated psychological discourse and practice in the twentieth century.

Psychology or the *Psychologies?*

The word *psychology* serves us well in the same way that the words *religion, philosophy, literature,* and *politics* serve. Each of these is a general term, locating us within a particular cosmos of conflicting ideas and ideals, where incommensurable points of view compete, where even the trajectories of inquiry diverge radically. Of course this is so, for these big words label realms of ultimate concern: Who am I? What is? What matters? Why does that happen? What should be? What must change and how? Each of these words is thus inescapably plural: There are *many* psychologies, *many* religions. In the singular, *psychology* names only the arena of concerns and controversies you are entering; it indicates nothing significant about either the questions or answers you will encounter.

The really interesting things only emerge as you get down to details and debates. Many qualitatively different points of view on the soul present themselves as teachers of the true and proclaim their attendant psychotherapies as agents of the good. We often hear generalizations such as "Psychology's research findings show . . ." or "Psychology is able to teach us that . . ." or "Psychology can help with . . ." But what do such phrases mean? There is no unitary psychology. The "findings" are usually either ratifications of common sense or doubtful, or of doubtful, significance. Whenever someone cites the teachings of magisterial and univocal psychology, we must always ask, at least quietly, Which one of the psychologies do you mean? How do you know it is true? So what? Whenever salvific psychology proffers life-altering insight and help, we must always ask persistently, Which one do you have in mind? What exactly does that particular one say and do? Why? Really? We are credulous to our peril because in the realm of psychology, as in religion, real people live and die in the details.

What then does the word *psychology* mean? How should we use this good word, and how should we think about the ways other people use it? The word is protean, the semantic field huge, the issues at stake momentous; so the potential for slippery semantics is high. I will discriminate the major uses by slicing the semantic pie into six pieces: (1) the functioning of the human soul, (2) knowledge emerging from close observation, (3) numerous theories of personality, often sharply at odds in how they interpret the soul, (4) numerous psychotherapeutic models to redress ills defined by particular theories, (5) current institutional arrangements for educating practitioners-to-be, housing professional practice, and publishing, and (6) an ethos pervading popular American culture. Though interrelated, these are quite different sorts of things—a living being's essential nature, knowledge, explanatory systems, interventive practices, social institutions, and a sociocultural characteristic.

Psychology *Per Se*
The bedrock meaning, psychology *per se*, simply refers to the functioning of the human soul itself. Persons operate heart, soul, mind, and might in relation to everything under the sun—and everything over the sun. Psychology *per se* is not the cancer ravaging your body, but it is the whole of your response to cancer and perhaps some factors contributing to the genesis and progress of your illness. Psychology *per se* is not the social conditions that you experience, but it is how you interpret and respond to those conditions and constraints. Psychology *per se* is neither the devil nor God but how you respond to the devil's sayings and doings, the things in you that make the lie natural or alien. And it is how you respond to what God says and does, the things in you that make for embracing or for evading truth. The core meaning of psychology is simply "you," a being who functions psychologically.

Your psychology is what you are *about*, the "functional" aspects of your life: belief, memory, emotion, conscience, identity, volition, attitude, action, speech, imagination, perception, desire, assumption, cognition, self-deception, anticipation, and so on, as well as the various dynamics and interrelationships existing within the whole. In addition, every context that impinges upon heart, soul, mind, and might, and with which you interact moment by moment, is fair game for psychological interest.

The soul's functions are wedded to somatic processes and heredity. We are embedded in social networks, multifaceted culture, economics, politics, language; we even inhabit the cycle of the seasons and changes in the weather! You-in-your-world is the subject matter.[1] Like all the modern Western psychologies (and all the world and local religions that do for psychology in nonwesternized places), the faith is busy with psychology *per se*. After all, we must know ourselves as we actually are if we are ever to live wisely. We must see God's gaze after him if we are to proceed wisely in intervening to change those things that need changing in every member of every nation, tribe, tongue, and people.

Psychology as Knowledge About Human Functioning

Psychology as knowledge refers to many sorts of close observations and descriptions of human psychological functioning, the "facts" noticed and portrayed. This is the thing about psychology books and psychologists in person that makes them the most interesting—at their best, they know a great deal about people. The ability to supply descriptive riches and a feel for how people work—case experience or research findings—is highly attractive. This can make a piece of psychological literature "ring bells" with human experience. Three factors contribute to the depth and breadth of knowledge one often finds in psychologists, whether theoreticians, researchers, or clinicians: (1) they intentionally go about acquiring knowledge,[2] (2) they spend time with others who are willing to open their lives, and (3) they are often willing to open their own lives to self-examination or outside scrutiny.

Of course, such a wealth of information and feel for people can be common property with many others besides psychologists. Psychological insight can be found in Shakespeare and suburban homemakers, in

---

[1]Of course, theories collide in their initial premises about the creature in view. I have biased my definition in the Christian direction by employing language such as "creature" and "heart, soul, mind and might" and "devil or God." Secular psychologies by definition look for causalities other than "the active heart vis-à-vis God," interpreting core functions of the soul as self-referential or as deriving deterministically from either body or society.

[2]Researchers acquire nomothetic knowledge arising from systematic investigation of populations (e.g., social science) or brain phenomena (e.g., cognitive neuroscience); clinicians acquire idiographic knowledge arising from case experience.

Augustine and drug addicts, in Freud and your pastor, in Puritans and feuding spouses, in Buddhists and small children. Human beings often size up human beings with stunning accuracy. There is an old saying that the village is never wrong in its opinion of a person's character. And sometimes the least likely see the most clearly whether or not the emperor wears clothes. The potential for obtuseness and self-deception is also common property, as is the potential to misinterpret and misuse what is seen so clearly. Psychologists are neither privileged to see nor exempt from blind foolishness. The knowledge component in a particular piece of psychology—a theory, a research study, a self-help book, a therapist's conversation, a projective test—may be rich or poor, accurate or skewed, realistically human or a caricature.

This aspect of psychology intuitively seems the most "objective," the most "neutral," the most "scientific," the most informative and descriptive. But psychological knowledge exhibits several striking qualities. First, the more important a piece of psychological knowledge is for living, the more it will be common property to all sorts of people and disciplines, and the more its meaning will be controversial; put the other way, the more distinctively "scientific" a bit of psychological knowledge is, the less "important" it will be. So the more important something is for understanding and influencing what makes people tick—the closer it gets to personality theory and applied psychology (see the two sections that follow)—the closer it will come to describing things that theologians, poets, and commonsense also know, discuss, and debate. Science and clinical observation supplement such knowledge and participate in such discussions but never solve the debates. Good parents and good elementary school teachers have always known tacitly what Piaget makes explicit and detailed about cognitive development in children (Piaget, 1952). When psychological researchers study pride, they may confirm numerous things about pride (Myers, 1981). Or in the name of developing a science of human nature, a clinician may seriously misconstrue the dynamics of pride (see, e.g., Adler, 1927). Christian and non-Christian will both ring the bells of experience with case-study details, but a world of difference exists between a "codependent's wounded inner child" (Bradshaw, 1990) and a person whose "fear of man" has replaced fear of God (Welch, 1997). As research moves further from knowledge that matters for everyday living, the significance of the knowledge generated diminishes, however fascinating the information discovered or perplexing the questions raised. Wisdom, a biblical understanding of the human condition and an ability to address that condition constructively, will not be significantly altered by a new theory about neural substrates of cognition and behavior or by a new model for how the brain processes, stores, and retrieves information.

A second characteristic is that psychological knowledge never presents "just the facts." Theory has multiple effects on observation and research: selecting, distorting, and fabricating facts. Even the so-called data level of psychology expresses the theoretical commitments of particular psychologies, not some abstract psychology in general or psychology-as-truth.

Knowledge arises from some principle of selectivity. A theory *selects* facts based on what it has determined to be significant. The best effect of theory is that it guides us to notice certain things, to bring them into focus and to magnify them. But the flip side of selectivity is that the data expresses a theory's blinkering effect on perception. Countless potential facts can be ignored—trees falling silently in the forest because no one is there to hear, perhaps whole forests falling. A telescope sees into deep space by narrowing the field of view. The very power that lets us examine one thing also has the potential to miss essential facts and to obscure the overall pattern and meaning. Gaze at a star in the Milky Way through a telescope and you do not know that a communications satellite just passed overhead or that there is a Milky Way in the first place. Secular psychological research does not see and report the most significant pieces of information about people, and it invariably misses the overall pattern of what is there. Certain facts cannot be seen or cannot be seen as significant. Only the Faith has a principle by which the magnifying power can be turned up without losing breadth: God's point of view, communicated to us.

Furthermore, because we humans see with a theory-informed gaze, a wrong theory distorts every fact, just as the truth rightly interprets every fact. A husband, falsely suspecting his wife of infidelity, has facts: He sees her rush in five minutes late for their lunch together, breathing heavily, with her makeup smeared. But he misinterprets every fact he has, just as he did not see other facts: her car broke down a half mile away on this sweltering day, and he never dealt with the guilt over his adultery three years ago. In a God-made, God-sustained, God-interpreted world, observational data will express the distorting effect of the secularity in any theory. Observations are always presented in a context of meanings, beliefs, values, priorities, goals. False theories misperceive what is there. The Pharisees and Peter had identical optical, auditory, and neural apparatus with which to see, hear, and consider Jesus. But the former saw and heard a charlatan and heretic, while the latter beheld and heeded his Savior and Lord. To give a simple example, when Karen Horney observes that people are driven to pursue human approval, power, pleasure, and safety (Horney, 1942), she *sees* "neurotic needs," not lusts of the flesh. In fact, neurotic needs do not exist; they are theoretical fictions, myths substituting for what God calls these same phenomena. Only the Faith has a principle by which our tendency to distort can be continually corrected: God's point of view.

All too often a theory will also even fabricate "facts," observing the figments of theory-guided imagination. All observations are constructed to a degree, but some observations may be pure artifacts. A theory tells us that certain things "have to be there"; the eye fills in the details wittingly or unwittingly. Sometimes people make things up. Research data is notoriously fluid and liable to be fudged; clinicians most often see what they expect to see. Sometimes dubious facts arise from complicity by the subjects studied (e.g., false memory syndrome). Sometimes bogus facts arise from biases built into testing instruments (e.g., tests purporting to measure aptitude or psychological characteristics generate theory-prejudiced "data"). In each case the fabrication may be calculated, but more often it simply just happens. Only the Faith has a principle by which our tendency to invent can be continually corrected.

Information and observation must always be subjected to analysis from the standpoint of the Faith. For example, Freud's observational and narrative abilities are dazzling. When he describes slips of the tongue or common character types or how nocturnal dreams are a playground of desires and fears, we recognize real people, ourselves included (Freud, 1900, 1901, 1916). But that knowledge comes with a strong fishy taste, the distinctively "Freudian" theory. He missed or dismissed crucial facts; every paragraph incarnates the same kink as his gaze; he free-associated ideas and jigged his illustrations and case studies to come out right. Freud's seeing, like that of Everyman who does not see with the Faith's eyes, was a powerful table saw set at a 75-degree angle. When he cuts a forest into boards, he cuts every board crooked. But the Faith sees true; it cuts boards at right angles.

All this is the old problem of the blind men and the elephant. Would-be students and doctors of the elephant portray the beast as a tree, snake, rope, wall, or leaf, and then, naturally enough, attempt to heal the problems they portray. Everybody sees many things, but who sees clearly what the thing is? If the interpretation is true, a corrective dynamic works against our tendency to ignore, misread, and invent facts; if the interpretation is false, a perverting dynamic works to undermine even the sharpest observations and best intentions.

Because of these epistemological effects, we must interact with secular knowledge with an intentional, self-conscious ambivalence, always learning but always debunking, always thinking through what we hear in the light of what we already know in the Faith, always expanding the scope of the Faith's application. Consider a concrete example. Alfred Adler's theory continues to exert a profound effect on modern psychologies. He is a progenitor of cognitive psychology, family systems, self-esteem theory and techniques of strategic intervention in counseling. His ideas permeate many books on child rearing and education. How useful is Adler's detailed and erudite portrayal of the "inferiority complex" in once-tiny people (Adler, 1927), when, from the standpoint of the Faith, a "desires-of-body-and-mind complex" enslaves and kills always-sinful people of any size (Eph 2:3)? Is Adler provocative, a catalyst? Maybe. If we have not thought long and hard from our own standpoint, he will spur us to get to work, as any alien theory does. Does he teach things analogous to biblical truth? Sure. A theory would babble if it did not speak in at least half-truths and formal similarities. Is he illustrative and informative? Does he enrich our knowledge base? If we do not know much about people, Adler gives us a lot of information. But we must reinterpret *everything*. His catalog of human depravity—vanity, jealousy, avarice, hatred, and faint-heartedness—ring true, except that every description is warped by his theory. He sees sin, but he calls it something else in order to solve it some other way. If we already know people well,

Adler adds little. Is he dangerous? Yes, Adler intends to convert us to his way of seeing. His methods of communicating his message—personal humility, the authority of science, vivid narrative—are skillful rhetorically. The bottom line? Adler sees the madness of the human heart through the eyes of that same madness. What he sees most accurately and cares about most deeply must be completely reconstrued. We would never integrate Adler and the Faith; the Faith makes better sense of Adler's best observations and best intentions. Our gaze "converts" his gaze, qualitatively changing all his "facts."

The Faith affirms that God sees it all, weighs it all properly, and controls it all for his own purposes. The Bible is intended to disciple us into seeing it all (or more of it) with God's gaze (or something more like God's gaze). Of course we who profess the Faith are not immune to the blinkering of our gaze, to distortions, and to fabrications. But God patiently teaches us—individually and corporately, over decades and centuries—how to see what we most need to see. Redemption exerts a correcting dynamic.

How then should we view psychological information? Bring it on; it is the stuff of life that only the Faith makes sense of and weighs properly. The scope and depth of our understanding increase as we become case-experienced. Especially bring on the "human documents"—real lives. Know yourself. The old prayer says, "We have followed too much the devices and desires of our own hearts." Watch where you go—in both senses of the word—and you will understand other people too. Know other people directly: rub shoulders, converse, care, notice. Bring on all sorts of other "documents" as well, portrayals of human life that also need interpretation through the Faith's eyes: imaginative literature, history, crosscultural studies, film, popular music, cultural anthropology, the daily newspaper, and lots of other things whose epistemological status is the same as the modern psychologies. With a careful caveat about the theory-ladenness of data and with a well-trained ability to think from our own point of view (Heb 5:14), we can learn from and interact with anything.

Psychology as Competing Philosophies of Life and Theories of Human Personality

Theory and worldview provide the intellectual center of the psychological enterprise, the "doctrinal core." We hinted at this doctrinal core under "Psychology *per se*" (see footnote 1, p. 199), and we were forced to reckon seriously with it when discussing psychology as knowledge. We will see later that the doctrinal core pervades psychology as therapy, as social institution, and as cultural ethos. Modern psychology in its most significant form is a marketplace of differing popular philosophies of life. Different schools of thought dispute each other (psychologies, not psychology). Each psychology's interpretive system is embodied in a set of categories and labels that map onto life lived. Norms and ideals set standards, against which diagnoses are made and toward which therapies aspire in seeking to alter life lived into something more worth living. The schema guides counseling conversations toward whatever "image" a human being is meant to be. As intellectual systems the personality theories are "alternative spiritualities" offering "rival 'words' about human nature"; they "mean their 'words' to be taken to heart, to shape our souls, and their therapies are potent methods for planting their ideas in us so that we may grow in the shapes that they ordain" (Roberts, 1993, pp. 4, 10). Just as there are many philosophies and many religions, it is no surprise that there will always be conflicting psychologies until the kingdom of God is established and everyone faces up to the final truth about our souls.

Psychological professionals often lament the clumsiness of their models, the slippage that occurs between life as it is and theoretical reconstructions. One of the pieces of folk wisdom in graduate education in psychology has always been, "If you want to really understand people, read Dostoyevsky and Shakespeare." A representative of Harry Stack Sullivan's psychology put the problem this way:

> The reader can see why psychiatry is so often charged with being reductive. For while the creatures described . . . may bear some resemblance to animals or to steam engines or robots or electronic brains, they do not sound like people. They are in fact constructs of theory, more humanoid than human. . . . It is just those qualities most distinctively human which seem to have been omitted. It is a matter of some irony, if one turns from psychology to one of Dostoyevsky's novels, to find that no matter how wretched, how puerile, or how dilapidated his characters may be, they all possess more humanity than the ideal man

who lives in the pages of psychiatry. (Farber, 1956, p. 110)[3]

Where does one find a psychological model where the characters in Dostoyevsky and Shakespeare would feel at home? Whatever the uncertainty and ambivalence about those authors' personal faith, they wrote about human life in distinctively human terms that mirror the universe of good and evil one finds in the Bible.

Psychological professionals also often lament that the chaos in their field seems unresolvable. Robert Coles writes, "This is all in a 'field,' as it is called, all too prone toward ideological splits and antagonisms, if not outright internecine war" (Coles, 1995, p. xxv). Carl Jung, who triggered the first split in the psychoanalytic movement, put an optimistic face on the fragmentation:

> The hard facts of reality [produced] an unwelcome widening of the horizon. In the first place, it was probably the fact that one had to admit the possibility of different interpretations of the observed material. Hence there grew up various schools with diametrically opposed views. . . .
>
> Thus we are faced in psychotherapy with a situation comparable to that in modern physics where, for instance, there are two contradictory theories of light. . . . The existence of many possible standpoints in psychology should not give grounds for assuming that the contradictions are irreconcilable and the various views merely subjective and therefore incommensurable. Contradictions in a department of science merely indicate that its subject displays characteristics which at present can be grasped only by means of antinomies. . . . Now the psyche is infinitely more complicated than light; hence a great number of antinomies is required to describe the nature of the psyche satisfactorily. (Jung, 1966, pp. 3-4)

These many decades later, no bridging theory has emerged that is able to reconcile antinomies. Instead, eclecticism is the order of our day. The

---

[3]Farber wrote at a time when psychotherapeutic practice and psychological theorizing were largely the province of psychiatrists. The clinical and counseling psychologies were nascent professionally. Now, more than forty years later, the social landscape has changed in such a way that we might easily substitute *psychology* for *psychiatry* in the first and last clauses without altering Farber's meaning.

only theory apparently capable of unifying the field in the near future is a ruthlessly antipsychological biopsychiatry that scoffs at all the fuss and bother that takes place in and about the psyche. It does not bridge antinomies; it bulldozes them away. Though eclecticism offers a pragmatic way to keep going on, it is an intellectual counsel of despair. The theoretical differences between secular psychologies are *not* reconcilable and complementary, as Jung believed. Such theories are truly incommensurable, as different as calling an elephant a tree or a snake. Tree and snake are not reconcilable perspectives but competing distortions. The bridging theory is the Faith that embeds us *coram Deo*. Our Grand Unified Theory (GUT) can understand how creatures who are thoroughly and inextinguishably elephantine can be described figuratively as having legs like an oak tree or a trunk as flexible and powerful as a python. But secular theories reify their metaphors—"It *is* a tree"—and lose the creature whom God made.

Other observers of modern psychological theorizing also express skepticism about the validity of the fruits. Historians take the long view of the enthusiasms that convulse a decade, a generation, a century. Thomas Kuhn (1970) thought psychology "prescientific" because it had never attained to any agreed-on paradigm: "Controversies over fundamentals seem endemic among psychologists," like the controversies in philosophy, art, religion, and politics (p. viii). Karl Popper (1965) thought that

> Marx's theory of history, Freud's psycho-analysis, and Alfred Adler's so-called "individual psychology," . . . though posing as sciences, had in fact more in common with primitive myths than with science; . . . they resembled astrology rather than astronomy. . . . "Clinical observations," like all other observations, are *interpretations in the light of theories*. . . . These theories describe some facts, but in the manner of myths. (pp. 34, 38)

Gerald Grob calls the search for the cause of troubled and troublesome people the "Holy Grail" of theory, but

> the problems of explaining human behavior, normal or abnormal, seemed beyond human capacity. The very concept of mental disease, for example, could not be separated from the deeper and more pro-

found problem of explaining the nature of human beings in general and their behavior in particular. (Grob, 1998, p. 203)

George Marsden speaks of further controversy intrinsic to the encounter between the Faith's psychology and psychological faiths: "the obviously Herculean task of integrating the largely opposed assumptions of modern psychology and evangelical theology" (Marsden, 1987, p. 238).

In the social sciences, particularly psychology (because it aims closest to the human heart), consensus is elusive and disagreement endemic. This is no quirk of our historical moment, resolvable if we will allow psychologists another twenty, fifty, or one hundred years to achieve theoretical harmony, a GUT. Fragmentation happens for a reason. The secular psychologies chase a rainbow: an explanation of what is wrong with us that is anything but sin against God, and a cure for the human condition that is anything but Christ. "The hearts of men are full of evil, and madness is in their hearts while they live" (Eccles 9:3 RSV). Madmen's theories about madmen cannot help but be touched with madness; sinners theorize sinfully about sinners.

But noting overtly incompatible points of view does not speak the final word. The Christian perspective does not rest on skepticism. Our point of view rests on the true paradigm that subjects all other explanations of human life to the deepest possible criticism. Thomas Kuhn's dismissal of the psychologies as "pre-paradigmatic" is only partially true. In fact, there *is* an underlying paradigm unifying the psychologies, however incompatible psychodynamic, behavioral, humanistic, existential, cognitive, and biological theories appear on the surface. Sin has typical effects on theorizing, and the secular psychologies manifest a profound paradigmatic commonality. All agree that human beings are autonomous rather than responsible to an objective God who acts and speaks. All agree that the problem with people is anything but sin, and problems can be explained in purely psychological, psychosocial, or psychosocial-somatic terms. All agree in positing some sort of determining factor to replace choice either for or against God as the central, specific, and pervasive issue of human existence. All agree that both answers and power to change reside either in the individual, in human relationships, or in medical chemistry. All agree that anything but Jesus Christ and the min-

istry of the Word will be the answer to sin and misery, that is, to our dysfunctions, dysphorias, and syndromes. All busy themselves trying to
prove that anything but Christianity's view of things is true. In the most
fundamental sense, all the varied psychologies are wrong in the same
way. However striking their observations or their effects, they impart a
false consciousness to their devotees. They must be subjected to radical
demythologizing by Christian presuppositions and invited to intelligent
repentance.

We often forget something very important. The Faith is a theory
whose view of human nature competes head-on with the personality theories. And it is a therapy whose cure of souls competes head-on with the
modern psychotherapies. In the twentieth century Christianity typically
has not been viewed—often not even presented—as a rational system. Its
persona is as a form of superstition, moralism, and irrationalism that has
been superseded by rational systems. One would certainly not find the
Bible, Augustine, Aquinas, Calvin, Baxter, Edwards, or Warfield agreeing
with *that* notion of the Faith! The persona is false. But we who hold to
Christian faith face two problems. The first is of our own making: we
tend to truncate the scope and depth of the Faith. We relegate it to "spiritual" matters; we view Scripture as a helpful "resource" to aid with problems that we allow others to define; we make it a source only of "control
beliefs" for our worldview, not specifics. We lose the detail, relevance,
purpose, and breadth of God's communication in the Bible. Scripture
does not discuss our soul's dynamics in the form of a psychology textbook, research study, or self-help book; it discusses us—and addresses
us—in a better form.

The second problem assails us from outside. Our theistic rational system is directly opposed by naturalistic rational systems. Secular theoreticians of the soul are among many moderns (including Christians!) who
believe that the Faith's perspective on the psyche does not extend
beyond prescribing behavioral morality, performing sacerdotal rituals,
eliciting religious experiences, battling demonic spooks, and professing
abstruse doctrines of little bottom-line value for the business of probing
the psyche and ameliorating its problems. But we who take the Christian
point of view must simply say, "On the contrary . . ." The psyche, rationally understood, operates the way God says it does, and it operates with

respect to God. Any theory explaining the psyche's essential operations as an encapsulated entity, or as a social construct or role within a social system, or as an epiphenomenon of biology, or as some combination of all three, is wrong—for rational reasons.

Granted, there has been a serious lack of fresh pastoral theological labor among Bible believers since the mid-1800s. Pastoral counseling has largely been a subset of secular psychologies and liberal theologies (Holifield, 1983). Those who hold to the Faith have been beleaguered intellectually and busy with other aspects of the church's mission. In the absence of our own well-articulated and skillfully practiced wisdom, the church has often been an uneasy borrower from the achievements of those committed to efface sin as the rational diagnosis and Christ as the rational cure. The Faith has had relatively little of significance to say or do about those phenomena, problems, and conflicts now labeled psychological, mental, social, emotional, behavioral, developmental, interpersonal, crosscultural, temperament, or adjustment. But even a cursory reading of the Bible shows a dominating concern for exactly those things. The modern psychologies have appropriated (or been granted) the heartland of the Faith. We have deferred and referred to secular wisdoms and neglected to cultivate our own wisdom. We need to reclaim the Faith's heartland.

We have a job to do. Adequate wisdom for the tasks of counseling is not a present possession of the church, and such wisdom is not acquired easily. It will be an individual and corporate achievement over the long haul. The Faith's incarnation into history is a work-in-progress and always will be. But our theory does not need to be created *ex nihilo*. A biblical psychology for the third millennium will break huge tracts of fresh ground but will cohere with extant orthodoxy, extending the scope of application of that orthodoxy.

Psychology as Psychotherapy

Mental health professionals talk to people, trying to help them solve their problems in living. Counseling practices and strategies are designed to facilitate change in beliefs, behaviors, feelings, attitudes, values, relationships, and the like. Functional things (not physiology, not social conditions), such as heart, soul, mind, and might are the target of conversational intervention. Just as theory shapes observation, so it guides intervention. One cannot intend to help another to change without an ideal for human functioning, usually explicit but easy to tease out when implicit. Ideals assert criteria of "good and evil," however much most practitioners recoil from acknowledging the moral nature of their ideals. The ideal is a mirror in which a practitioner identifies failures to match up—problems, dysfunctions, illnesses, syndromes, sins. With diagnosis made, the ideal then serves as a beacon toward which an intentional conversation will aim. Such conversations are the stock-in-trade of the psychotherapeutic professions that have emerged in Western culture in the twentieth century.

We easily forget that counseling has become part of the defined roles of psychiatrist, social worker, and psychologist only over the past fifty to one hundred years. The roles and functions of "mental health professionals" are not givens of the natural order but social-cultural creations. In America counseling conversation became associated with psychiatrists in the 1910s, clinical social workers in the 1920s, and clinical psychologists in the 1940s. Previously, psychiatrists acted as M.D.s and administrators, social workers tackled community conditions, and psychologists did research and testing.[4] Twentieth-century America has seen an explosion of professions claiming to help people with their problems by talking with them, and further claiming such conversations as their professional prerogative. Prior to the twentieth century constructive conversation was something done informally with family, friends, and mentors, while only pastors had any rationale for and history of intentional interventive conversation. But pastors lost their leadership role in counseling troubled people between the Civil War and the 1920s because "clergy analysis remained primitive" during the very time that powerful competing models and competing professions arose outside the church (Abbott, 1988, p. 282).

---

[4]Interestingly, to this day social work and schools of social work remain divided between two essentially different kinds of professionals: psychotherapeutic case workers and community workers (the original "charity work" from which the profession emerged). In another of those fluidities of history, since about 1970 psychiatrists have been turning away from psychotherapy and toward biopsychiatry, responding to the expansion of competing counseling professions.

What is this exotic thing termed *psychotherapy?* Here is how Freud described the interaction between counselor and counseled:

> Nothing takes place between them except that they talk to each other. . . . [The therapist gets the patient] to talk, listens to him, talks to him in his turn, and gets him to listen. . . . "So it is a kind of magic, . . . you talk, and blow away his ailments." Quite true. It *would* be magic if it worked rather quicker. . . . Magic that is so slow loses its miraculous character. And incidentally do not let us despise the *word.* After all it is a powerful instrument; it is the means by which we convey our feelings to one another, our method of influencing other people. (Freud, 1926, pp. 187-188)

Psychotherapy is conversation in which the "therapist" seeks to "heal" the "patient" (the medical metaphor is singularly inapt for describing what transpires but singularly useful ideologically). Such conversations occur "under the guidance of the therapist" who "plays the part of this effective outsider; he makes use of the influence which one human being exercises over another." The whole thing is an "educative process," a remedial "after-education" under the leadership of an authoritative and caring expert who strategically intervenes in another's life (Freud, 1916, p. 312). Something similar could be said by representatives of any other counseling school: cognitive, behavioral, existential, Adlerian, family systems, nouthetic, and so on. Even Carl Rogers ought to have said it, because his purportedly "nondirective" counseling actually *did* very directive things covertly.[5]

To put this in words from the Faith, *all* counseling attempts to be pastoral, shepherding the souls of wandering sheep. The basic tools of all counseling are the same: "speaking the truth in love," with all the ingredients of any effective and ethical attempt to persuade others. Personal integrity, humility, generosity, patience, and candor create trust and cred-

---

[5]Rogers's directiveness is now acknowledged by academic psychologists, but the myth that psychotherapy ought to be and can be value-neutral, rather than value-laden, continues to dominate both popular conceptions of the process and most introductory level training in counseling offered to those who are not mental health professionals (e.g., managers, physical therapists, lay counselors, peer counselors, nurses).

ibility. Accountability, creativity, metaphor, repetition, narrative, and the appropriateness that arises from having gathered your facts make communication vivid and relevant. A message—some "truth" about what is wrong, what should be, and how to get there—bids to restructure and reeducate the soul. Modern psychotherapy is simply the attempt to do face-to-face pastoral work in service to different gods, different ideals, different diagnoses, a different gospel. Secular psychotherapy is "pastoral work" done by "secular pastoral workers" (Freud, 1926, pp. 255-256). The Faith has its own version of pastoral work—the original, the best, the always renewable, however impotent and obscured in any particular historical moment.[6]

The Faith teaches us to make a searching criticism of psychotherapeutic activities, theorizing about persons, and psychological information. But what about the instances of good sense and insight one finds scattered in psychology books—the precisely accurate observations, the caring and helpful things done in psychotherapies, the winsome personal characteristics of individual psychologists? The most accurate way to put it is that these are not intrinsic to the logic of any secular psychological model, just as foolishness, ignorance, bumbling, and disagreeable personal characteristics are not intrinsic to the Faith. The former are happy contradictions, the latter unhappy contradictions. The former arise not from what is distinctly secular psychological but from the remnant image of God, and God's providential common grace scattering blessings and restraining evils. The latter arise not from what is distinctly biblical but from remnant sin, and the incompleteness of redemption both individually and corporately until the day Christ completes the good work he has begun in us.

Again consider Alfred Adler as a case in point, not because he is so unusual, but because he is so typical. Christianity rebuts his theory that the drive train of the soul is compensation for childhood inferiorities. But Adler was a sharp observer of human nature and sought to avoid the pitfalls of Freud's particular reductionism. He was also a caring man who worked extensively with poor children. He knew that love—"social feel-

---

[6]A critique of the competency of the *church's* pastoral counseling theory, training, and practice during the twentieth century—and remedial proposals—lies beyond the scope of this article. See Powlison, 1992, 1996, 1997, 1999.

ing"—is better than hate, isolation, manipulation, and fear. He saw some things accurately and he cared about some things intensely.

Here are four complementary perspectives on Adler's relative goodness. First, it is a common grace of God. Slum children are better served by kindly concern than by brutality and neglect, and Freud's model needs critiquing. We can say, "Thank you, God, for your goodness to children, that you restrain many evils and shower many goods." Second, Adler's relative goodness unwittingly points to something better. His best insights and most pressing concerns only come into their own within the fuller model of the Faith. "Common sense" and "common humanity" always whisper hints of biblical truth when they are in fact sense and care. The Faith is always better than the best of other models; God shouts clearly what others mumble. We can say, "That's so insightful! (or caring, or skillful, or humble). Why, he almost sees, says, and does it as well as the Bible. Praise you, living God, for the perfection of your ways and words." Third, Adler's relative goodness is a rebuke to us who profess the Faith. Where we are ignorant about people, remote from human need and obtuse when it comes to helping, God uses Adler's example to reprove us. This is not that we would become Adlerians but that we would grow more committed to the Faith. We can say, "Mea culpa; teach me your ways, O Lord." Finally, Adler's relative goodness is dangerous. His very brilliance and care are bent to serve a godless model. He exhibits the skills of a counterfeiter and charms of a con man, the winsome characteristics of anyone who would be persuasive. That he rings the bells of experience and labors to meliorate the human condition hides the perverse intentionality of his system. We can say, "Beware. He's wrong, however attractive he seems. God, help us to live lovingly, skillfully, and winsomely as we proclaim what is True."[7]

---

[7]The modern psychologies provide only the latest instance of an old problem, the relationship between "Jerusalem and Athens." For example, the Greek and Roman philosophers—Dante's first circle of hell—were often stunningly observant about human nature and quite skillful in effecting change in the direction of a morally excellent life. Ancient philosophy was intended for living, and it was closely wedded to arts of persuasion aiming to catalyze a conversion and carry on a discipleship process (Nussbaum, 1994). At the same time, their rendition of human life was "foolishness with God," to be argued with by Christian truth and practice (1 Cor 1; Acts 17).

Psychology as a System of Institutional Arrangements

Ideas and practices do not exist in a vacuum; they happen somewhere. Practitioners-to-be are trained in educational departments that claim disciplinary turf. Psychotherapeutic activity occurs in clinics, hospitals, and offices. Boards examine, accredit, and supervise, legitimating both education and practice. Licensing laws and courts reinforce (or destabilize) the social structure of professional practice. Patients link with psychotherapeutic practitioners through a referral system that routinely connects mental health professionals to each other and to various other institutions: educational, medical, judicial, social service, business, and, frequently, ecclesiastical. If you need to talk to someone, the pathways are in place that lead you to a mental health professional. Health insurance companies reimburse the conversations of only certain kinds of practitioners. Publishers select and publish textbooks, self-help books, newspaper columns, and training videos. Drug companies advertise the salvific effects of Prozac in major magazines and flood M.D.s with inducements to prescribe. In all these ways and more, psychology is a "mental health system." The power that the psychologies wield in our society does not occur because modern theories are intrinsically more plausible than outmoded religious ideas, or because modern therapies are demonstrably more effective than outmoded religious practices, or because the church is not potentially a far superior institutional setting for curing souls. Power is wielded because theories and therapies are institutionalized. Let me give two examples.

Several years ago a group of teenaged boys in the suburbs of Philadelphia beat another boy to death with baseball bats. This incident caused a tremendous uproar in the community. Teams of counselors came into the high school to help students and teachers deal with their shock, grief, anger, guilt, confusion, and fear. The counselors sought to help their clientele face what had happened, find comfort in grief, balance the competing demands of justice and mercy, find forgiveness, achieve clarity, and go forward with courage. The designated experts in these garden-

---

Calvin expressed the dual response well in his *Institutes*. He commends the pagan philosophers for their brilliant perceptions and high ethical intentions; he condemns them as benighted and perverted. He is not contradictory but sees the way the Faith enables us to see.

variety troubles of the soul were not agents and representatives of the Faith that is about just such things. Instead, secular mental health professionals ministered secular cures. A subplot occurred in the religious community. A clergy task force was created, not to do the frontline counseling but as an auxiliary support for the professionals. Representative Catholic, mainline Protestant, and Jewish leaders formed a steering committee; conservative Protestant pastors were pointedly excluded. No one said as much, but the most plausible explanation is that no one wanted to run the risk of hearing words such as *Jesus* or *sin* injected into discussions of the soul's garden-variety troubles. This is psychology in action as a system of institutional arrangements.

Institutional structures tacitly shape many assumptions that work against the Faith. They are not givens, of course. The institutional structures in Islamic nations work like those in the United States, only they exclude the voice and presence of the Faith even more effectively. But Christian workers in Africa, India, or Korea have tremendous freedoms, opportunities, and invitations to address the psychological problems of struggling people. A friend of mine from India—a pastor with counseling interests and experience—attended a large conference of Christian mental health professionals in the United States. He was troubled by the squeamishness and intimidation that professing Christians felt about inserting the Faith into the counseling process. They feared being thought unprofessional by clients, or incurring disapproval from colleagues or supervisors, or even facing professional censure for imposing their values on vulnerable people—as if every psychotherapy does not intrude its values at every point. He disliked the preoccupation with "professional issues": licensure, establishing lines of referral from local church pastors, doing life-issues seminars in local churches to cultivate a paying clientele, charging $115 per hour for conversation. He was appalled at how pastors and laity were condescended to by mental health professionals: "In India normal Christians know people best, freely reach out to help, and know how to help." He was dismayed that basic biblical categories such as sin, God's sovereignty, repentance, faith, obedience, and the Holy Spirit were inconspicuous in comparison to DSM-IV labeling, locating causality in a person's history of victimization, and the presumption that counseling healed illnesses. "If people want to see victimization, let them come to India. But we bring people the gospel of Jesus and he changes them, giving them hope and new life." His upset—unenculturated to our sociocultural air—provides snapshots of the power of institutionalization.

Institutional structures are not givens of the natural order. They are functional. The Faith critiques the working of the various forces—personal, social, professional, political, cultural, economic—that create and sustain such structures. The Faith has as much to say about normative institutional structures and professional roles as it does about theory of personality and counseling methodology. The classic summary passage is Ephesians 3:14—5:2, where the entire people of God is called to mobilize as a transformative countercultural community. When the church falls short of God's will, the solution is not to change the goal and take recourse in an autonomous mental health professionalism that in its fundamental structure counterfeits the church's ministry. The Faith intends to exercise authority and oversight in the counseling field, both over the practice of personal ministry (theory and therapy) and over the institutional arrangements that deliver care (education, accreditation, licensing, counseling, and supervision). Both church and parachurch must come squarely under such oversight, and parachurch must energize rather than enervate church ministry. An autonomous counseling profession ordained by the state is unconscionable when the church is called to counsel as an instrument of Christ's grace and wisdom.

Psychology as a Mass Ethos

Psychology in this final sense is the Zeitgeist of a therapeutic society. The very categories of experience have become "psychologized" and, because the modern psychologies are heavy borrowers of medical prestige and metaphors, "medicalized." The existential and relational realities of life—pointedly addressed by the Faith—are often interpreted as a medical and therapeutic drama. Terms such as *alcoholism* and *dysfunctionality,* a proliferation of syndromes, the explosion of Ritalin and Prozac use, and psychologized legal defenses are among the most obvious signposts of the phenomenon. Life turns on whether we feel good, on health and disease, not on what God thinks of us. The spirit of the age is the pervasive foe of the Faith, the air we breathe, a mass religion that has "no fear of God before its eyes."

Robert Coles describes the psychological ethos as "a dominant theme, if not an obsession, in our national life. . . . [It] means a concentration, persistent, if not feverish, upon one's thoughts, feelings, wishes, worries—bordering on, if not embracing, solipsism: the self as the only or main form of (existential) reality." The ethos entails "intense hope and great (messianic) faith," and evidences a "sadly instructive and desperate gullibility" (Coles, 1995, pp. 99-101). The therapeutic has infiltrated Christianity. When James Hunter evaluated trends in evangelical publishing in 1980, even before the massive "recovery movement" later in the decade, he concluded that evangelical faith was being deluged by a psychotherapeutic, narcissistic, and hedonistic preoccupation with the "sensitivities and 'needs' of modern man," and that it had lost touch with the traditional Protestant form of self-examination that was concerned with "the rule of sin in the life and the process of mortification and sanctification" (Hunter, 1983, pp. 99, 94; cf. Wells, 1993). It is not surprising to hear people talking in the church foyer about "her dysfunctional family upbringing," "his self-esteem," and "my needs not being met." They read their lives in terms of the therapeutic rather than through God's gaze on the same phenomena. Os Guinness called the modern psychologies carriers of idolatry and heresy. The therapeutic is "a substitute theology designed to replace faith in God. . . . Psychology supplies us with alternative priests. Sincere counselors may bridle at this point, but there is no question that psychology itself has become an ideology—a set of ideas that serves the interests of an entire industry" (Guinness, 1992, pp. 114, 126).

The Faith will draw converts from among the multitude who imbibe psychology as ethos, as well as from the more self-consciously psychologized. Those converts need continual discipleship into the radically different thought forms and practices taught and modeled in Scripture. Much of the ongoing work of counseling and discipleship involves the progressive reshaping of psychologized people into the shape of biblical wisdom. By cultural habituation, people simply assume a Ptolemaic universe where the drama of life, including "god" and "spirituality," circles around the self with its feelings and desires. The Faith teaches us to breathe the fresh air and see the bright light of a Copernican universe, where the drama of life circles around God in Christ.

Conclusion

There has been a logic to the order in which I have presented these six meanings of the word *psychology*, a crescendo of significance. The most significant effects of the secular psychologies lie not in any particular research findings, not even in the passing parade of theories in academia and therapies in professional circles. We live, move, and have our being within the institutional structures and cultural Zeitgeist of a psychologized society. Our fellow human beings—too often, we ourselves—are well-socialized and deeply enculturated into a false system that is bigger than the particular models that pass in and out of fashion intellectually and professionally. Grasp this rightly, grasp the radical contents and implications of the Faith's psychology, and we begin to seize the day for the Faith.

What is the seemingly elusive thing that I have termed "the Faith's psychology"? It is as systematic as any personality theory but far more comprehensive, recognizing entire dimensions to which secularity is blind. It is as practical as any psychotherapy but far more comprehensive, embedding private conversations within community life and resources. It is as distinctive as the Bible's view of the human condition and Christ's cure. To portray the Faith's psychology in detail lies far beyond the scope of this article.[8] But in its briefest form our psychology says the following. Human beings live actively accountable to the true God who knows and weighs us. Life has to do with God. We are innately and thoroughly worshipers, lovers, fearers, trusters, believers, obeyers, refugees, hopers, seekers, desirers of something or other. This is not a general background truth but a specific foreground truth, playing out in every motion of the soul. The human heart and the intricate multitude of responses—behavior, emotion, cognition, memory, anticipation, attitude,

---

[8]In addition to classic theological writings (e.g., Augustine, Luther, Calvin, Owen, Edwards) and contemporary writing on the Christian life (e.g., John Piper, Joni Eareckson Tada, Jerry Bridges, Sinclair Ferguson), see such counseling oriented books as Welch (1997, 1998), Powlison (1997), Adams (1979), and numerous articles in the *Journal of Biblical Counseling*.

and so on—are *ruled*. We heed either the true God, Savior, and Lord, or a host of identifiable lies, lusts, idols, voices, and pretenders. Human beings are thus fundamentally "depraved": morally bent, dark, insane, and unholy vis-à-vis the God who made, sustains, sees, and evaluates us. He must personally intervene to straighten, enlighten, make sane, and sanctify.

We are moral responders, but we do not live in a vacuum. Numerous significant forces impinge upon us, to some degree constraining and shaping us, but never determining our fundamental direction. These forces set the stage on which we live, operating within God's sovereign government and providing the context in which hearts are revealed and loyalties play out. Everything around us matters: the varied trials and temptations that make for misery and happiness; the deviancies and wisdoms of sociocultural voices and models; the sufferings of being sinned against and the joys of being loved; the abilities and disabilities of genetic inheritance and physiological functioning; the blessings and curses of economic, political, and technological conditions; the opportunities and constraints of each historical moment; the devil and the angels; and so forth. In the Bible's view, such things—nature and nurture, material cause and efficient cause—never name the final cause of our soul's pervasive moral insanity, the big WHY? that anchors every theory (see Welch, 1991). The human heart is an active agent with respect to the one true and living God. So we humans are not fundamentally deprived, as if nature or nurture explained the most significant things about us. We are not products of conditioned drives (behavioral psychology), unmet needs (humanistic psychology), physiological dysfunctions (bio-psychiatry), or instincts either traumatized or conflicted (psychodynamic psychology). Such theories merely shuffle the deck of nature and nurture, fabricating humanoids. Secular "responsibility" models are equally confused. We are not self-determining, whether responsible to ourselves (per philosophical psychologies such as existential, logotherapeutic, rational-emotive, and cognitive) or responsible to society (per moralistic psychologies). The Bible teaches a theocentric view of both the inward springs of life and outward influences on life.

When problems of person and situation are conceived vis-à-vis God, then Christ as the Bible presents him offers the only sufficient and logical solution. Understand the specifics of the human condition rightly, and the specifics of the person and work of Jesus are the only key that fits the lock. In the deepest sense, then, the Faith does not offer merely a "better, truer" psychological model competing with other models. The Faith offers the true, redeeming Person who competes with finally vacuous and misleading models. In the Faith's view, then, "counseling" is fundamentally personalized, a face-to-face ministry of this Christ within the context of his redeemed and redeeming community. Ephesians 3:14—5:2 offers a compact, six-hundred-word summary of the Faith's psychology.

I realize that the Bible words I have used in the previous three paragraphs often function in our thinking like a snow cone with all the juice sucked out: flavorless, colorless, cold, unappealing. Yet, in God's own speaking, these words carry a freight of vivid meanings. The problem is ours, not the Bible's. We must rediscover the depth and breadth, the taste and hue, and so redeem good words to do what God intends them to do. These are the words of the Faith's psychology, however cobwebbed or arid our current understanding of them. Every reformation and renewal of Christian thought and practice does something similar: the overly familiar takes on electrifying new relevance. Desiccated and truncated "truths" come to life like a desert in bloom. As we who profess faith unfold Ephesians 3:14—5:2 afresh, our own "psychology" will flourish in all six meanings of the word.

As we have seen, the Faith's psychology engages a multiform "psychology" that can mean six quite different things: from the essential you to your times, from observations to institutions, from various theories to various therapies. The Faith's coherent and comprehensive model says different things in each area, but there is a common theme. Only a psychology faithful to the Faith—the only true psychology—will understand and cure the madness in our hearts, because the madness expressed throughout our lives registers specific, identifiable realities that have to do with God. The psychological faiths are finally further instances of the madness they hope to cure. They systematically suppress both the truth about our souls and the truth of the Shepherd who finds lost souls.

Accurate thinking about the Faith's psychology and the psychological faiths enables three very good things. First, we will grow into wiser human beings. Grow wiser as persons, and we will grow wiser as counselors, more mature as pastoral theologians, more skillful in the cure of souls by the grace of Jesus. We fall far short of the fullness of biblical wisdom, each and all, even when our commitments are true. But knowing our Lord's will more clearly brings the goal into focus. All of God's people, individually and collectively, will grow up into the form of counseling wisdom peculiar to the church.

Second, we will become able to edify the quasi-psychologized church. Believing Christianity in our time and place embraces a great deal of secular psychology, just as the Christianity in other times and other places has embraced superstitious animism, pagan philosophies, or political agendas. Psychology is in our pores, not just in our classrooms, offices, and bookstores. Though we may sometimes live our faith better than we think it, there is always a cost to syncretism, however witting or unwitting. (There is a corresponding cost to hypocrisy, when we live our faith worse than we think it.) Sometimes the Faith's medicine goes down easily. Many Christians sense the inherent conflict between the Faith and the modern psychologies. Yet they find parts of these psychologies "helpful," or they do not see how the Faith addresses particular counseling problems. They have not been able to articulate how modern psychologies can be simultaneously insightful and wrong-headed, how psychotherapies can be well intended but misleading. When they are taught and counseled in the Faith's better way, they prove joyfully receptive. Other times the medicine will be tougher to swallow. Efforts to recast the Faith into the theories, methods, and institutions of the secular psychologies need to be opposed frankly, lucidly, and humbly, with the riches of positive, biblical alternatives in hand. In either case, we must develop the gentleness, discernment, clarity, and toughness to edify our brothers and sisters.

Third, we will gain the goods to bring good news to this psychologized world. Jesus calls people to far more than individual piety and a reformation of morals. There is intellectual change, methodological change, institutional change. The Faith calls for the radical reorientation demanded by God-centered, God-interpreted, God-ruled reality. As Christians grow to intellectual, practical, and institutional maturity in practicing our own distinctive psychology, the Faith will drop a bombshell in the playground of the psychologians. The therapeutic society is futile. Each latest and greatest insight, each newest cure, is a more elaborate form of the disease. There is no exit from the labyrinth, when the knowledge, theories, practices, and institutions bear the stamp of the labyrinth. A Redeemer, an outside truth, must break in. The futility of the alternatives to Christianity is a powerful point of contact for the Truth. We are called to become "radical reformers" with respect to the psychologies (Jeeves, 1997, p. 151). Even better, we are called to become well-tuned instruments of Christ's grace to the dissatisfied, uneasy, needy, wandering, and confused.

A host of psychologized people have already had their world turned upside down, inside out, and backwards by God's very different psychology. Countless more will come. As we develop and hone the Faith's distinctive message, methods, and institutional structures, we will make it easier for them to come because our light will burn brighter. The ultimate test of any model for relating the Faith to psychology is its ability to animate and guide intelligent evangelism of those committed to the psychological faiths.

During the past hundred years countless observers have noted that the psychological mode has trumped and subordinated the theological mode. Discourse about life has been conducted as if the human soul lived under psychological stars, breathing purely psychological air. The psychological faiths have no outside point of reference for human existence. There is no fear of God intrinsic to either theory or practice, theoretician or practitioner. There is no God of any weight, no One with whom we have to do. The church was once that hidebound institution charged to do a particular theory-driven psychotherapy (Tit 2:11—3:8), but not very competent at the job (Adams, 1970). The secular psychologists successfully revolted and have sustained a long hegemony over the cure of souls (Abbott, 1988, pp. 308-314). But the Faith is not intrinsically hidebound, malingering, or inept. The human soul lives under brighter stars and breathes fresher air: christological stars, revelatory air. The God who lives does not let his people rest easy when one of their mandated tasks is being done by others. As we do our job right, the Faith's psychology will again be seen as radical, satisfying, true, good, radiant—and formidable enough to be worth pointed opposition. And it will carry the day. "The Faith is always converting the age, not as an old religion, but as a new religion. . . . At least five times the Faith has to all appearance gone to the dogs. In each of these five cases it was the dog that died" (Chesterton, 1925, pp. 255, 260-261). When the Faith meets the psychologies, we must lead with our own psychology, calling all others to repentance. Chesterton put the result this way: "In my vision the heavenly chariot flies thundering through the ages, the dull heresies sprawling and prostrate, the wild truth reeling but erect" (Chesterton, 1908, p. 101).

References

Abbott, A. (1988). *The system of professions.* Chicago: University of Chicago Press.

Adams, J. (1970). *Competent to counsel.* Grand Rapids, MI: Zondervan.

Adams, J. (1979). *A theology of Christian counseling: More than redemption.* Grand Rapids, MI: Zondervan.

Adler, A. (1927/1992). *Understanding human nature* (C. Brett, Trans.). Oxford: Oneworld Publications.

Bradshaw, J. (1990). *Homecoming.* New York: Bantam.

Chesterton, G. K. (1908/1959). *Orthodoxy.* Garden City, NY: Image.

Chesterton, G. K. (1925/1955). *The everlasting man.* Garden City, NY: Image.

Coles, R. (1995). *The mind's fate: A psychiatrist looks at his profession.* Boston: Little, Brown.

Farber, L. (1956). Martin Buber and psychiatry. *Psychiatry: A Journal for the Study of Interpersonal Processes, 19,* 109-120.

Freud, S. (1900/1976). The interpretation of dreams. In J. Strachey (Trans. and Ed.), *The complete psychological works of Sigmund Freud* (Vols. 4-5). New York: W. W. Norton.

Freud, S. (1901/1971). *The psychopathology of everyday life* (A. Tyson, Trans.). New York: W. W. Norton.

Freud, S. (1916/1976). Some character-types met with in psycho-analytic work. *In The complete psychological works of Sigmund Freud* (Vol. 14). New York: W. W. Norton.

Freud, S. (1926/1976). The question of lay analysis. *The complete psychological works of Sigmund Freud* (Vol. 20). New York: W. W. Norton.

Grob, G. (1998). Psychiatry's Holy Grail: The search for the mechanisms of mental diseases. *Bulletin of the History of Medicine, 72*(2), 189-219.

Guinness, O. (1992). America's last men and their magnificent talking cure. In O. Guinness and J. Seel (Eds.), *No God but God.* Chicago: Moody Press.

Holifield, E. B. (1983). *A history of pastoral care in America: From salvation to self-*

realization. Nashville: Abingdon.

Horney, K. (1942). *Self-analysis*. New York: W. W. Norton.

Hunter, J. (1983). *American evangelicalism*. New Brunswick, NJ: Rutgers University Press.

Jeeves, M. (1997). *Human nature at the millennium*. Grand Rapids, MI: Baker.

Jung, C. (1966). The practice of psychotherapy. In *The collected works of C. G. Jung* (Vol. 16). Princeton, NJ: Princeton University Press.

Kuhn, T. (1970). *The structure of scientific revolutions*. Chicago: University of Chicago Press.

Marsden, G. (1987). *Reforming fundamentalism: Fuller Seminary and the new evangelicalism*. Grand Rapids, MI: Eerdmans.

Myers, D. (1981). *The inflated self*. New York: Seabury Press.

Nussbaum, M. (1994). *The therapy of desire: Theory and practice in Hellenistic ethics*. Princeton, NJ: Princeton University Press.

Piaget, J. (1952). *The origins of intelligence in children*. New York: International University Press.

Popper, K. (1963/1965). *Conjectures and refutations: The growth of scientific knowledge*. New York: Harper & Row.

Powlison, D. (1992). Integration or inundation. In M. Horton (Ed.), *Power religion*. Chicago: Moody Press.

Powlison, D. (1996). *Competent to counsel? The history of a conservative Protestant anti-psychiatry movement*. Unpublished doctoral dissertation, University of Pennsylvania.

Powlison, D. (Ed.). (1997). *Counsel the Word: A selection from the Journal of Biblical Counseling*. Glenside, PA: CCEF.

Powlison, D. (in press). Questions at the crossroads: The cure of souls and modern psychotherapies. In M. McMinn and T. Phillips (Eds.), *Care for the soul: Exploring the intersection of psychology and theology*. Downers Grove, IL: InterVarsity Press.

Roberts, R. (1993). *Taking the word to heart: Self and other in an age of therapies*. Grand Rapids, MI: Eerdmans.

Welch, E. (1991). Why ask "why?": Four types of causes in counseling. *Journal of Biblical Counseling, 10*(3), 40-47.

Welch, E. (1997). *When people are big and God is small*. Phillipsburg, NJ: Presbyterian & Reformed.

Welch, E. (1998). *Blame it on the brain*. Phillipsburg, NJ: Presbyterian & Reformed.

Wells, D. (1993). *No place for truth, or Whatever happened to evangelical theology?* Grand Rapids, MI: Eerdmans.

A Levels-of-Explanation Response

David G. Myers

David Powlison's skepticism of secular psychology and psychotherapy echoes some criticisms made in earlier years by the Marxist and feminist left. On this much they all agree: Psychology is theory-laden. "A theory tells us that certain things 'have to be there'; the eye fills in the details wittingly or unwittingly," says Powlison. This has also been the more recent critique of postmodernists. So even if his fellow critics feel like strange bedfellows, he has much company.

As I emphasize in my chapter for this volume, considerable evidence supports this aspect of the Powlison critique (which, of course, also applies to all this book's chapters). Belief guides perception. I concur strongly enough to have titled an earlier book *Psychology Through the Eyes of Faith*. Indeed, one of the *purposes* of any theory is to organize disconnected observations into a coherent system and to make predictions that allow us to test and apply it. And contrary to the extreme subjectivists and postmodernists who say psychology is nothing but assumptions and biases, many ideas and theories *have* been overturned by convincing research findings. It was new evidence, for example, that, for better or worse, challenged and changed my preconceived ideas about sexual orientation.

But of course there is more to contemporary psychology than the theories of the long-dead personality theorists discussed in this chapter (and who, with the exception of Freud, merit no more than a paragraph or two each in any current introductory psychology textbook). The psychological science that I represent is that which appears in the journals of the American Psychological Association, the American Psychological Society, and the British Psychological Society. It is also the psychology that is summarized in today's college psychology textbooks, taught in today's schools, and examined by the Advanced Placement psychology exam and Graduate Record Examination psychology exam. For those of us in what Robert Roberts calls "establishment psychology" (or what Gary Collins calls "mainstream psychology"), psychology is the science of behavior and mental processes. For Powlison psychology is instead "the whole of your response to cancer . . . how you respond to the devil's sayings and doings. . . . The core meaning of psychology is simply 'you,' a being who functions psychologically."

It is difficult to know what to make of this and later statements about psychology. But this much can be comfortably said: When he and I use the word *psychology,* we are not talking about the same thing. Readers of this book may therefore feel rather like Alice in Wonderland as she spoke to Humpty Dumpty: "The question is whether you can make words mean so many different things."

Whatever Powlison takes "secular psychology" to be, this much is clear: it is bad. He represents, I infer, what Gary Collins describes as the Jay Adams tradition of "vehement attacks on psychology." Psychology, we are told, drains away the "lifeblood of humanness . . . leaving a figment, a beast, an automaton, a humanoid, a counterfeit, a corpse." For those of us who have not previously encountered the Jay Adams tradition, these "psychophobic" words (Collins's phrase) will be puzzling. They would be similarly puzzling to anyone who has participated in psychology since the cognitive revolution of the 1970s or since the awe-inspiring neuroscience revelations of the 1990s—and surely also to anyone who has witnessed the more recent upsurge in research on emotions, stress, and the self.

Moreover, Powlison contends, "the more important a piece of psychological knowledge is for living, the more it will be common property to all sorts of people and disciplines. . . . Good parents and good elementary teachers have always known tacitly what Piaget makes explicit and detailed about cognitive development in children." So Piaget didn't teach us anything new, nor, one presumes, has the new generation of cognitive scientists. We knew it all along (which is what people always say, once they know the outcome of any investigation, sporting event, political election, or other historical happening). Indeed we have commonsense proverbs to cover many alternative outcomes—whether it should turn out that "birds of a feather flock together" or that "opposites attract." Does "absence make the heart grow fonder" or is "out of sight, out of mind"? Are "two heads better than one" or do "too many cooks spoil the broth"? Is it true that "you can't teach an old dog new tricks" or are you "never too old to learn"? As the philosopher Alfred North White-head (1861-1947) once remarked, "Everything important has been said before."

But some research findings *do* jolt our common sense. Sometimes Grandmother's intuition has it wrong. Informed by countless casual observations, our intuition may tell us that familiarity breeds contempt, that dreams predict the future, that birth order predicts personality outside the home, and that emotional reactions coincide with menstrual phase. But the available evidence now suggests that these commonsense ideas are wrong. Sometimes commonsense ideas—rooted in repeated everyday observations—prove accurate. Other times, research overturns popular ideas—about aging, about sleep and dreams, about personality. And it certainly has surprised us with discoveries about how the brain's chemical messengers control our moods and memories, about animal abilities, about the effects of stress on our capacity to fight disease. As Agatha Christie's Miss Marple explained, "It wasn't what I expected. But facts are facts, and if I am proved to be wrong, I must just be humble about it and start again."

A striking example of the power of evidence to overwhelm the pre-conceptions of those open to it comes from the challenge to the common-sensical and popular psychology assumption that parental nurture shapes children's personalities and language. We observe that gentle parents tend to have gentle children and that children talk with their parents' accents, and so we assume that parental nurture has done its job. Or so we assumed until behavior geneticists accumulated study after study showing, for instance, that adopted siblings who share the same parents are hardly more alike than any two children paired at random.

Judy Harris, a home-bound woman with no Ph.D., assembled the evidence documenting that parents matter less and peers matter more than nearly everyone has supposed. (Immigrant kids, for example, always end up talking like their peers, not their parents.) Then she dared to submit her thesis to psychology's most prestigious review journal, *Psychological Review*. Impressed by the strength of this challenge to conventional thinking, the editor accepted it. Similarly impressed, MIT psychologist Steven Pinker alerted his agent, leading to its provocative book version: *The Nurture Assumption* (Free Press, 1998). Also impressed, I struck up a correspondence with Harris and ended up critiquing all her draft chapters and nominating the book for the annual American Psychological Association-related George Miller book award, which it won. Again, it wasn't what I expected—and further research will surely further modify our understandings—but this much is plainly true: the bright light of evidence, even when marshaled by previously unknown scholars, has a way of shining through the darkest glasses.

Not only is secular psychology, in Powlison's antipsychology view, nothing more than plain old common sense, it "does not see and report the most significant pieces of information about people. . . . Only the Faith has a principle by which the magnifying power can be turned up without losing breadth: God's point of view, communicated to us." Faith, he grants, is not immune to distortions. "But God patiently teaches us—individually and corporately, over decades and centuries—how to see what we most need to see. Redemption exerts a correcting dynamic. . . . Our point of view rests on the true paradigm."

This I take to be a close approximation of the prescientific view against which the Christian founders of science reacted. They instead saw *humility* as an ideal. They distrusted anyone who presumed to have a corner on God's truth or special access to God. Galileo's church *knew* that the sun revolved around a stationary earth, because the Bible (it seemed) told them so. But when Galileo found the book of God's works telling a different story than what the church fathers took to be God's words, he let the truth of God's works be known. "Ever reforming" became a later motto of the Reformed Christian tradition.

If some people nevertheless claim, like the church fathers of Galileo's day, to have "God's point of view communicated to us," how are we to evaluate whether their claim is an authentic message of divine wisdom or the prideful pronouncement of a false prophet? I recall the words of Moses: "If a prophet speaks in the name of the Lord and what he says does not come true, then it is not the Lord's message" (Deut 18:22 TEV).

If people of faith can bypass the hard work of investigation and go straight to the answers, . . . well, why not? Just tell us how many neurotransmitters the body has; why electroconvulsive therapy is therapeutic for so many depressed people; what genes contribute to schizophrenia; whether hypnosis and multiple personality reflect dissociated states of consciousness; to what extent children's developing personalities, language, and values, respectively, are shaped by genes, parents, and peers; how best to understand the function of dreams; what long-term consequences (if any) there are to various forms of child abuse; and how one might best help someone conquer anorexia. Or how about "one of the basic and important questions of human existence" as posed (and tentatively answered) by John Bargh and Tanya Chartrand in the July 1999 *American Psychologist:* To what extent are our judgments, emotions, and behaviors a product of conscious (self-controlled, explicit) versus nonconscious (automatic, implicit) thinking?

These are but a few off-the-top-of-the-head examples of nontrivial current issues. If God indeed gives inside answers to us people of faith, then let's speak up. Yet ought not we also consider our limitations? Both history and the Bible's own witness show that all people—including people of faith—are fallible, fallen creatures. The rains of truth and illusion fall on both the just and the unjust.

In sum, David Powlison and I could hardly differ more in our understanding of psychology and of whether God beckons his disciples to wholeheartedly participate in scientific exploration of the human creation. But we do agree that all forms of psychology are theory laden. Indeed, who any longer wants psychology to be deprived of theory? Our theories distill and organize observations into a shorter list of principles that guide research and application. Christian teachers, scholars, and writers will therefore want not only to be true to observed reality, they will also want to be true to their own values, mindful of hidden values, and able to view the human creature through the lens of Christian ideas such as pride, evil, and love as articulated in Robert Roberts's and Gary Collins's chapters.

"The ultimate test of any model for relating the Christian faith to psychology," Powlison concludes, "is its ability to animate and guide intelligent evangelism of those committed to the psychological faiths." Good words, which I take to mean that people of faith are called not to isolate themselves in separatist enclaves, talking only to each other. In the tradition of the apostle Paul, who was Greek to the Greeks and Jew to the Jews, people of faith also are called to be in the world—understanding it, engaging it, talking its language, and winsomely leavening its discourse.

An Integration Response

Gary R. Collins

Not long ago I found myself seated next to David Powlison at a luncheon for Christian counselors. I was reminded again what a pleasant person he is—gracious and friendly. He and his associates represent a new generation that has come out of the nouthetic-counseling tradition. These are people who retain their strong and admirable commitment to the authority and inerrancy of Scripture but who are more gentle and less abrasive then some of their predecessors.

As I read this chapter I often found myself nodding in agreement. I agree completely that the Christian faith and the Bible give distinctive assertions about God that are intended to apply to real people in every situation of real life. I agree too that no person can be completely understood or aided if we drain away the biblically based "distinctive and comprehensive point of view about our souls and the cure for what ails us." I appreciated the assertion, made more than once, that no human being lives in a vacuum; we are shaped by biology, heredity, society, economics, politics, contemporary morality. As a psychologist I agree that my profession has given us a depth and breadth of knowledge about human beings drawn from our observations, interviews, case experiences, and research findings. I agree, as well, that secular psychologists have been too inclined to dismiss faith's perspectives on the psyche and that churches have become too fascinated with psychology. Most in my field would agree that psychology has a potential for "obtuseness and self-deception," that it sometimes misinterprets facts and that often it has limited impact in helping the hurting.

I am surprised, however, that when Powlison criticizes psychology, he fails to stress that many of his criticisms apply equally well to theology, to biblical interpreters, and to what he calls "Faith's psychology." Throughout the chapter, for example, he is critical of the diversified nature of psychology. He correctly shows that psychology is not a unified field, that it is more accurate to talk about *psychologies* than about *psychology*. As the chapter progresses, however, he implies (at least to me) that the alternative to this—faith or "Faith's psychology"—is unified and cohesive. Repeatedly throughout the chapter I pick up a unified-us-versus-fractured-them type of thinking. *They* are the bad guys who are scattered and floundering. *We* are the good guys (and gals) who have it all together because we follow Jesus. Compared to secular psychologists, there surely is less diversity among those of us who are Christ followers, who take the Bible seriously, and who seek to be led in our lives and our work by the Holy Spirit. But on this side of eternity we are all fallible creatures and many of the author's criticisms of psychology, including its diversity, apply as well to people of faith.

Powlison gives a different criticism of psychology in the section titled "Psychology as Knowledge About Human Functioning." He suggests that the "more distinctively 'scientific' a bit of psychological knowledge is . . . the closer it will come to describing things that theologians, poets, and common sense also know, discuss, and debate." He cites cognitive development in children and the dynamics of pride as examples. Then he dismisses the practical significance of research on the "neural substrates of cognition and behavior" or on how the brain "processes, stores, and retrieves information." I wonder if Powlison has ever had to deal with a hyperactive child or an adult who cannot focus his or her attention because of the effects of attention deficit disorder? We have learned about this not from the Bible but from our knowledge of neurological influences in the brain that have been discovered through careful research, which Powlison dismisses as irrelevant to life and something that theologians and poets already know.

He then writes that psychological knowledge never presents "just the facts," that there is always a selecting of facts based on one's preconceived theory. I concede that despite their efforts to avoid this, psychologists sometimes do select facts to fit their preconceived conclusions. I did this in the last two sentences of the preceding paragraph. We pick the examples to prove our points. But Powlison does the same throughout his chapter. All of us do this all of the time, including those who seek to analyze behavior from the standpoint of faith. The chapter acknowledges that none of us are immune to the "blinkering of our gaze, to distortions, and to fabrications." So why is psychology criticized for the intended or unintended selective perception that characterizes everybody, theologians included?

I agree with Powlison that we need to bring on and examine all the knowledge we can find about human life. Surely we need to evaluate every theory or psychological finding with caution and care. But that is what psychologists seek to do. We Christians, including those of us who counsel or write, may criticize psychological theorists who appear to be selective and biased in their choice of data, but let's be honest enough to admit that we are guilty of the same thing. Then in our work let's strive to be as unbiased as possible.

Powlison's section on "Psychology as Competing Philosophies of Life" never mentions *worldviews*, but this is what he is discussing. Every one of us has a view of the world—its people, pathologies, potential for change, ultimate purpose—the universe and the existence or nonexistence of a divine being. For some, their worldview is fuzzy and poorly articulated. For others, including many Christians, it is clear, guiding their beliefs and giving principles for living. Like others before him, Powlison correctly points out that secular worldviews, including the worldviews of most psychologies, in many ways are opposed to biblically based worldviews.[1] We must never forget this in our efforts to understand and counsel people.

But this raises an issue that is not mentioned directly in the chapter: Can Christian people-helpers learn from and utilize the findings of secular therapists whose work comes out of nonbiblical, competing philosophies of life? I think the answer is yes. The Bible, God's Word, is his

---

[1]This is a theme that I tried to emphasize throughout my book *The Biblical Basis of Christian Counseling for People Helpers* (Colorado Springs: NavPress, 1993).

clearest and only written form of communication with human beings. But God communicates in other ways as well, sometimes through the insights, research findings, and conclusions of people who do not know him but who bear a remnant of his image, and whom he graciously uses for his purposes. Powlison acknowledges this. He criticizes Adler, for example, but recognizes that Adler also has some perspectives that are admirable, even rebuking to those of us who profess the faith. Powlison quotes from people like Thomas Kuhn, Robert Coles, and others who do not write from a Christian perspective. To ignore these writers would be to cut ourselves off from a huge body of knowledge that can be useful. If we were to cut ourselves off completely from secular writers, to be consistent we would also have to stop reading newspapers or avoid reading those novelists who show such insights into human behavior.

Nevertheless, in our study of secular thought we must be careful. I agree that the theories of secular psychologies can be very persuasive. For the psychologist or other reader who is neither grounded in biblical teaching nor growing in a daily walk with God, it is easy to be deceived, to deceive others, and to do more harm than good with our therapies. It is important, then, that Christians "make a searching criticism of psychotherapeutic activities, of theorizing about persons, and of psychological information," even as we learn from these secular writers.

What about the profession of these secular psychologists? Powlison is not the first or the only one to challenge the field. From within the profession many psychologists, both Christian and non-Christian, have been critical even before their work began to be shaped by the mental health industry. Some, like the author of a secular book titled *House of Cards: Psychology and Psychotherapy Built on Myth,* have been sensational and perceived as mavericks. Others have done careful, admirable, high-quality research demonstrating what works in therapy but showing as well what does not work. In recent years Christian counselors have watched as many in their profession continue to criticize "the Faith" even as they embrace a fuzzy Eastern-mystical spirituality propagated by people who "do not understand the things of the Spirit." Many of us would agree with that pastor from India who was troubled by the squeamishness and intimidation of professing Christians who are reluctant to bring their faith into their counseling practices.

As his chapter ends Powlison seeks to articulate his "seemingly elusive . . . Faith's psychology" by outlining its parameters and distinctive features. Apart from my conviction that this is not as unitary a force as the author seems to imply, I have no great disagreements with what is written. But I do have problems with a return of the us-versus-them mentality that pits "the Faith" against muddling psychologies that are dismissed as irrelevant, despite the author's more open attitudes earlier in the chapter. Consider again the sad story about the boy who was beaten to death with a baseball bat. Did those counseling teams who went into the high school serve no useful purpose because they were ignorant of the Christian faith and only giving secular cures? Did God refuse to use them to bring help and healing? Did those who tried to understand what happened completely miss the mark despite what they had learned about active listening, cognitive-behavioral interventions, the impact of television, and the role of abuse and pathology in the families of violent kids? Is none of this relevant to our culture or to the needs of people who have desperate psychospiritual needs but who have no contact with churches?

I agree that the Faith is the better way, but does our knowledge of conditioned drives, physiological dysfunction, trauma, depression, or loneliness have no bearing on the hurting community that experienced murder in its midst? Many Christian mental health professionals would agree with Powlison and others that in the Faith's view counseling is "fundamentally personalized, a face-to-face ministry of . . . Christ, within the context of his redeemed and redeeming community." But how does this apply in practice to the kid who wielded the bat and presumably is now with other out-of-control kids in an explosive adolescent treatment center someplace far from any redeeming community? God has given us the ideal psychology. Perceptive observers like David Powlison see much of this as they look at Scripture. But we live in a fallen world that shuns, ignores, and dismisses divine truth. Maybe God in his mercy and grace has allowed us to discover other truths about human behavior, truths consistent with biblical teaching but discovered by other means for use by those who don't know the Savior. Maybe God uses even imperfect psychology—like he uses imperfect Christians—to influence this world until his Son returns in his glory.

Resources

Dawes, Robyn M. (1994). *House of cards: Psychology and psychotherapy built on myth.* New York: Free Press.

A Christian Psychology Response

Robert C. Roberts

Integration is problematic not because it absolutely cannot be done but because the snares and pitfalls awaiting those who try it are so insidious. The therapies and personality theories that compete with Christianity for hearts and minds are enormously seductive. They often speak fetchingly to our desire for simple and easily plausible answers, for indulgence of our wrongdoing and license to self-indulgence, to our yearning for attention and permission to gaze at our precious navels. They flatter by intimating that our problems come from what others have done to us, from not being kind enough to our dear self or from being out of touch with that innocent, pure, and beautiful little thing. To such moral temptations are added the intellectual difficulties. Our cultural air is saturated with "psychological" terms and concepts, so that the plausibility of the theories can seem absolutely patent, like $1 + 1 = 2$. Part of what's in the air is the false belief that professional psychology is scientific in something like the sense in which professional chemistry is scientific. (*Some* professional psychology *is* scientific, and Powlison may underestimate this fact.) And as Powlison forcefully points out, we are not well armed with a clear conception of the Christian alternative. Many Christian professionals who sincerely desire to be faithful witnesses to Christ in their teaching or clinical work have only the vaguest impressions of what Christianity has to say about the psyche. They have advanced degrees in aspects of twentieth-century psychology and barely a Sunday school conception of the faith. And again as Powlison points out, this lamentable situation is not due to mere individual dereliction. We are reaping the harvest of more than a century of communal dereliction: the church has neglected and forgotten its own psychological resources and handed over the tasks of counseling and therapy to "professionals" professing other and opposing faiths. But if the snares were immobilized and the pitfalls uncovered, integration would seem to be a modestly important enterprise for a Christian psychologist. As Powlison comments, "With a careful caveat about the theory-ladenness of data and with a well-trained ability to think from our own point of view (Heb 5:14), we can learn from and interact with anything."

The rub is, of course, that "well-trained ability" we lack, but it seems highly unlikely that after more than a century of development of non-Christian psychotherapies, they would contain nothing of any interest to Christians. Despite the comment I just quoted, one drift of Powlison's chapter seems to be that integration is a *conceptually impossible* enterprise, and I want to indicate why that is not true.

Most therapeutic techniques can be detached from the philosophies of life in which their originators (or rediscoverers) embed them. The empathic listening of a Carl Rogers (or something recognizably like it) is not *conceptually* or *inextricably* tied to his theory that psychological dysfunction derives from introjected conditions of personal worth imposed by the social environment. Christians may have their own biblical reasons for using this powerful technique and may embed it in a therapy that has no tendency to produce the amoral and narcissistic attitudes for which Rogerian therapy is justly famous. In Jungian therapy, dream analysis is intimately tied up with a theory about individuation and the healing effect of getting in touch with universal archetypal (mythical) ideas that are supposedly found in the unconscious self. (These ideas are said to come out in dreams.) In Jung's conception of psychic well-being, it is dysfunctional to derive any religious consciousness from doctrines. (It all needs to be discovered within oneself.) But something *like* Jung's dream analysis might be practiced with a very different theory of what is being accomplished by it. C. S. Lewis has a theory of mythological consciousness similar to Jung's, but he holds strongly to Christian doctrines, and in particular he thinks of the incarnation as a historical fulfillment of a mythic theme found throughout the world (Lewis, 1970). A dream analysis along these lines might be used in support of personality formation around a belief in Christ as the historically incarnate Lord. A technique used by cognitive therapists is that of arguing their clients out of beliefs that create emotional problems for them. The beliefs with which the therapist proposes to replace the "irrational" beliefs are sometimes ones that Christians could not endorse—for example, the belief that nothing has any ultimate importance. But arguing, as a technique, can surely be separated from particular ideological conclusions like this one. Christian therapists can use this technique to argue their clients into Christian beliefs or, at any rate, beliefs that are healthy by Christian standards. These are just three examples. Twentieth-century psychologies are full of techniques for changing people's attitudes and behavior, and in many if not all cases the techniques can be adapted for Christian use.

You might object that Christians could very well have thought up such generic "techniques" as listening empathetically, talking to people about their dreams, and arguing them out of their unhealthy beliefs on their own and without pagan aid. Who needs help from Rogers and Jung and Beck? And of course you are right. But it is a fact that techniques like these have been developed in the non-Christian psychologies and have become powerful influences in the interest of those pagan spiritualities. Maybe we would have developed the techniques in the absence of these psychologies; maybe not. But there they are, and it seems a matter of Christian justice to give credit where credit is due. Furthermore, as Powlison points out, psychological learning is often importantly "in the details," and these psychologists do not *just* listen empathically and argue and talk about dreams; they do these things *in their own way* and *with great skill* that bears careful observation on our part. As he says, "We can learn from anything," and here is something especially well developed and of psychological interest to learn from.

I have focused on techniques because they are rather easy to detach from the objectionable ideologies that are the central mechanism of integration snares. But theoretical elements in psychologies can be integrated as well. Freud's idea of defense mechanisms is detachable from his atheism and his naturalism; the defense mechanisms might be allowable in Christian psychology both as an explanation in normal development and as a way in which sin manifests itself.

So there is a modest place for integration, and in saying this I am agreeing with one drift of Powlison's chapter. But as I said, there is an anti-integration drift as well, premised not just on integration's snares and pitfalls but on a certain view about how conceptual systems work. The relationship between theory and fact is an issue fundamental to Powlison's chapter, and he says things that may seem to conflict with one another. In this he is like most others who talk about this difficult issue and want to do justice to two true claims that seem to be in tension with one another: (1) Psychological theories pervade and affect the facts (observations) over which they range ("wrong theory distorts every fact"). (2) The same facts can be observed through the lenses of various theories ("Christian and non-Christian will both ring the bells of experience with case-study details"; "At their best, [secular psychologists] know a great deal about people"). Since statement 2 is true, statement 1 must not be taken to imply that psychologists of different theoretical orientations cannot talk rationally to one another, or that each must be blind to the facts that the other identifies in his theory. Some theorists have held such a radical view, but it is not borne out by what happens when people with very different theories talk to one another. By the same token, since 1 is true, 2 must not be taken to imply that psychologists of different theoretical orientations "mean the same things" when they refer to the same facts. We might say that they refer to the same facts but conceptualize them (somewhat) differently.

When Powlison says, "We would never integrate Adler and the Faith," it is significant that he does not say, "We would never integrate any of Adler's insights or observations or any element of Adler's theory." The incommensurability is not between these *pieces* of Adler's psychology and the Christian psychology but between Adler's whole *system* and the Christian one. The pieces, whether they be facts or theoretical elements, can be understood and possibly acknowledged cross-theoretically, and what is understood can be detached and possibly integrated into another system of thought and practice. Claim 2 makes integration possible; claim 1 makes it crucial that integration be careful and sophisticated.

Thus it is unclear whether I am disagreeing with Powlison about the possibility of integration. But I am certainly agreeing with the emphasis of his well-written essay. Present-day Christian psychology needs not primarily integration but a careful and profound retrieval of the psychology that is native to the Christian faith. Only when we are well grounded in that psychology will we be able to walk among the psychological snares and pitfalls of the twentieth century with fair confidence that we are not betraying the biblical faith.

References

Lewis. C. S. (1970). Myth becomes fact. In W. Hooper (Ed.), *God in the dock: Essays on theology and ethics.* Grand Rapids, MI: Eerdmans.

6 Finding One Truth in Four Views

Eric L. Johnson & Stanton L. Jones

After reading a book like this, it's easy to come away feeling frustrated: four sincere and intelligent Christians expressing four different views, on some points saying virtually opposite things as they work out answers to difficult problems (for example, the tension that seems to exist between psychology and the testimony of the Scriptures). In the extreme it can lead to a kind of despair or at least indifference—apparently it doesn't really matter what Christians think. "It's all simply a matter of personal opinion or taste. To each his own."

Such a conclusion would be too easy. There surely are topics that are shaped mostly by personal preference: what music we enjoy, what clothes we like. But the underlying goal of psychology is loftier than affirming personal preference: it aims at truth. Moreover, through the ages Christians have assumed that God created our minds and the universe in such a way that we can understand something of the way the universe really is (a philosophical position termed *realism* [see Alston, 1996; Plantinga, 1983, 2000], which we believe all the authors of this book adhere to). So though intelligent Christians differ, it doesn't mean there is no point in pursuing the truth. Before we conclude the book, we want to explore how to make sense of these four approaches to the relation of Christianity and psychology.

A Fifth Approach?

Before we do that, however, we need to address the likely concern of some Christians in psychology that an important approach to the relation of faith and psychology has been left out. Over the past few decades, a few authors have focused on how Christians live out their Christianity in the field of psychology and argued that this *ethical* (embodied, experiential, practical, personal) dimension of the Christian's involvement in psychology is of fundamental importance (Bouma-Prediger, 1990; De Vries, 1982; Dueck, 1995; Farnsworth, 1982, 1985; Sorenson, 1996a, 1996b). Though likely all of these authors support the intellectual task of relating faith and psychology, all have raised awareness about the relation of Christian practice to psychology. One can legitimately question the penchant evangelicals have for spending so much time and so many resources on abstractions, doing psychology "in the head," when it's clear from the Bible that God is more concerned with how we live our lives—the actual state of our own souls and our relationship with God and others. Some have even questioned whether the whole task of intellectually relating faith to psychology is seriously flawed. For one thing, it seems to perpetuate the modern idolization of knowledge and intellect over other aspects of human life (including the spiritual). Second, it could be a sort of defense mechanism, focusing on intellectual reflection to keep our minds off our insecurities and the great limitations we feel in our hearts regarding our relationships with God and others.

Clearly, such ethical-religious concerns are of fundamental importance. The centrality of living in the love and for the glory of God in our relationships with others (with personal integrity and authenticity) cannot be stated forcefully enough. This applies to all Christians at all times and certainly to Christians who study human nature. Mere intellectual, abstract exercises that relate propositions of theology and psychology have limited value and can be a form of escapism that unwittingly leads us away from Christ (see Sorenson, 1996a, for a delightful parody on such waywardness).

Nevertheless, we are not treating this ethical awareness as a distinct approach to psychology for two reasons. First, we think that to do so would actually undermine its very point. The ethical insight into the personal, existential, relational, religious quality of psychology applies equally to all the approaches that Christians take to psychology.[1] It is foundational to all of life. All knowing and acting is fundamentally ethical and religious (Frame, 1987; O'Donovan, 1985). The personal, relational, moral, and spiritual dimensions of life pervade all human activity, including the research, teaching, counseling, advocating, writing, reading, and understanding that constitute psychological activity. As a result, this awareness is not so much another Christian approach to psychology as it is a preeminent realization calling Christians to faithful worship and service in all of life. To treat it as a separate approach would be to pit existential, relational, moral, religious existence against understanding, to treat it as constituting one optional approach alongside other "choices" (as if there were any options to faithful integrity). On the contrary, this ethical awareness is of ultimate importance and grounds all theoretical options as a call to live all of life together unto the Lord with integrity.

Second, while this realization casts a hue over every square inch of psychology, of itself it provides little help in understanding and treating human nature from the standpoint of the Christian faith, the goal of this book. It is necessary that students and professionals spend time personally working out their own faith privately and with others and God. Yet this ethical-spiritual-experiential work cannot replace the search for truth, that is, the *intellectual* task of relating faith to the science of psychology and to therapy. We conclude then that this ethical call does not constitute a separate approach (alongside the others).

Unfortunately, it is not uncommon for individuals to sense this ethical call and, combined with the confusion that results from seeing the various approaches Christians have taken to psychology, conclude that there is no point in developing a Christian understanding of psychology; they opt instead for the ethical solution: "the only thing that matters is how you live." Yet we contend in the strongest possible terms that this not an either-or proposition. Just as surely as psychological activity is pervaded by these ethical-religious dimensions, so is all psychological activity shaped by our understanding of human nature. Neglecting the cognitive dimension (e.g., thinking Christianly about things like psychology) while

---

[1]Though it must be admitted that this theme is especially emphasized in this book by Collins, who has shifted in his view of integration since his earlier writing, making this theme a main pillar in his present model of integration.

emphasizing the ethical usually leads to inconsistency and incongruence between life and faith.

Truth Is Larger Than We Can Think

This book, then, is concerned with the search for truth. The Christian tradition has typically maintained that humans can discern the truth about the universe (though the favored means of this search have changed over the centuries). In addition, Christians have assumed the Bible offers truth about reality that is also possible to discern. Back of such beliefs are the core Christian beliefs that God created all things and knows all things, and that he has created us in such a way that we can similarly know things (Plantinga, 1983, 1993). As mentioned above, Christians typically have been *realists,* an approach to knowledge shared with many non-Christians (though by no means all). But Christians also have been *revelationists;* that is, they have believed the Bible is a special source of truth—a special revelation of God—that provides some truths we could not obtain in any other way. (Some have gone even further, contending that God is the ultimate source of truth found in all truth-seeking endeavors, e.g., science, technology, and literature; see Is 28:23-29; Gilson, 1940, ch. 12). The goal of all understanding from a Christian standpoint is to understand things the way God does. As Jonathan Edwards (1980) suggested, true knowledge is "the consistency and agreement of our ideas with the ideas of God" (p. 341). He knows everything perfectly, and our goal is to know everything like he does. Put another way: his understanding is the "landscape" that we, in our science, try to paint on the canvas of our discipline. There is one truth—God's understanding of reality, the way things really are—and the goal of science is to do our best to comprehend it and reproduce it.

Yet the best Christian thinking about such things recognizes that human understanding is limited and partial. We see in a glass darkly, and standing in one place we can only see from one standpoint; as a result, under the best of circumstances we finite creatures can never hope to obtain God's perfect understanding. Even worse, depending on the limitations of our motives, methods, and sources, we can easily get things wrong. So while Christians seek God's understanding, they acknowledge that God's understanding alone is comprehensive and perfect, and that theirs is only a partial reflection or reproduction of the whole.

The result of our human limitations in knowing is that no human knows everything. No human perspective can capture all the truth. The truth is too big and our minds are too small. One response to this state of affairs is to fall into a kind of intellectual apathy called *relativism:* "There are all these different approaches out there, so it doesn't matter what a person believes." But as we continue to reflect on things, we start to recognize that thoughts do matter; some beliefs do seem to be a more accurate reflection of reality than others; some writers seem to have a better grasp of things than others. This realization encourages us to harken to the advice of the father in Proverbs:

> Turn . . . your ear to wisdom
>   and apply . . . your heart to understanding,
> and if you call out for insight
>   and cry aloud for understanding,
> and if you look for it as for silver
>   and search for it as for hidden treasure,
> then you will understand the fear of the LORD
>   and find the knowledge of God.
> For the LORD gives wisdom,
>   and from his mouth come knowledge and understanding.
> (Prov 2:2-6)

The task of developing a fuller, richer understanding is not easy; it requires much effort, but it is very rewarding.

The fact is that the truth, the "landscape," is so big that many perspectives are required to get the fullest "picture" possible (Frame, 1987). And the more complex the truth, the more likely it will require different perspectives. In the modern era of psychology there always have been multiple schools of thought regarding human nature. In the early days there were the structuralists, functionalists, behaviorists, psychoanalysts, and gestalt psychologists (Boring, 1950). In the 1960s there were the mainstream (natural science), psychoanalytic, and humanistic approaches (Bugental, 1964). Today there still are the mainstream empirical approach (by far the largest, and composed of dozens of subgroups), evolutionary psychology, object relations, and social constructivism, and so it goes. Part of the reason these "schools" tend to arise is due to socio-historical changes in the beliefs of a culture, part is the individual differences of psychologists (thinking styles, interests, and passions), part is the variety of approaches taken to understand different key "problems" or phenomena (and different approaches work better on some problems than others), and part of it is due to the training students receive (the direction they are pointed in) when in graduate school (when these perspectives tend to sink in). But doubtless a large part of the reason (as is the case for all the human sciences) is the sheer complexity of human nature. Humans have an inner, conscious side and an outer, behavioral side; they think and process information and also seem to harbor unconscious motives and desires; they are biological creatures as well as spiritual beings; they are determined by social and biological forces, but they also exercise free agency. Such complexity seems to require different approaches of study.

In addition, psychology in the modern era has been pulled in two directions: science and therapy. Some have focused on the nature of individual human beings—their functional characteristics in such areas as memory, behavior, cognition, and emotion—and others have focused on how to repair the damage to this human nature. Different foci affect what is seen and what is deemed important. (Such differences have figured prominently in this book: two of the authors are counselors, one a researcher, and the other a philosopher.)

As all our authors acknowledged, our understanding also develops within communities. Scholars and scientists (as mentioned above) are trained (and socialized) in certain ways of approaching their topic. These people in turn join certain associations or divisions and contribute to certain journals and avoid others. These social-institutional realities affect what counts as knowledge and how individuals approach their object of study (Danziger, 1990). If the physical sciences are affected by these influences (Kuhn, 1962), it seems even more likely that the human sciences (like psychology) would as well, a supposition that has received a good deal of documentation (e.g., Ash & Woodward, 1987; Buss, 1979; Campbell, 1979; Foucault, 1965; Rose, 1990). As a result, when trying to understand an author it's usually helpful to inquire into what "community of scholars" he or she is a part of. What are the assumptions of that community? What is this scholar's academic background? For whom is he or she writing? Writing for pastors or for non-Christian audiences will have an effect on what is considered important. Such an awareness doesn't minimize the value of an author's approach; it puts it in context.

To complicate things even more, in this book we are concerned with the relation of psychology and Christianity (itself a bit of a mystery). Each of the authors has a different perspective on how faith contributes to the topics of psychology and counseling. Given the complexity of both faith and psychology, such variety is not only inevitable, it is good. It provides us with a broader vista than any one perspective could.

So different perspectives on human nature are to be expected. But we must add that all perspectives are not necessarily of equal value. Some approaches (e.g., phrenology) have died an appropriate death because they were of little or no value. They did so poorly at capturing truth, of faithfully representing God's landscape as the Creator had structured it, that their portrayal was of no use to future truth seekers. Other models may be only partially helpful in capturing truth.

Moreover, it is not merely that one's perspective may be limited. Error is possible. Each system may fail to accurately or faithfully interpret Scripture or may misjudge psychological research or both (a point we must all take to heart). To take sides on an issue in the text, Dr. Myers argues that biological factors provide the sole cause of homosexuality, that homosexual orientation may be impossible to change, that Scripture is somehow ambiguous on this issue. He also infers that it is therefore a morally neutral option for sexual expression. We believe that these positions are not entailed by his levels-of-explanation approach, and a fair reading of both Scripture and of the available empirical evidence contradicts the conclusions he draws.[2] But the possibility of such error remains for us all.

In spite of all these difficulties, how do we bring these different perspectives together in order to understand the relation of Christianity to psychology as fully, as comprehensively, as is humanly possible?

---

[2]For a fuller elaboration of the editors' views see Johnson, 1992; and especially Jones and Yarhouse, 2000.

Toward a Comprehensive Understanding

A systems evaluation. The first thing to be done is to evaluate each of the approaches on its own terms. Each view we have been exposed to is a system of thought, and it can be evaluated individually for its strengths and weaknesses. Admittedly, the goal of objective analysis is an ideal. The reality is that we can never analyze models without some prejudgments. Whenever we read or think about anything, we come with a preunderstanding that guides our present reflections, formed through previous experiences, training, and study, that often predisposes us to a certain model. So the analysis of each model "on its own terms" is actually somewhat idealistic. Yet this still is an important goal. Though we all have to start somewhere (beginning with our prior understanding), we nevertheless strive to be as fair an evaluator as we can be. Truth seems to be disclosed best when we assume this stance (while praying that God would give us understanding). Aware of our pre-understanding, we nevertheless maintain an attitude of fairness and openness to the truth, trusting that there is likely something of value in each model, being mindful of how our pre-understanding might warp our interpretation of the different models.

When analyzing these approaches, we suggest that there are two important sets of questions to ask. First, how comprehensive is it? How much of human nature and the Christian life is being described with this approach? What things about human nature and salvation are clarified or illuminated by it? Each approach likely has something to offer (rarely are well-thought-out positions without any value), and we should be able to summarize the breadth of its viewpoint of the "landscape" of the truth. It can be useful to ask the reverse of this question. How much is being left out by this perspective? What aspects of human nature and the Christian life are neglected or overlooked because of the limitations of this particular way of looking at Christianity and psychology? These limitations too should be stated. Nevertheless, while a model's narrower scope may limit its overall usefulness, its own unique contributions to the "big picture" we're seeking can be appreciated.

The second set of questions we should ask is, How faithful to Scripture is each model? Is the biblical revelation respected in every sense of the word? Does the psychologist resist the temptation to twist Scripture to fit a tidy scheme by ignoring other passages of Scripture or using inappropriate or unsophisticated methods of interpreting its message? Does the author seem to rely in an appropriate way on the totality of scriptural revelation in framing this view of the psychological phenomenon?

When evaluating each model on its own terms, in reference to comprehensiveness and fidelity to Scripture, we likely will be left with a preference for one or more models (a preference usually influenced by our previous pre-understanding). Still, such preferences are necessary, for they help us to make our way around complex subjects, providing the inevitable and necessary means for further understanding (Gadamer, 1988; Polanyi, 1958).

Building a metasystem. Assuming that each of these different models portrays some of the truth, our next step is to develop a way of appropriating as much of the truth as possible from all the systems. This requires developing some sort of "metasystem." To help us figure out how to do that, we're going to use some psychology. Researchers in the field of early-adult cognitive development have documented that some adults seem to develop in the quality of their thinking over time (Basseches, 1984; King & Kitchener, 1994; Kramer, 1990; Richards & Commons, 1984, 1990; Rybash, Hoyer, & Roodin, 1986).[3]

Broadly speaking, there appear to be three stages of thought. Piaget, the great cognitive-developmental psychologist, studied the first two. The first we'll call "prelogical" or "presystemic." (Piaget actually divided this stage in two [preoperational and concrete operational] but for our purposes we'll treat them as one stage). The thinking of children (and most adults when we don't need or want to think more complexly about a topic) is presystemic. Their thinking is prelogical or presystemic because it's prior to or "beneath" logical or systemic thinking (that is, thinking structured as a formal system of logic). They are incapable of thinking about their thoughts; they cannot organize their thoughts into a logical system. Instead, their understanding is inconsistent, composed of

---

[3]This is called "postformal" thought in the psychological literature. For more analysis of postformal theory, see Johnson (1996a; 1996b; 1998). Certain philosophers have also recognized and used this type of thinking (e.g., Kierkegaard and Ricoeur) and so have some evangelical theologians like D. A. Carson (1981), Frame (1987), and Poythress (1987). (The latter two were influenced by C. Van Til [1972].)

many different beliefs, some of which contradict other beliefs. Children are unable to recognize logical inconsistencies because they do not have the mental ability to evaluate them.

Piaget found that only in adolescence did people begin to develop the ability to think logically or systemically (Piaget's stage of formal operations).[4] Persons in this stage can think abstractly. They can think about their thoughts, organizing, comparing, and evaluating them. As a result, they are able to develop a logically consistent system of thought.

Such thinking is profoundly important to modern life. Without such logical abilities, scientific research would not have developed, for in order to devise a meaningful experiment the scientist must be able to abstract a number of variables that are relevant to the research question and hypothesize how they might be related. So the scientist must be able to abstractly organize the variables of interest and devise a "system" of relations between them. But it's not just scientists who use systemic thinking. Such thinking is required to understand any abstract system of thought, for example, complex mathematics (like calculus), government systems (like democracy and fascism), economic systems (like capitalism and communism), and theological systems (like Islam and Eastern Orthodoxy). That's why students typically don't study such topics until late high school or college; before then, they usually do not have the reasoning ability to understand such purely mental systems of propositions or beliefs.

However, in spite of its tremendous power, systemic thought has limitations. It has a hard time grasping what happens when systems change and when variables (and systems) interact with each other (like in the weather or in complex social interactions); systemic thought struggles in real-life problem-solving contexts where all the information necessary to solve the problem in a clear-cut way isn't available (e.g., should I talk to the boss about problems with my immediate supervisor?); and most important for our "problem" in this book, systemic thinking has difficulty synthesizing a number of single systems into a bigger picture, a metasystem (Richards & Commons, 1984; see also Basseches, 1984; King & Kitchener, 1994).

---

[4]Though it is probably in college that students really develop in this way of thinking and only in some areas. In fact, research has found that only about 50 percent of college seniors use formal operations consistently on tasks devised to assess such thinking (Pascarella & Terenzini, 1991).

In addition to the above difficulties for systemic thinking, it appears that the world we live in contains "things" that are not capable of being grasped within a single, logical system. For example, how can light be both a wave and a particle? How can an adult child best show love to a verbally abusive mother? How can God be both three and one? How do we best help the poor—by giving them assistance or by encouraging them to help themselves? The nature of reality itself seems to require metasystemic thinking. Such complex topics seem to defy human formal logic abilities. Hearty debates in college dorms often result when two systemic thinkers get together (something like a debate between Rush Limbaugh and Jesse Jackson). Holding to opposite sides of an issue, both are logically consistent within their own belief system. As long as they only see the topic from within their own system, they are logically incapable of seeing the insights found in the other position. Of course, a goal of a good debater is to expose the logical inconsistencies of the *other* person's thinking. But systemic thinkers stuck in their own system are genuinely unable to grasp the truth in another system insofar as those truths contradict *their own* system of thought. Debates between rigidly systemic thinkers are sometimes productive, but most often they end in frustration. (Although we usually can benefit from exposure to the thinking of extremely logical thinkers since their consistency often reveals unwarranted inconsistencies and resistances in our own thinking.) But what if the "opposing" position actually has some truth as well? After all, other systems usually are based on some evidence and developed with some rationale. This creates a "logic problem" for a systemic thinker.

One response to such problems is to revert back to presystemic thinking and ignore them. Another approach is actually more thoughtful but has the same outcome. It recognizes the logic problem and concludes that solving it is impossible, the solution of relativism. Either of these two ways out can lead a person to become "eclectic," that is, to choose whatever beliefs (or practices) he or she wishes without attempting to fit them together into a larger system of thought. Certainly, this can be done, but it often leads to inconsistencies that undermine important truths; it also forecloses on growth in understanding, keeping the individual from moving to higher, more complex levels of thinking that can embrace more of the truth.

A third faulty response to logic problems is to cling rigidly to a formal system and deny the insights and benefits of other approaches. Many Christians who view relativism as the ultimate evil lapse into this pattern, resulting in the tendency to draw very sharp dividing lines between their entirely correct system and the entirely false opposing system and to defend their views at all costs. They're unwilling to admit that their views have any drawbacks or points of weakness; thus a deeper grasp of the truth is beyond their reach. But there is a fourth, possible reaction.

Early-adult cognitive-developmental researchers have found that some adults move beyond presystemic, systemic, and relativistic thinking. They move to thinking in a "metasystemic" way that transcends the limits of a single logical system. Metasystemic thought synthesizes the truths of multiple systems that are apparently contradictory (at the level of systemic thought). This happens as the genuine insights of the different systems are understood and accepted, forging a new "synthesis" of ideas without regressing into invalid, unsubstantiated, irrational conclusions.

Metasystemic thinking is the goal set before us in this book, and it is a Christian goal. The Christian has been freed from a "party" spirit to embrace the truth wherever it is found. And that, after all, is the goal of Christian understanding: to get at the truth, to describe the "big picture" as best we can, to get as close as possible to God's comprehensive, meta-metasystemic understanding of things.

Moving Toward the One Truth Through Studying Four Views

So, back to this book. Each of the contributors has presented a largely coherent, logically consistent system for approaching psychology in light of one's faith. Yet it is clear that there are striking differences between these systems. As suggested above, one approach to these differences is the systemic approach: pick one and stick to that one, arguing against all others where they seem to contradict the favored system. However, a metasystemic approach pushes us to embrace more of the truth than can be found in one system, yet without reverting either to relativism or unreflective, logical inconsistency. A fair reading of each of the authors reveals that each is uniquely pointing to important truths. All truth is from God and needs to be embraced. Somehow, each of us readers must move beyond our own present, limited understanding of such things and, in dependence on God's spirit of wisdom, seek to embrace all the truth we can.

Our predicament reminds us of the very familiar story, apparently from India, of a group of blind men who were asked to decide what object was before them (an elephant). One held the tail and said it was a rope, another touched a leg and said it was a tree, yet another felt the elephant's side and said it was a wall, and the last held the trunk and said it was a large snake. The discerning reader will recognize that this example need in no way belittle the work of our contributors. Each of them is an outstanding expert who possesses a deep understanding of his specialty. In fact, without the differing perspectives of specialists, it would be nearly impossible to get a better, bigger picture. Rather, the story of the blind men reveals everyone's predicament. We all have a limited perspective; no one but God can grasp the whole vista of reality. Consequently, we need to hear "reports" from others in order to paint the biggest picture possible and compose the most accurate understanding of reality.

Contrary to how this story has been used by some, such a task does not necessarily relativize all of the views. It doesn't require that we treat all views as equally valid and accept all beliefs without critical reflection. On the contrary, metasystemic thinking requires a great deal of contemplation (really, it's a life-long reasoning process) and involves deep reflection, in light of our present understanding, on the systems presented. Perhaps we'll see things in a light different from the that of a particular contributor, but still we must try to do justice to the key insights of the contributor in order to get as close as possible to God's comprehensive understanding. The fact is, there are usually limitations in every complex system. Everyone's understanding likely has some error. So we must critique each system and its beliefs; if we don't, falsehoods will inevitably creep into our understanding. The goal is to develop as comprehensive an understanding as possible, and the hindrance is our tendency to embrace an unnecessarily restrictive bias that excludes the truth in other systems. As we work through a particular approach, a clue to discovering our own bias is to ask, how am I dealing with its assertions? Systemic thinkers rashly reject thoughts that do not fit neatly into their present system regardless of the evidence. Metasystemic thinkers use their present understanding as a guide while they listen intently to other perspectives, attempting to hear and incorporate compelling evidence of truth, even if it seems contradictory to a formal approach at first.

Nevertheless, relativism is a danger here, especially in a postmodern era when the notion of truth is frequently being called into question. Consequently, to help safeguard the realism we have been advocating and to steer clear of relativism, we want to conclude with a few qualifications regarding metasystemic thinking.[5]

The Ultimate Truth of Christianity

The first qualification is that in Christ, God and his revelation of himself in the Old and New Testaments is *the* ultimate truth. As the story of the blind men and the elephant is usually told, there is a sighted king or wise man watching their attempt to identify the elephant. Often, proponents of particular philosophies or religions (such as Christians) who claim to have all of the truth are compared to the blind men, while the storyteller is the king/wise man with a "God's-eye view" who sees the pathetic limitations of those claiming their view alone is right. The storyteller sees the whole; we, the blind people, see only in part. Using this story to refute the particular and exclusive truth of Christianity creates a major problem: the person arguing for the new, improved universal religion or spiritual truth (who takes the role of the king in the story) only "explains" or incorporates Christianity by robbing it of its core essence, that is, by destroying the uniqueness of Christianity.

Christianity, we believe, is the faith system that alone has the potential to do justice to all of the complexity of both our human experience and that of the entire world. This is not to say that individual Christians have answers to every question life poses but rather that Christianity as a total system of life and thought has the breadth and complexity to deal with all of reality, including the most difficult human problems, while revealing, most centrally, the way God chose to intervene in human life to save us from our sin. Christianity embodies a breadth that allows it to be what some call a "world and life view." At the same time, it is defined at its

---

[5]This may be especially appropriate given that the story of the blind men and the elephant is often used against orthodox Christian belief and either in support of relativism and pluralism, or in support of some grand religious doctrine that (supposedly) refutes the exclusive truthfulness and reliability of the core Christian message.

core by the offensive (to some) particularity of the way that God acted to give us eternal life in the life, death, and resurrection of Jesus Christ.

Hence, metasystemic thinking ceases to be legitimate for Christians when it embraces elements of thought that contradict core Christian belief. Here we again face a difficult judgment call—what sorts of ideas contradict core Christian belief? And how can we guard against rejecting ideas that are legitimate and valuable which we mistakenly judge to be non-Christian (like the argument of Galileo that the earth rotates around the sun)? Balancing a vigorous affirmation of core Christian beliefs with an openness to novel ideas that stretch us and open up vistas we have not yet explored can be difficult. But that is a necessary tension bound up in the calling of the Christian who seeks the truth.

Genuine Versus Apparent Contradictions

The second qualification is that openness to metasystemic complementarity must stop when the ideas we are comparing are deeply incompatible, that is, when they are truly (not just apparently) contradictory; that is, they are contradictory for God. Openness to metasystemic thinking is not license to believe mutually incompatible things. "All crows are black," says Professor A, to which the metasystemic student replies, "My knowledge has grown!" "But all crows are white!" exclaims Professor B, to which the metasystemic student must not reply, "Ah, this too must be true!"

Learning to distinguish when ideas are actually incompatible versus when they are only incompatible in appearance but possibly harmonious at a deeper level is a difficult but essential reasoning skill for the Christian thinker. The law of noncontradiction still holds in metasystemic thinking. A statement cannot be true and its opposite (its contradictory), rightly understood, also be true. However, metasystemic thinking can permit us to identify that some apparent contradictions can be harmonized (e.g., that God is both three and one), leading us to develop new ways of describing something very complex (e.g., God is of one substance and three persons) without resorting to genuinely contradictory statements. Some of the beliefs of our authors are truly incompatible with some of the beliefs of the others; we cannot use metasystemic magic to put together what logic genuinely renders asunder. However, if the evidence demands it, the metasystemic thinker is willing to hold two beliefs that appear to be contradictory with the hope that further seeking may lead to greater clarity with the confidence that God's understanding contains no genuine contradictions.

Invalid Conclusions Are Still Wrong

Another valuable reasoning skill for the metasystemic thinker is learning how to recognize when theorists or researchers generalize beyond the real value of their work and make extravagant and universal claims about their particular approach, theory, or finding. An example of this is the researcher who convincingly demonstrates that certain environmental variables influence the development of a personality trait or pattern (in this case, a justified assertion based on the evidence) and then claims (without evidence) that the research establishes the universal truth of environmental determinism (i.e., the teaching that humans are completely programmed by their environments). We have good reason to believe that environmental variables influence development, yet the entire cumulative weight of all those studies has never proved the grand hypothesis of environmental determinism. "Influences" does not equal "determines." Metasystemic thinking still utilizes formal logical analysis in which an invalid conclusion is simply wrong. So the discerning metasystemic thinker embraces the more limited findings of the researcher while rejecting the unwarranted, broader claim that is also being made.

In another context, one of us tried to provide a model of such thinking (but without applying the "metasystemic" label) in analyzing psychotherapeutic models (Jones & Butman, 1991). It was suggested, for example, that the Christian has something to learn from a psychotherapeutic system that emphasizes the importance that contextual/environmental variables can have in shaping human behavior (such as traditional behavior therapy) but also from one that emphasizes human rationality (such as cognitive therapy) and even from one that emphasizes irrational, primitive, and emotional motives in human life (such as classic psychoanalysis). The value of each can be appreciated as the Christian contemplates the theoretical elegance of each model and the empirical effectiveness of each model with certain types of clients. What we reject in our metasystemic thinking are the exclusionary claims of the more extreme proponents who argue that their model is absolutely true to the exclusion of the views of their competitors. Even more important, we do not argue that these models should be wholly appreciated despite their deep incompatibility with Christian thought. Rather, we study them because each model picks up certain elements of understanding of the human person that either is explicitly present in or at least fits with (i.e., is not genuinely logically contradictory with) the scriptural revelation we have from God.

So, metasystemic thinking provides no license to think sloppily, that is, *il*-logically. Metasystemic thought is not illogical; it is supralogical. It integrates simple logics into a higher order without abandoning logic's laws. Logic is valuable, in fact essential, for complex thought. Many things in life are best understood with systemic thinking, and all human thought requires a respect for the laws of logic. But when the available evidence compels us (as when we are presented with four coherent approaches to faith and psychology), we are bidden to develop a more comprehensive understanding than a systemic understanding alone could accomplish.

"Regions" of Study

The final qualification, which picks up on a theme introduced earlier, is that psychological theories and systems (and different approaches to faith and psychology such as the four portrayed in this book) are often better suited for dealing with certain types of problems and not others. One of us has argued elsewhere (Jones, 1996) that the task of bringing distinctively Christian modes of analysis to bear on psychology differs when the Christian psychologist strives to understand and perhaps influence various aspects of human and animal experience. It was suggested that "as we move across the spectrum from neuroscience and animal learning to personality theory, the necessary role of . . . distinctively Christian control beliefs" for the Christian scholar becomes more and more evident and influential (p. 135). In other words, the role that distinctively Christian beliefs play in developing a Christian understanding of psychology grows as we move from topics in which Christian belief seems to have little bearing (animal learning; neuroscience) to issues that deal with the core of human character and existence. Why is this so?

Because "as we move along that spectrum of psychological topics toward the more molar and more uniquely human, we . . . move into an arena which is more obviously the preoccupation of biblical revelation" (pp. 135-136).

Topics that are closer to the core of our being and those aspects of human nature that are more directly influenced by sin and by redemption will benefit more from Christian (and will suffer more from non-Christian) reflection and interpretation, whereas further-removed topics in psychology will be less affected.

Look carefully at the areas of focus of the proponents of the four models in this book. It is no accident that many of the scholars who advocate the levels-of-explanation approach to integration are academic psychologists who study more tightly defined and closely specified aspects of human behavior. Myers, our "levels" author, is a social psychologist whose earlier empirical work focused on studying the behavior of individuals in small groups. His frequent coauthor and equally distinguished advocate of the "levels" approach, Malcolm Jeeves, is one of the world's foremost neuroscientists. These are areas (group dynamics and brain function) about which the Bible has little to say. It is no accident, equally, that many of the advocates of the biblical-counseling approach are those trained in and committed to pastoral counseling and counseling within the Christian community, dealing with concrete problems that are the "bread and butter" of practical ministry. Powlison, our biblical-counseling author, is theologically trained and most concerned about the strategies and tactics that should be used in the ministry to deal with the concrete sins and problems of living of the people of God. These are precisely the types of concerns (problems) to which Scripture speaks with the most clarity.

Our fourth lesson, then, is that the different models outlined in this book may each make the most sense, be the most compelling, when applied to different "regions" of study. We should not ask simply "Is this the right model?" but rather make the question just a bit more complicated: "Is this the right model for understanding how my Christian faith relates to this specific problem or understanding this particular phenomenon?" Take two fundamental questions from different ends of the psychological spectrum: How do animals remember and learn? and What are the most basic motivations of the human being? Surely Christian belief will bear on the two questions in different ways and to differing degrees. If you agree with us in this, you are doing metasystemic thinking.

Legitimate Preferences

The last clarification regarding metasystemic thinking concerns the legitimate and necessary role that values play in our thinking. Because of our limited understanding (compared to God), we need to listen reflectively to those who have other views in order to develop as comprehensive an understanding as we can. These different views can help us embrace more of the truth than we would if left to our own present system of thought, and it also helps to reduce the limitations and minimize the weaknesses of any one system. However, this doesn't mean that we won't find one (or more) of these approaches especially attractive. As suggested before, metasystemic thinking does not equalize all systems. It may be that one system, or model, is actually more valid, more comprehensive, than the others. Most systems are actually to some extent already metasystems and have already synthesized the truth of other systems to some extent. So we may find one approach is more helpful than another, describing more of the vista, providing more of a map. In our search for God's understanding, we all simply aim to do the best we can wherever we're at.

We suspect that most of the readers of this book have found themselves gravitating toward one or another of the models. The two editors themselves differ regarding the relative strengths and weaknesses of these views and find themselves at different places on the continuum. Yet we're also convinced that each of the views has value for the overall project of relating Christianty and psychology.

A Two-Track Model for Christians in Psychology

One more thing. As already suggested, the debate expressed in this book is shaped to some extent by the communities that the respective authors participate in as psychologists or counselors. Though well-known among Christians in psychology, Myers primarily writes within the perspective of what has been called "modern," "mainstream," or "establishment" psychology, while the other authors primarily have written about psychology and counseling to explicitly Christian audiences.[6] Clearly this difference in audience and professional context has colored some of the conversation to which we have listened. And it raises questions regarding the goals of Christians in psychology. Should Christians work toward the creation of a common body of knowledge, acceptable to all interested parties (a distinctly *modern* goal), or should Christians work on a uniquely *Christian* understanding of psychology and counseling (a rather *premodern* or *postmodern* goal)? Though arguments for only one path can be made, we want to suggest that both options should be pursued (in good metasystemic fashion). As Myers has cogently argued, there is a need for Christians to work within the context of (modern) psychology, contributing to it with excellence (and we would add, even though at present certain considerations are not allowed in to the discourse, e.g., reference to the work of the Holy Spirit). When entering into another community's "game" (in this case, the modern secular), it's necessary to play by their rules (aiming to do so without compromise). At the same time, Christians need to work at developing an understanding of human nature and therapy that is increasingly consistent with Scripture and Christian belief for use within the Christian community (a task that is unrealizable as long as only one option is perceived). Engaging in such a two-track approach to psychology challenges us to be active professionals in the majority culture, leavening the discourse where possible, yet free to view and help humans within the church in light of God's redemption and revelation (using both Scripture and research).

We conclude by acknowledging what you may already have concluded, that there's no simple formula for developing metasystemic understanding, except to keep seeking and pursuing wisdom, which, it must be said, entails calling on God, the source of all wisdom. We leave this tremendous and gratifying task to the reader to work through in their quest to think Christianly about psychology, and to develop the fullest understanding possible of psychology from a Christian standpoint. Done in faith, all of this simply draws us to Christ, in whom are

---

[6]The exception being Roberts, whose philosophical work has sometimes been addressed to mainstream readers.

hidden all the treasures of wisdom and knowledge (Col 2:3). As Jonathan Edwards (1980) suggested, "All the arts and sciences, the more they are perfected, the more they issue in divinity, and coincide with it, and appear to be as parts of it" (p. 397). The science of psychology and the art of counseling are both fundamentally religious enterprises (as is all of life). May God get glory from our journey together.

References

Alston, W. (1996). *A realist conception of truth.* Ithaca, NY: Cornell University Press.

Ash, M. G., & Woodward, W. R. (Eds.). (1987). *Psychology in twentieth-century thought and society.* Cambridge: Cambridge University Press.

Basseches, M. (1984). *Dialectical thinking and adult development.* Norwood, NJ: Ablex.

Boring, E. G. (1950). *A history of experimental psychology.* New York: McGraw-Hill.

Bouma-Prediger, S. (1990). The task of integration: A modest proposal. *Journal of Psychology and Theology, 18,* 21-31.

Bugental, J. F. T. (1964). The third force in psychology. *Journal of Humanistic Psychology, 4,* 19-26.

Buss, A. R. (Ed.). (1979). *Psychology in social context.* New York: Irvington.

Campbell, D. T. (1979). A tribal model of the social system vehicle carrying scientific knowledge. *Knowledge: Creation, Diffusion, Utilization, 1,* 181-201.

Carson, D. A. (1981). *Divine sovereignty and human responsibility: Biblical perspectives in tension.* Atlanta: John Knox Press.

Danziger, K. (1990). *Constructing the subject: Historical origins of psychological research.* Cambridge: Cambridge University Press.

De Vries, M. (1982). Beyond integration. *Journal of Psychology and Christianity, 2,* 320-325.

Dueck, A. (1995). *Between Jerusalem and Athens: Ethical perspectives on culture, religion, and psychotherapy.* Grand Rapids, MI: Baker.

Edwards, J. (1980). *The works of Jonathan Edwards: Scientific and philosophical writings* (Vol. 6). (W. E. Anderson, Ed.). New Haven: Yale University Press.

Farnsworth, K. E. (1982). The conduct of integration. *Journal of Psychology and Theology, 10,* 308-319.

Farnsworth, K. E. (1985). *Whole-hearted integration: Harmonizing psychology and Christianity through word and deed.* Grand Rapids, MI: Baker.

Foucault, M. (1965). *Madness and civilization* (R. Howard, Trans.). New York:

Random House.

Frame, J. (1987). *The doctrine of the knowledge of God.* Phillipsburg, NJ: Presbyterian & Reformed.

Gadamer, H. G. (1988). *Truth and method.* New York: Crossroad.

Johnson, E. L. (1992). A place for the Bible within psychological science. *Journal of Psychology and Theology, 20,* 346-355.

Gilson, E. (1940). *The spirit of medieval philosophy.* New York: Charles Scribner's Sons.

Johnson, E. L. (1992). A place for the Bible within psychological science. *Journal of Psychology and Theology, 20,* 346-355.

Johnson, E. L. (1996a). The call of wisdom: Adult development within Christian community, Part I: The crisis of modern theories of post-formal development. *Journal of Psychology and Theology, 24,* 85-92.

Johnson, E. L. (1996b). The call of wisdom: Adult development within Christian community, Part II: Towards a covenantal constructivist model of post-formal development. *Journal of Psychology and Theology, 24,* 93-103.

Johnson, E. L. (1998). Growing in wisdom in Christian community: Toward measures of Christian postformal development. *Journal of Psychology and Theology, 26,* 365-381.

Jones, S. (1996). Reflections on the nature and future of the Christian psychologies. *Journal of Psychology and Christianity, 15*(2), 133-142.

Jones, S., & Butman, R. (1991). *Modern psychotherapies: A comprehensive Christian appraisal.* Downers Grove, IL: InterVarsity Press.

Jones, S. L., and Yarhouse, M. A. (2000). *Homosexuality: The use of scientific research in the church's moral debate.* Downers Grove, IL: InterVarsity Press.

King, P. M., & Kitchener, K. S. (1994). *Developing reflective judgment: Understanding and promoting intellectual growth and critical thinking in adolescents and adults.* San Francisco: Jossey-Bass.

Kramer, D. A. (1990). Conceptualizing wisdom: The primacy of affect-cognitive relations. In R. J. Sternberg (Ed.), *Wisdom: Its nature, origins, and development* (pp. 279-313). New York: Cambridge University Press.

Kuhn, T. (1962). *The structure of scientific revolutions.* Chicago: University of Chicago Press.

O'Donovan, O. (1985). *Resurrection and moral order.* Grand Rapids, MI: Eerdmans.

Pascarella, E. T., & Terenzini, P. T. (1991). *How college affects students.* SanFrancisco: Jossey-Bass.

Plantinga, A. (1983). Reason and belief in God. In A. Plantinga & N. Wolterstorff (Eds.), *Faith and rationality: Reason and belief in God* (pp. 16-92). South

Bend, IN: University of Notre Dame Press.

Plantinga, A. (1993). *Warrant and proper function.* Oxford: Oxford University Press.

Plantinga, A. (in press). *Warranted Christian belief.* Oxford: Oxford University Press.

Polanyi, M. (1958). *Personal knowledge: Toward a post-critical philosophy.* Chicago: University of Chicago Press.

Poythress, V. (1987). *Symphonic theology.* Grand Rapids, MI: Zondervan.

Richards, F. A., & Commons, M. L. (1984). Systematic, metasystematic, and cross-paradigmatic reasoning: A case for stages of reasoning beyond formal operations. In M. L. Commons, F. A. Richards, & C. Armon (Eds.), *Beyond formal operations: Late adolescent and adult cognitive development* (pp. 92-119). New York: Praeger.

Richards, F. A., & Commons, M. L. (1990). Postformal cognitive-developmental theory and research: A review of its current status. In C. N. Alexander & E. J. Langer (Eds.), *Higher stages of human development: Perspectives on adult growth* (pp. 139-161). New York: Oxford University Press.

Rose, N. (1990). Psychology as a 'social' science. In J. Shotter & I. Parker (Eds.), *Deconstructing social psychology* (pp. 103-116). London: Routledge.

Rybash, J. M., Hoyer, W. J., & Roodin, P. A. (1986). *Adult cognition and aging: Developmental changes in processing, knowing and thinking.* New York: Pergamon.

Sorenson, R. L. (1996a). Where are the nine? *Journal of Psychology and Theology, 24,* 179-196.

Sorenson, R. L. (1996b). The tenth leper. *Journal of Psychology and Theology, 24,* 197-211.

Van Til, C. (1972). *Common grace and the gospel.* Phillipsburg, NJ: Presbyterian & Reformed.

Name Index

Subject Index